With expert readings and forecasts, you can chart a course to romance, adventure, good health, or career opportunities while gaining valuable insight into yourself and others. Offering a daily outlook for 18 full months, this fascinating guide shows you:

- The important dates in your life
- What to expect from an astrological reading
- How the stars can help you stay healthy and fit
  And more!

Let this sound advice guide you through a year of heavenly possibilities—for today and for every day of 2010!

SYDNEY OMARR'S® DAY-BY-DAY ASTROLOGICAL GUIDE FOR

ARIES—March 21–April 19
TAURUS—April 20–May 20
GEMINI—May 21–June 20
CANCER—June 21–July 22
LEO—July 23–August 22
VIRGO—August 23–September 22
LIBRA—September 23–October 22
SCORPIO—October 23–November 21
SAGITTARIUS—November 22–December 21
CAPRICORN—December 22–January 19
AQUARIUS—January 20–February 18
PISCES—February 19–March 20

IN 2010

Sydney Omarr's®

DAY-BY-DAY ASTROLOGICAL GUIDE FOR

CANCER

JUNE 21–JULY 22

2010

by Trish MacGregor
with Carol Tonsing

A SIGNET BOOK

SIGNET
Published by New American Library, a division of
Penguin Group (USA) Inc., 375 Hudson Street,
New York, New York 10014, USA
Penguin Group (Canada), 90 Eglinton Avenue East, Suite 700, Toronto,
Ontario M4P 2Y3, Canada (a division of Pearson Penguin Canada Inc.)
Penguin Books Ltd., 80 Strand, London WC2R 0RL, England
Penguin Ireland, 25 St. Stephen's Green, Dublin 2,
Ireland (a division of Penguin Books Ltd.)
Penguin Group (Australia), 250 Camberwell Road, Camberwell, Victoria 3124,
Australia (a division of Pearson Australia Group Pty. Ltd.)
Penguin Books India Pvt. Ltd., 11 Community Centre, Panchsheel Park,
New Delhi - 110 017, India
Penguin Group (NZ), 67 Apollo Drive, Rosedale, North Shore 0645
New Zealand (a division of Pearson New Zealand Ltd.)
Penguin Books (South Africa) (Pty.) Ltd., 24 Sturdee Avenue,
Rosebank, Johannesburg 2196, South Africa

Penguin Books Ltd., Registered Offices:
80 Strand, London WC2R 0RL, England

First Printing, June 2009
10 9 8 7 6 5 4 3 2 1

First published by Signet, an imprint of New American Library,
a division of Penguin Group (USA) Inc.

CONTENTS

INTRODUCTION

Seize the Moment

"Timing is everything" is a saying worth repeating this year. Astrology is the art of interpreting moments in time, and astrology fans from the rich and famous to the readers of daily horoscope columns realize that some moments are more favorable for certain actions than others. Knowing that they can plan their actions in tune with the rhythm of the cosmic cycles gives them confidence that they are making wise choices. This could be a challenging year for many, so let this guide help you seize the moment and turn those challenges into opportunities by using the tools astrology provides.

In our toolbox for 2010, you'll find secrets of astrological timing—how to find the most auspicious dates this year. For those who are new to astrology or would like to know more about it, we offer easy techniques to start using astrology in your daily life. You'll learn all about your sun sign and how to interpret the mysterious symbols on a horoscope chart. You can use the convenient tables in this book to look up other planets in your horoscope, each of which sheds light on a different facet of your personality.

Many people turn to astrology to help them find love or figure out what went wrong with a relationship. At your service is the world's oldest dating and mating coach, ready to help you decide whether that new passion has potential or might burn out fast. We'll go through the pros and cons of all the possible sun-sign combinations, with celebrities to illustrate the romantic chemistry.

Contemplating a career change? Our sun-sign chapters can help you build your confidence and focus your job search in the most fulfilling direction by highlighting your natural talents and abilities.

Many readers have explored astrology on the Internet, where there are a mind-boggling variety of sites. Our suggestions are well worth your surfing time. We show you where to get free horoscopes, connect with other astrology fans, find the right astrology software for your ability, and even find an accredited college that specializes in astrological studies.

Whether it's money matters, fashion tips, or ideas for vacation getaways, we'll provide ways to use astrology in your life every day. Before giving yourself or your home a makeover, be sure to consult your sun sign, for the colors and styles that will complement your personality.

To make the most of each day, there are eighteen months of on-target daily horoscopes. So here's hoping this year's guide will help you use your star power wisely to make 2010 a happy, successful year!

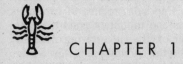

CHAPTER 1

The Top Trends of 2010: Transition Times

Astrologers judge the trends of a year by following the slow-moving planets, from Jupiter through Pluto. A change in sign indicates a new cycle, with new emphasis. The farthest planets (Uranus, Neptune, and Pluto) which stay in a sign for at least seven years, cause a very significant change in the atmosphere when they change signs. Shifts in Jupiter, which changes every year, and Saturn, every two years, are more obvious in current events and daily lives. Jupiter generally brings a fortunate, expansive emphasis to its new sign, while Saturn's two-year cycle is a reality check, bringing tests of maturity, discipline, and responsibility. This year, Jupiter in Pisces and Saturn in Libra are in auspicious signs for most of the year, which should act as a balance to more volatile elements in the comos.

Little Pluto—The Mighty Mite

Though astronomers have demoted tiny Pluto from being a full-fledged planet to a dwarf planet, astrologers have been tracking its influence since Pluto was discovered in 1930 and have witnessed that this minuscule celestial body has a powerful effect on both a personal and global level. So Pluto, which moved into the sign of Capricorn in 2008, will still be called a "planet" by astrologers and will be given just as much importance as before.

Until 2024, Pluto will exert its influence in this practical, building, healing earth sign. Capricorn relates to structures, institutions, order, mountains and mountain countries, mineral rights, issues involving the elderly and growing older—all of which will be emphasized in the coming years. It is the sign of established order, corporations, big business—all of which will be accented. Possibly, it will fall to business structures to create a new sense of order in the world.

You should now feel the rumblings of change in the Capricorn area of your horoscope and in the world at large. The last time Pluto was in Capricorn was the years up to and during the Revolutionary War; therefore this should be an important time in the U.S. political scene, as well as a reflection of the aging and maturing of American society in general. Both the rise and the fall of the Ottoman Empire happened under Pluto in Capricorn.

The Pisces Factor

This year, Jupiter moves from experimental, humanitarian Aquarius to creative, imaginative Pisces. Jupiter is the coruler of Pisces, along with Neptune, so this is a particularly auspicious place for the planet of luck and expansion to be. During the year that Jupiter remains in a sign, the fields associated with that sign are the ones that currently arouse excitement and enthusiasm, usually providing excellent opportunities.

Jupiter in Pisces expands the influence of Neptune in Aquarius; there should be many artistic and scientific breakthroughs. International politics also comes under this influence, as Neptune in Aquarius raises issues of global boundaries and political structures not being as solid as they seem. This could continue to produce rebellion and chaos in the environment. However, with the generally benevolent force of Jupiter backing up the creative side of Neptune, it is possible that highly original and effective solutions to global problems will be found, which could transcend the current social and cultural barriers.

Another place we notice the Jupiter influence is in fashion,

4

which should veer into a Pisces fantasy mood, with more theatrical, dramatic styles and a special emphasis on footwear. Look for exciting beachwear and seaside resorts that appeal to our desire to escape reality.

Those born under Pisces should have many opportunities during the year. However, the key is to keep your feet on the ground. The flip side of Jupiter is that there are no limits. You can expand off the planet under a Jupiter transit, which is why the planet is often called the "Gateway to Heaven." If something is going to burst (such as an artery) or overextend or go over the top in some way, it could happen under a supposedly lucky Jupiter transit, so be aware.

Those born under Virgo may find their best opportunities working with partners this year, as Jupiter will be transiting their seventh house of relationships.

During the summer months, Jupiter dips into Aries, which should give us a preview of happenings next year. In this headstrong fire sign, Jupiter promotes pioneering ventures, start-ups, all that is new and exciting. It can also promote impatience with more conservative forces, especially in early summer, which looks like the most volatile time this year. Jupiter returns to Pisces in September for the rest of the year.

Saturn in Libra

Saturn, the planet of limitation, testing, and restriction, will be moving through Libra, the sign of its exaltation and one of its most auspicious signs, this year. In Libra, Saturn can steady the scales of justice and promote balanced, responsible judgment. There should be much deliberation over duty, honor, and fairness, which will be ongoing for the next two years, balancing the more impulsive energy of other planets. Far-reaching new legislation and diplomatic moves are possible, perhaps resolving difficult international standoffs. As this placement works well with the humanitarian Aquarius influence of Neptune, there should be new hope of resolving conflicts. Previously, Saturn was in Libra during the early 1920s, the early 1950s, and again in the early 1980s.

Continuing Trends

Uranus and Neptune continue to do a kind of astrological dance called a "mutual reception." This is a supportive relationship where Uranus is in Pisces, the sign ruled by Neptune, while Neptune is in Aquarius, the sign ruled by Uranus. When this dance is over in 2011, it is likely that we will be living under very different political and social circumstances.

Uranus in Pisces and Aries

Uranus, known as the Great Awakener, tends to cause both upheaval and innovation in the sign it transits. This year, it is accompanied by Jupiter, as it is preparing to leave Pisces and dip its toe into Aries from June to mid-August. However, the Pisces influence will predominate, since Jupiter will be in Pisces most of the year.

During previous episodes of Uranus in Pisces, great religions and spiritual movements have come into being, most recently Mormonism and Christian Fundamentalism. In its most positive mode, Pisces promotes imagination and creativity, the art of illusion in theater and film, and the inspiration of great artists.

A water sign, Pisces is naturally associated with all things liquid—such as oceans, oil, and alcohol—and with those creatures that live in the water—fish, the fishing industry, fish habitats, and fish farming. Currently there is a great debate going on about overfishing, contamination of fish, and fish farming. The underdogs, the enslaved, and the disenfranchised should also benefit from Uranus in Pisces. Since Uranus is a disruptive influence that aims to challenge the status quo, the forces of nature that manifest now will most likely be in the Pisces area—the oceans, seas, and rivers. We have so far seen unprecedented rainy seasons, floods, mud slides, and disastrous hurricanes. Note that 2005's devastating Hurricane Katrina hit an area known for both the oil and fishing industries.

Pisces is associated with the prenatal phase of life, which is related to regenerative medicine. The controversy over embryonic stem cell research will continue to be debated, but recent developments may make the arguments moot. Petroleum issues, both in the oil-producing countries and offshore oil drilling, will come to a head. Uranus in Pisces suggests that development of new hydroelectric sources may provide the power we need to continue our current power-thirsty lifestyle.

As in previous eras, there should continue to be a flourishing of the arts. We are seeing many new artistic forms developing now, such as computer-created actors and special effects. The sky's the limit on this influence.

Those who have problems with Uranus are those who resist change, so the key is to embrace the future.

As Uranus prepares to enter Aries, an active fire sign, we should have a preview of coming influences over the summer.

Neptune in Aquarius

Neptune is a planet of imagination and creativity, but also of deception and illusion. Neptune is associated with hospitals, which have been the subject of much controversy. On the positive side, hospitals are acquiring cutting-edge technology. The atmosphere of many hospitals is already changing from the intimidating and sterile environment of the past to that of a health-promoting spa. Alternative therapies, such as massage, diet counseling, and aromatherapy, are becoming commonplace, which expresses this Neptune trend. New procedures in plastic surgery, also a Neptune glamour field, and antiaging therapies are giving the illusion of youth.

However, issues involving the expense and quality of health care, medication, and the evolving relationship between doctors, drug companies, and HMOs reflect a darker side of this trend.

Neptune is finishing up its stay in Aquarius and will begin its transit of Pisces, which it rules, in 2011. So this should be a time of transition into a much more Neptunian era, when Pisces-related issues will be of paramount importance.

Lunar Eclipses Are Movers and Shakers

Eclipses could shake up the financial markets and rock your world in 2010. The eclipses in late June and July are the ones to watch as they coincide with a close contact of Jupiter and Uranus in Aries. This is a potentially volatile time, so it would be wise to be prepared. As several recent studies have shown the stock market to be linked to the lunar cycle, track investments more carefully during this time.

New Celestial Bodies

Our solar system is getting crowded, as astronomers continue to discover new objects circling the sun. In addition to the familiar planets, there are dwarf planets, comets, cometoids, asteroids, and strange icy bodies in the Kuiper Belt beyond Neptune. A dwarf planet christened Eris, discovered in 2005, is now being observed and analyzed by astrologers. Eris was named after a goddess of discord and strife. In mythology, she was a troublemaker who made men think their opinions were right and others wrong. What an appropriate name for a planet discovered during a time of discord in the Middle East and elsewhere! Eris has a companion moon named Dysnomia for her daughter, described as a demon spirit of lawlessness. With mythological associations like these, we wonder what the effect of this mother-daughter duo will be. Once Eris's orbit is established, astrologers will track the impact of this planet on our horoscopes. Eris takes about 560 years to orbit the sun, which means its emphasis in a given astrological sign will affect several generations.

CHAPTER 2

How to Find Your Best Times This Year

It's no secret that some of the most powerful and famous people, from Julius Caesar to Queen Elizabeth I, from financier J. P. Morgan to Ronald Reagan, have consulted astrologers before they made their moves. If astrology helps the rich and famous stay on course through life's ups and downs, why not put it to work for you? Anyone can follow the planetary movements, and once you know how to interpret them, you won't need an expert to grasp the overall trends and make use of them.

For instance, when mischievous Mercury creates havoc with communications, it's time to back up your vital computer files, read between the lines of contracts, and be very patient with coworkers. When Venus passes through your sign, you're more alluring, so it's time to try out a new outfit or hairstyle, and then ask someone you'd like to know better to dinner. Venus timing can also help you charm clients with a stunning sales pitch or make an offer they won't refuse.

In this chapter you will find the tricks of astrological time management. You can find your red-letter days as well as which times to avoid. You will also learn how to make the magic of the moon work for you. Use the information in this chapter and the planet tables in this book and also the moon sign listings in your daily forecasts.

Here are the happenings to note on your agenda:

- Dates of your sun sign (high-energy period)
- The month previous to your sun sign (low-energy time)

- Dates of planets in your sign this year
- Full and new moons (Pay special attention when these fall in your sun sign!)
- Eclipses
- Moon in your sun sign every month, as well as moon in the opposite sign (listed in daily forecast)
- Mercury retrogrades
- Other retrograde periods

Your Most Proactive Time

Every birthday starts off a new cycle of solar energy for you. You should feel a new surge of vitality as the powerful sun enters your sign. This is the time when predominant energies are most favorable to you. So go for it! Start new projects, and make your big moves (especially when the new moon is in your sign, doubling your charisma). You'll get the recognition you deserve now, when everyone is attuned to your sun sign. Look in the tables in this book to see if other planets will also be passing through your sun sign at this time. Venus (love, beauty), Mars (energy, drive), and Mercury (communication, mental sharpness) reinforce the sun and give an extra boost to your life in the areas they affect. Venus will rev up your social and love life, making you seem especially attractive. Mars amplifies your energy and drive. Mercury fuels your brainpower and helps you communicate. Jupiter signals an especially lucky period of expansion.

There are two downtimes related to the sun. During the month before your birthday period, when you are winding up your annual cycle, you could be feeling especially vulnerable and depleted. So at that time get extra rest, watch your diet, and take it easy. Don't overstress yourself. Use this time to gear up for a big push when the sun enters your sign.

Another downtime is when the sun is in the sign opposite your sun sign (six months from your birthday). This is a reactive time, when the prevailing energies are very different from yours. You may feel at odds with the world. You'll have to work harder for recognition because people are not on your wavelength. However, this could be a good time to work on a team, in cooperation with others, or behind the scenes.

Be a Moon Watcher

The moon is a powerful tool to divine the mood of the moment. You can work with the moon in two ways. Plan by the sign the moon is in; plan by the phase of the moon. The sign will tell you the kind of activities that suit the moon's mood. The phase will tell you the best time to start or finish a certain activity.

Working with the phases of the moon is as easy as looking up at the night sky. During the new moon, when both the sun and moon are in the same sign, begin new ventures—especially activities that are favored by that sign. Then you'll utilize the powerful energies pulling you in the same direction. You'll be focused outward, toward action, and in a doing mode. Postpone breaking off, terminating, deliberating, or reflecting— activities that require introspection and passive work. These are better suited to a later moon phase.

Get your project under way during the first quarter. Then go public at the full moon, a time of high intensity, when feelings come out into the open. This is your time to shine—to express yourself. Be aware, however, that because pressures are being released, other people will also be letting off steam. Since confrontations are possible, take advantage of this time either to air grievances or to avoid arguments.

About three days after the full moon comes the disseminating phase, a time when the energy of the cycle begins to wind down. From the last quarter of the moon to the next new moon, it's a time to cut off unproductive relationships, do serious thinking, and focus on inward-directed activities.

You'll feel some new and full moons more strongly than others, especially when they fall in your sun sign. That full moon happens at your low-energy time of year, and is likely to be an especially stressful time in a relationship, when any hidden problems or unexpressed emotions could surface.

11

Full and New Moons in 2010

All dates are calculated for eastern standard time and eastern daylight time.

New Moon—January 15 in Capricorn (solar eclipse)
Full Moon—January 30 in Leo

New Moon—February 13 in Aquarius
Full Moon—February 28 in Virgo

New Moon—March 15 in Pisces
Full Moon—March 29 in Libra

New Moon—April 14 in Aries
Full Moon—April 28 in Scorpio

New Moon—May 13 in Taurus
Full Moon—May 27 in Sagittarius

New Moon—June 12 in Gemini
Full Moon—June 26 in Capricorn (lunar eclipse)

New Moon—July 11 in Cancer (solar eclipse)
Full Moon—July 25 in Aquarius

New Moon—August 9 in Leo
Full Moon—August 24 in Pisces

New Moon—September 8 in Virgo
Full Moon—September 23 in Aries

New Moon—October 7 in Libra
Full Moon—October 22 in Aries

New Moon—November 5 in Scorpio
Full Moon—November 21 in Taurus

New Moon—December 5 in Sagittarius
Full Moon—December 21 in Gemini (lunar eclipse)

Timing by the Moon's Sign

To forecast the daily emotional "weather," to determine your monthly high and low days, or to synchronize your activities with the cycles of the moon, take note of the moon's sign under your daily forecast at the end of the book. Here are some of the activities favored and the moods you are likely to encounter under each moon sign.

Moon in Aries: Get Moving

The new moon in Aries is an ideal time to start new projects. Everyone is pushy, raring to go, rather impatient, and short-tempered. Leave details and follow-up for later. Competitive sports or martial arts are great ways to let off steam. Quiet types could use some assertiveness, but it's a great day for dynamos. Be careful not to step on too many toes.

Moon in Taurus: Lay the Foundations for Success

Do solid, methodical tasks like follow-through or backup work. Make investments, buy real estate, do appraisals, or do some hard bargaining. Attend to your property. Get out in the country or spend some time in your garden. Enjoy creature comforts, music, a good dinner, or sensual lovemaking. Forget starting a diet—this is a day when you'll feel self-indulgent.

Moon in Gemini: Communicate

Talk means action today. Telephone, write letters, and fax! Make new contacts; stay in touch with steady customers. You can juggle lots of tasks today. It's a great time for mental activity of any kind. Don't try to pin people down—they too are feeling restless. Keep it light. Flirtations and socializing are good. Watch gossip—and don't give away secrets.

13

Moon in Cancer: Pay Attention to Loved Ones

This is a moody, sensitive, emotional time. People respond to personal attention and mothering. Stay at home, have a family dinner, or call your mother. Nostalgia, memories, and psychic powers are heightened. You'll want to hang on to people and things (don't clean out your closets now). You could have shrewd insights into what others really need and want. Pay attention to dreams, intuition, and gut reactions.

Moon in Leo: Be Confident

Everybody is in a much more confident, warm, generous mood. It's a good day to ask for a raise, show what you can do, or dress like a star. People will respond to flattery and enjoy a bit of drama and theater. You may be extravagant, treat yourself royally, and show off a bit—but don't break the bank! Be careful not to promise more than you can deliver.

Moon in Virgo: Be Practical

Do practical, down-to-earth chores. Review your budget, make repairs, or be an efficiency expert. Not a day to ask for a raise. Tend to personal care and maintenance. Have a health checkup, go on a diet, or buy vitamins or health food. Make your home spotless. Take care of details and piled-up chores. Reorganize your work and life so they run more smoothly and efficiently. Save money. Be prepared for others to be in critical, fault-finding moods.

Moon in Libra: Be Diplomatic

Attend to legal matters. Negotiate contracts. Arbitrate. Do things with your favorite partner. Socialize. Be romantic. Buy a special gift or a beautiful object. Decorate yourself or your surroundings. Buy new clothes. Throw a party. Have an elegant, romantic evening. Smooth over any ruffled feathers. Avoid confrontations. Stick to civilized discussions.

Moon in Scorpio: Solve Problems

This is a day to do things with passion. You'll have excellent concentration and focus. Try not to get too intense emotionally. Avoid sharp exchanges with loved ones. Others may tend to go to extremes, get jealous, or overreact. Great for troubleshooting, problem solving, research, scientific work—and making love. Pay attention to those psychic vibes.

Moon in Sagittarius: Sell and Motivate

A great time for travel, philosophical discussions, or setting long-range career goals. Work out, do sports, or buy athletic equipment. Others will be feeling upbeat, exuberant, and adventurous. Taking risks is favored. You may feel like gambling, betting on the horses, visiting a local casino, or buying a lottery ticket. Teaching, writing, and spiritual activities also get the green light. Relax outdoors. Take care of animals.

Moon in Capricorn: Get Organized

You can accomplish a lot now, so get on the ball! Attend to business. Issues concerning your basic responsibilities, duties, family, and elderly parents could crop up. You'll be expected to deliver on promises. Weed out the deadwood from your life. Get a dental checkup. Not a good day for gambling or taking risks.

Moon in Aquarius: Join the Group

A great day for doing things with groups—clubs, meetings, outings, politics, or parties. Campaign for your candidate. Work for a worthy cause. Deal with larger issues that affect humanity—the environment and metaphysical questions. Buy a computer or electronic gadget. Watch TV. Wear something outrageous. Try something you've never done before. Present an original idea. Don't stick to a rigid schedule; go with the flow. Take a class in meditation, mind control, or yoga.

Moon in Pisces: Be Creative

This can be a very creative day, so let your imagination work overtime. Film, theater, music, and ballet could inspire you. Spend some time resting and reflecting, reading, or writing poetry. Daydreams can also be profitable. Help those less fortunate. Lend a listening ear to someone who may be feeling blue. Don't overindulge in self-pity or escapism. People are especially vulnerable to substance abuse. Turn your thoughts to romance and someone special.

Eclipses Clear the Air

Eclipses can bring on milestones in your life, if they aspect a key point in your horoscope. In general, they shake up the status quo, bringing hidden areas out into the open. During this time, problems you've been avoiding or have brushed aside can surface to demand your attention. A good coping strategy is to accept whatever comes up as a challenge that could make a positive difference in your life. And don't forget the power of your sense of humor. If you can laugh at something, you'll never be afraid of it.

When the natural rhythms of the sun and moon are disturbed, it's best to postpone important activities. Be sure to mark eclipse days on your calendar, especially if the eclipse falls in your birth sign. This year, those born under Capricorn, Cancer, and Gemini should take special note of the feelings that arise. If your moon is in one of these signs, you may be especially affected. With lunar eclipses, some possibilities could be a break from attachments, or the healing of an illness or substance abuse that was triggered by the subconscious. The temporary event could be a healing time, when you gain perspective. During solar eclipses, when you might be in a highly subjective state, pay attention to the hidden subconscious patterns that surface, the emotional truth that is revealed at this time.

The effect of the eclipse can reverberate for some time, often months after the event. But it is especially important to stay cool and make no major moves during the period known as the shadow of the eclipse, which begins about a week before and lasts until at least three days after the eclipse. After three days, the daily rhythms should return to normal, and you can proceed with business as usual.

This Year's Eclipse Dates

January 15: Solar Eclipse in Capricorn
June 26: Lunar Eclipse in Capricorn
July 11: Solar Eclipse in Cancer
December 21: Lunar Eclipse in Gemini

Retrogrades: When the Planets Seem to Backstep

All the planets, except for the sun and moon, have times when they appear to move backward—or retrograde—as it seems from our point of view on Earth. At these times, planets do not work as they normally do. So it's best to "take a break" from that planet's energies in our life and to do some work on an inner level.

Mercury Retrograde: The Key Is in "Re"

Mercury goes into retrograde most often, and its effects can be especially irritating. When it reaches a short distance ahead of the sun several times a year, it seems to move backward from our point of view. Astrologers often compare retrograde motion to the optical illusion that occurs when we ride on a train that passes another train traveling at a different speed—the second train appears to be moving in reverse.

What this means to you is that the Mercury-ruled areas of your life—analytical thought processes, communications, scheduling—are subject to all kinds of confusion. Be prepared. Communications equipment can break down. Schedules may be changed on short notice. People are late for appointments or don't show up at all. Traffic is terrible. Major purchases malfunction, don't work out, or get delivered in the wrong color. Letters don't arrive or are delivered to the wrong address. Employees will make errors that have to be corrected later. Contracts don't work out or must be renegotiated.

Since most of us can't put our lives on "hold" during Mercury retrogrades, we should learn to tame the trickster and make it work for us. The key is in the prefix re-. This is the time to go back over things in your life, reflect on what you've done during the previous months. Now you can get deeper insights, and spot errors you've missed. So take time to review and re-evaluate what has happened. Rest and reward yourself—it's a good time to take a vacation, especially if you revisit a favorite place. Reorganize your work and finish up projects that are backed up. Clean out your desk and closets. Throw away what you can't recycle. If you must sign contracts or agreements, do so with a contingency clause that lets you reevaluate the terms later.

Postpone major purchases or commitments for the time being. Don't get married (unless you're remarrying the same person). Try not to rely on other people keeping appointments, contracts, or agreements to the letter; have several alternatives. Double-check and read between the lines. Don't buy anything connected with communications or transportation (if you must, be sure to cover yourself).

Mercury retrograding through your sun sign will intensify its effect on your life.

If Mercury was retrograde when you were born, you may be one of the lucky people who don't suffer the frustrations of this period. If so, your mind probably works in a very intuitive, insightful way.

The sign in which Mercury is retrograding can give you an idea of what's in store—as well as the sun signs that will be especially challenged.

Mercury Retrogrades in 2010

Mercury has four retrograde periods this year, since it will be retrograde as the year begins. During the retrograde periods, it will be especially important to watch all activities which involve mental processes and communication.

December 26, 2009, to January 15 in Capricorn
April 17 to May 11 in Taurus
August 20 to September 12 in Virgo
December 10 to December 30 from Capricorn to Sagittarius

Venus Retrograde: Relationships Are Affected

Retrograding Venus can cause your relationships to take a backward step, or you may feel that a key relationship is on hold. Singles may be especially lonely, yet find it difficult to connect with someone special. If you wish to make amends in an already troubled relationship, make peaceful overtures at this time. You may feel more extravagant or overindulge in shopping or sweet treats. Shopping till you drop and buying what you cannot afford are bad at this time. It's *not* a good time to redecorate—you'll hate the color of the walls later. Postpone getting a new hairstyle. It only lasts for a relatively short time this year; however, Scorpio and Libra should take special note.

Venus Retrogrades in 2010

Venus retrogrades from October 8 to November 18, from Scorpio to Libra.

Use the Power of Mars

Mars shows how and when to get where you want to go. Timing your moves with Mars on your side can give you a big push. On the other hand, pushing Mars the wrong way can guarantee that you'll run into frustrations around every corner. Your best times to forge ahead are during the weeks when Mars is traveling through your sun sign or your Mars sign (look these up in the planet tables in this book). Also consider times when Mars is in a compatible sign (fire signs with air signs, or earth signs with water signs). You'll be sure to have planetary power on your side.

Mars began a lengthy retrograde in extravagant Leo on December 20, 2009. Your patience may have been tested more than usual during last year's festivities. The Mars retrograde in Leo will last until March 10, during which time there are sure to be repercussions on the international level.

Mars Retrogrades in 2010

Mars turns retrograde in Leo on December 20, 2009, until March 10, 2010.

When Other Planets Retrograde

The slower-moving planets stay retrograde for many months at a time (Jupiter, Saturn, Neptune, Uranus, and Pluto).

When Saturn is retrograde, it's an uphill battle with self-discipline. You may not be in the mood for work. You may feel more like hanging out at the beach than getting things done.

Neptune retrograde promotes a dreamy escapism from reality, when you may feel you're in a fog (Pisces will feel this, especially).

Uranus retrograde may mean setbacks in areas where there have been sudden changes, when you may be forced to regroup or reevaluate the situation.

Pluto retrograde is a time to work on establishing proportion and balance in areas where there have been recent dramatic transformations.

When the planets move forward again, there's a shift in the atmosphere. Activities connected with each planet start moving ahead; plans that were stalled get rolling. Make a special note of those days on your calendar and proceed accordingly.

Other Retrogrades in 2010

The five slower-moving planets all go retrograde in 2010.

Jupiter retrogrades from July 23 in Aries to November 18 in Pisces.

Saturn retrogrades from January 13 in Libra to May 30 in Virgo.

Uranus retrogrades from July 5 in Aries to December 5 in Pisces.

Neptune retrogrades from May 31 to November 7 in Aquarius.

Pluto retrogrades from April 6 to September 13 in Capricorn.

CHAPTER 3

Introduction to Astrology

Astrology is a powerful tool that can help you discover and access your personal potential, understand others and interpret events in your life and the world at large. You don't have to be an expert in astrology to put it to work for you. It's easy to pick up enough basic knowledge to go beyond the realm of your sun sign into the deeper areas of this fascinating subject, which combines science, art, spirituality, and psychology. Perhaps from here you'll upgrade your knowledge with computer software that calculates charts for everyone you know in a nanosecond or join an astrology group in your city.

In this chapter, we'll introduce you to the basics of astrology. You'll be able to define a sign and figure out why astrologers say what they do about each sign. As you look at your astrological chart, you'll have a good idea of what's going on in each portion of the horoscope. Let's get started.

Know the Difference Between Signs and Constellations

Most readers know their signs, but many often confuse them with constellations. *Signs* are actually a type of celestial real estate, located on the *zodiac*, an imaginary 360-degree belt circling the earth. This belt is divided into twelve equal 30-degree portions, which are the *signs*. There's a lot of confusion about the difference between the *signs* and the *constellations* of the zodiac, patterns of stars which originally marked the twelve divisions, like signposts. Though a *sign* is named after the *constellation* that once marked the same area, the constellations are no longer in the same place relative to the earth that they were many centuries ago. Over hundreds of years, the earth's orbit has shifted, so that from our point of view here on earth, the constellations seem to have moved. However, the signs remain in place. (Most Western astrology uses the twelve-equal-part division of the zodiac, though there are some other methods of astrology that still use the constellations instead of the signs.)

Most people think of themselves in terms of their sun sign. A *sun sign* refers to the sign the sun is orbiting through at a given moment (from our point of view here on earth). For instance, if someone says, "I'm an Aries," the sun was passing through Aries when that person was born. However, there are nine other planets (plus asteroids, fixed stars, and sensitive points) that also form our total astrological personality, and some or many of these will be located in other signs. No one is completely "Aries," with all their astrological components in one sign! (Please note that, in astrology, the sun and moon are usually referred to as "planets," though of course they're not. Though there is some controversy over Pluto, it is still called a "planet" by astrologers.)

As we mentioned before, the sun signs are *places* on the zodiac. They do not *do* anything (the planets are the doers). However, they are associated with many things, depending on their location on the zodiac.

How Do We Define a Sign's Characteristics?

The definitions of the signs evolved systematically from four interrelated components: a sign's element, its quality, its polarity or sex, and its order in the progression of the zodiac. All these factors work together to tell us what the sign is like.

The system is magically mathematical: the number 12—as in the twelve signs of the zodiac—is divisible by 4, by 3, and by

2. There are four elements, three qualities, and two polarities, which follow one another in sequence around the zodiac.

The four elements (earth, air, fire, and water) are the building blocks of astrology. The use of an element to describe a sign probably dates from man's first attempts to categorize what he saw. Ancient sages believed that all things were composed of combinations of these basic elements—earth, air, fire, and water. This included the human character, which was fiery/choleric, earthy/melancholy, airy/sanguine, or watery/phlegmatic. The elements also correspond to our emotional (water), physical (earth), mental (air), and spiritual (fire) natures. The energies of each of the elements were then observed to relate to the time of year when the sun was passing through a certain segment of the zodiac.

Those born with the sun in fire signs—Aries, Leo, Sagittarius—embody the characteristics of that element. Optimism, warmth, hot tempers, enthusiasm, and "spirit" are typical of these signs. Taurus, Virgo, and Capricorn are "earthy"—more grounded, physical, materialistic, organized, and deliberate than fire sign people. Air sign people—Gemini, Libra, and Aquarius—are mentally oriented communicators. Water signs—Cancer, Scorpio, and Pisces—are emotional, sensitive, and creative.

Think of what each element does to the others: water puts out fire or evaporates under heat. Air fans the flames or blows them out. Earth smothers fire, drifts and erodes with too much wind, and becomes mud or fertile soil with water. Those are often perfect analogies for the relationships between people of different sun-sign elements. This astrochemistry was one of the first ways man described his relationships. Fortunately, no one is entirely "air" or "water." We all have a bit, or a lot, of each element in our horoscopes. It is this unique mix that defines each astrological personality.

Within each element, there are three qualities that describe types of behavior associated with the sign. Those of cardinal signs are activists, go-getters. These four signs—Aries, Cancer, Libra, and Capricorn—begin each season. Fixed signs, which happen in the middle of the season, are associated with builders and stabilizers. You'll find that Taurus, Leo, Scorpio, and Aquarius are usually gifted with concentration, stamina, and focus. Mutable signs—Gemini, Virgo, Sagittarius, and Pisces—fall at the end of each season and thus are considered catalysts for change. People born under mutable signs are flexible and adaptable.

The polarity of a sign is either its positive or negative "charge." It can be masculine, active, positive, and yang, like air or fire signs, or it can be feminine, reactive, negative, and yin, like the water and earth signs. The polarities alternate, moving energy around the zodiac like the poles of a battery.

Finally, we consider the sign's place in the order of the zodiac. This is vital to the balance of all the forces and the transmission of energy moving through the signs. You may have noticed that your sign is quite different from your neighboring sign on either side. Yet each seems to grow out of its predecessor like links in a chain and transmits a synthesis of energy gathered along the "chain" to the following sign, beginning with the fire-powered positive charge of Aries.

How the Signs Add Up

SIGN	ELEMENT	QUALITY	POLARITY	PLACE
Aries	fire	cardinal	masculine	first
Taurus	earth	fixed	feminine	second
Gemini	air	mutable	masculine	third
Cancer	water	cardinal	feminine	fourth
Leo	fire	fixed	masculine	fifth
Virgo	earth	mutable	feminine	sixth
Libra	air	cardinal	masculine	seventh
Scorpio	water	fixed	feminine	eighth
Sagittarius	fire	mutable	masculine	ninth
Capricorn	earth	cardinal	feminine	tenth
Aquarius	air	fixed	masculine	eleventh
Pisces	water	mutable	feminine	twelfth

Each Sign Has a Special Planet

Each sign has a "ruling" planet that is most compatible with its energies. Mars adds its fiery assertive characteristics to Aries. The sensual beauty and comfort-loving side of Venus rules Taurus, whereas the idealistic side of Venus rules Libra. Quick-moving Mercury rules two mutable signs, Gemini and Virgo. Its mental agility belongs to Gemini while its analytical side is best expressed in Virgo. The changeable emotional moon is associated with Cancer, while the outgoing Leo personality is ruled by the sun. Scorpio originally shared Mars, but when Pluto was discovered in the last century, its powerful magnetic energies were deemed more suitable to the intense vibrations of the fixed water sign Scorpio. Though Pluto has, as of this writing, been downgraded, it is still considered by astrologers to be a powerful force in the horoscope. Disciplined Capricorn is ruled by Saturn, and expansive Sagittarius by Jupiter. Unpredictable Aquarius is ruled by Uranus and creative, imaginative Pisces by Neptune. In a horoscope, if a planet is placed in the sign it rules, it is sure to be especially powerful.

The Layout of a Horoscope Chart

A horoscope chart is a map of the heavens at a given moment in time. It looks like a wheel with twelve spokes. In between each of the "spokes" is a section called a *house*.

Each house deals with a different area of life and is influenced by a special sign and a planet. Astrologers look at the houses to tell in what area of life an event is happening or about to happen.

The house is governed by the sign passing over the spoke (or cusp of the house) at that particular moment. Though the first house is naturally associated with Aries and Mars, it would also have an additional Capricorn influence if that sign was passing over the house cusp at the time the chart was cast. The sequence of the houses starts with the first house located at the left center spoke (or the number 9 position, if you were reading a clock). The houses are then read *counterclockwise* around the chart, with the fourth house at the bottom of the chart, the tenth house at the top or twelve o'clock position.

Where do the planets belong? Around the horoscope, planets are placed within the houses according to their location at the time of the chart. That is why it is so important to have an accurate time; with no specific time, the planets have no specific location in the houses and one cannot determine which area of life they will apply to. Since the signs move across the houses as the earth turns, planets in a house will naturally intensify the importance of that house. The house that contains the sun is naturally one of the most prominent.

The First House: Self

The sign passing over the first house at the time of your birth is known as your ascendant, or rising sign. The first house is the house of "firsts"—the first impression you make, how you initiate matters, the image you choose to project. This is where you advertise yourself, where you project your personality. Planets that fall here will intensify the way you come across to others. It is the home of Aries and the planet Mars.

The Second House: The Material You

This house is where you experience the material world, what you value. Here are your attitudes about money, possessions, and finances, as well as your earning and spending capacity. On a deeper level, this house reveals your sense of self-worth, the inner values that draw wealth in various forms. It is the natural home of Taurus and the planet Venus.

The Third House: Your Thinking Process

This house describes how you communicate with others, how you reach out to others nearby and interact with the immediate environment. It shows how your thinking process works and the way you express your thoughts. Are you articulate or tongue-tied? Can you think on your feet? This house also shows your first relationships, your experiences with brothers and sisters, as well as how you deal with people close to you, such as your neighbors or pals. It's where you take short trips, write letters, or use the telephone. It shows how your mind works in terms of left-brain logical and analytical functions. It is the home of Gemini and the planet Mercury.

The Fourth House: Your Home Life

The fourth house shows the foundation of life, the psychological underpinnings. Located at the bottom of the chart, this house shows how you are nurtured and made to feel secure—your roots! It shows your early home environment and the circumstances at the end of your life (your final "home"), as well as the place you call home now. Astrologers look here for information about the parental nurturers in your life. It is the home of Cancer and the moon.

The Fifth House: Your Self-Expression

The Leo house is where the creative potential develops. Here you express yourself and procreate, in the sense that children are outgrowths of your creative ability. But this house most represents your inner childlike self, who delights in play. If your inner security has been established by the time you reach this house, you are now free to have fun, romance, and love affairs and to give of yourself. This is also the place astrologers look for playful love affairs, flirtations, and brief romantic encounters (rather than long-term commitments). It is the home of Leo and the sun.

The Sixth House: Care and Maintenance

The sixth house has been called the "care and maintenance" department. This house shows how you take care of your body and organize yourself to perform efficiently in the world. Here is where you get things done, where you look after others and fulfill service duties, such as taking care of pets. Here is what you do to survive on a day-to-day basis. The sixth house demands order in your life; otherwise there would be chaos. The house is your "job" (as opposed to your career, which is the domain of the tenth house), your diet, and your health and fitness regimens. It is the home of Virgo and the planet Mercury.

The Seventh House: Your Relationships

This house shows your attitude toward your partners and those with whom you enter commitments, contracts, or agreements. Here is the way you relate to others, as well as your close, intimate, one-on-one relationships (including open enemies—those you "face off" with). Open hostilities, lawsuits, divorces, and marriages happen here. If the first house represents the "I," the seventh or opposite house is the "not I"—the complementary partner you attract by the way you come across. If you are having trouble with partnerships, consider what you are attracting by the energies of your first and seventh house. It is the home of Libra and the planet Venus.

The Eighth House: Your Power House

The eighth house refers to how you merge with something or someone, and how you handle power and control. This is one of the most mysterious and powerful houses, where your energy transforms itself from "I" to "we." As you give up power and control by uniting with something or someone, two kinds of energies merge and become something greater, leading to a regeneration of the self on a higher level. Here are your attitudes toward sex, shared resources, and taxes (what you share with the government). Because this house involves what belongs to others, you face issues of control and power struggles, or undergo a deep psychological transformation as you bond with another. Here you transcend yourself through dreams, drugs, and occult or psychic experiences that reflect the collective unconscious. It is the home of Scorpio and the planet Pluto.

The Ninth House: Your Worldview

The ninth house shows your search for wisdom and higher knowledge: your belief system. As the third house represents the "lower mind," its opposite on the wheel, the ninth house, is the "higher mind," the abstract, intuitive, spiritual mind that asks "big" questions, like "Why we are here?" After the third house has explored what was close at hand, the ninth stretches out to broaden you mentally with higher education and travel. Here you stretch spiritually with religious activity. Since you are concerned with how everything is related, you tend to push boundaries and take risks. Here is where you express your ideas in a book or thesis, where you pontificate, philosophize, or preach. It is the home of Sagittarius and the planet Jupiter.

The Tenth House: Your Public Life

The tenth house is associated with your public life and high-profile activities. Located directly overhead at the "high noon" position on the horoscope wheel, this is the most "visible" house in the chart, the one where the world sees you. It deals with your career (but not your routine "job") and your reputation. Here is where you go public, take on responsibilities (as opposed to the fourth house, where you stay home). This will affect the career you choose and your "public relations." This house is also associated with your father figure or the main authority figure in your life. It is the home of Capricorn and the planet Saturn.

The Eleventh House: Your Social Concerns

The eleventh house is where you extend yourself to a group, a goal, or a belief system. This house is where you define what you really want: the kinds of friends you have, your political affiliations, and the kind of groups you identify with as an equal. Here is where you become concerned with "what other people think" or where you rebel against social conventions. It's where you become a socially conscious humanitarian or a partying social butterfly. It's where you look to others to stimulate you and discover your kinship to the rest of humanity. The sign on this house can help you understand what you gain and lose from friendships. It is the home of Aquarius and the planet Uranus.

The Twelfth House:
Where You Become Selfless

Old-fashioned astrologers used to put a rather negative spin on this house, calling it the "house of self-undoing." When we "undo ourselves," we surrender control, boundaries, limits, and rules. The twelfth house is where the boundaries between yourself and others become blurred and you become selfless. But instead of being self-undoing, the twelfth house can be a place of great creativity and talent. It is the place where you can tap into the collective unconscious, where your imagination is limitless.

In your trip around the zodiac, you've gone from the "I" of self-assertion in the first house to the final house, which symbolizes the dissolution that happens before rebirth. The twelfth house is where accumulated experiences are processed in the unconscious. Spiritually oriented astrologers look to this house for evidence of past lives and karma. Places where we go for solitude or to do spiritual or reparatory work belong here, such as retreats, religious institutions, or hospitals. Here is also where we withdraw from society voluntarily or involuntarily, and where we are put in prison because of antisocial activity. Selfless giving through charitable acts is part of this house, as is helpless receiving or dependence on charity.

In your daily life, the twelfth house reveals your deepest intimacies, your best-kept secrets, especially those you hide from yourself and repress deep in the unconscious. It is where we surrender a sense of a separate self to a deep feeling of wholeness, such as selfless service in religion or any activity that involves merging with the greater whole. Many sports stars have important planets in the twelfth house, which enable them to play in the zone, finding an inner, almost mystical, strength that transcends their limits. The twelfth house is the home of Pisces and the planet Neptune.

Which Are the Most Powerful Houses?

Houses are stronger or weaker depending on how many planets are inhabiting them. If there are many planets in a given house, it follows that the activities of that house will be especially important in your life. If the planet that rules the house is also located there, this too adds power to the house. The most powerful houses are the first, fourth, seventh, and tenth. These are the houses on "the angles" of a horoscope.

CHAPTER 4

The Moon: Your Inner Light

In some astrology-conscious lands, the moon is given as much importance in a horoscope as the sun. Astrologers often refer to these two bodies as the "lights," an appropriate description, since the sun and moon are not planets, but a star and a satellite. But it is also true that these two bodies shed the most "light" on a horoscope reading.

As the sun shines *out* in a horoscope, revealing the personality, the moon shines *in*. The sign the moon was transiting at the time of your birth reveals much about the inner you, secrets like what you really care about, what makes you feel comfortable and secure. It represents the receptive, reflective, female, nurturing self. It also reflects the one who nurtured you, the mother or mother figure in your chart. In a man's chart, the moon position describes his receptive, emotional, yin side, as well as the woman in his life who will have the deepest effect, usually his mother. (Venus reveals the kind of woman who will attract him physically.)

The moon is more at home in some signs than in others. It rules maternal Cancer and is exalted in Taurus—both comforting, home-loving signs where the natural emotional energies of the moon are easily and productively expressed. But when the moon is in the opposite signs—Capricorn and Scorpio—it leaves the comfortable nest and deals with emotional issues of power and achievement in the outside world. If you were born with the moon in one of these signs, you may find your emotional role in life more challenging.

To determine your moon sign, it is worthwhile to have an accurate horoscope cast, either by an astrologer, a computer program, or one of the online astrology sites that offer free charts. Since detailed moon tables are too extensive for this book, check through the following listing to find the moon sign that feels most familiar.

Moon in Aries

This placement makes you both independent and ardent. You are an idealist, and you tend to fall in and out of love easily. You love a challenge but could cool once your quarry is captured. Your emotional reactions are fast and fiery, quickly expressed and quickly forgotten. You may not think before expressing your feelings. It's not easy to hide how you feel. Channeling all your emotional energy could be one of your big challenges.

    Celebrity example: Angelina Jolie

Moon in Taurus

You are a sentimental soul who is very fond of the good life and gravitates toward solid, secure relationships. You like displays of affection and creature comforts—all the tangible trappings of a cozy, safe, calm atmosphere. You are sensual and steady emotionally, but very stubborn, possessive, and determined. You can't be pushed and tend to dislike changes. You should make an effort to broaden your horizons and to take a risk sometimes. You may become very attached to your home turf, your garden, and your possessions. You may also be a collector of objects that are meaningful to you.

    Celebrity example: Prince Charles

Moon in Gemini

You crave mental stimulation and variety in life, which you usually get via a varied social life, the excitement of flirtation, or multiple professional involvements. You may marry more than once and have a rather chaotic emotional life due to your difficulty with commitment and settling down, as well as your need to be constantly on the go. (Be sure to find a partner who is as outgoing as you are.) You will have to learn at some point to focus your energies because you tend to be somewhat fragmented—to do two things at once, to have two homes, or even to have two lovers. If you can find a creative way to express your many-faceted nature, you'll be ahead of the game.

Celebrity example: Jim Carrey

Moon in Cancer

This is the most powerful lunar position, which is sure to make a deep imprint on your character. Your needs are very much associated with your reaction to the needs of others. You are very sensitive, caring, and self-protective, though some of you may mask this with a hard shell, like the moon-sensitive crab. This placement also gives an excellent memory, keen intuition, and an uncanny ability to perceive the needs of others. All of the lunar phases will affect you, especially full moons and eclipses, so you would do well to mark them on your calendar. Because you're happiest at home, you may work at home or turn your office into a second home, where you can nurture and comfort people. (You may tend to mother the world.) With natural psychic, intuitive ability, you might be drawn to occult work in some way. Or you may get professionally involved with providing food and shelter to others.

Celebrity example: Tom Cruise

Moon in Leo

This warm, passionate moon takes everything to heart. You are attracted to all that is noble, generous, and aristocratic in life (and you may be a bit of a snob). You have an innate ability to take command emotionally, but you do need strong support, loyalty, and loud applause from those you love. You are possessive of your loved ones and your turf and will roar if anyone threatens to take over your territory.

Celebrity example: Paul McCartney

Moon in Virgo

You are rather cool until you decide if others measure up. But once someone or something meets your high standards, you hold up your end of the arrangement perfectly. You may, in fact, drive yourself too hard to attain some notion of perfection. Try to be a bit easier on yourself and others. Don't always act the censor! You love to be the teacher; you are drawn to situations where you can change others for the better, but sometimes you must learn to accept others for what they are—enjoy what you have!

Celebrity example: John F. Kennedy

Moon in Libra

Like other air-sign moons, you think before you feel. Therefore, you may not immediately recognize the emotional needs of others. However, you are relationship-oriented and may find it difficult to be alone or to do things alone. After you have learned emotional balance by leaning on yourself first, you can have excellent partnerships. It is best for you to avoid extremes, which set your scales swinging and can make your love life precarious. You thrive in a rather conservative, traditional, romantic relationship, where you receive attention and flattery—but not possessiveness—from your partner. You'll be your most charming in an elegant, harmonious atmosphere.

Celebrity example: Leonardo DiCaprio

Moon in Scorpio

This is a moon that enjoys and responds to intense, passionate feelings. You may go to extremes and have a very dramatic emotional life, full of ardor, suspicion, jealousy, and obsession. It would be much healthier to channel your need for power and control into meaningful work. This is a good position for anyone in the fields of medicine, police work, research, the occult, psychoanalysis, or intuitive work, because life-and-death situations don't faze you. However, you do take personal disappointments very hard.

Celebrity example: Elizabeth Taylor

Moon in Sagittarius

You take life's ups and downs with good humor and the proverbial grain of salt. You'll love 'em and leave 'em or take off on a great adventure at a moment's notice. "Born free" could be your slogan. Attracted by the exotic, you have mental and physical wanderlust. You may be too much in search of new mental and spiritual stimulation to ever settle down.

Celebrity example: Donald Trump

Moon in Capricorn

Are you ever accused of being too cool and calculating? You have an earthy side, but you take prestige and position very seriously. Your strong drive to succeed extends to your romantic life, where you will be devoted to improving your lifestyle and rising to the top. A structured situation where you can advance methodically makes you feel wonderfully secure. You may be attracted to someone older or very much younger or from a different social world. It may be difficult to look at the lighter side of emotional relationships. Though this moon is placed in the sign to your detriment, the good news is that you tend to be very dutiful and responsible to those you care for.

Celebrity example: Brad Pitt

Moon in Aquarius

You are a people collector with many friends of all backgrounds. You are happiest surrounded by people, and you may feel uneasy when left alone. Though you usually stay friends with lovers, intense emotions and demanding one-on-one relationships turn you off. You don't like anything to be too rigid or scheduled. Though tolerant and understanding, you can be emotionally unpredictable; you may opt for an unconventional love life. With plenty of space, you will be able to sustain relationships with liberal, freedom-loving types.

Celebrity example: Princess Diana

Moon in Pisces

You are very responsive and empathetic to others, especially if they have problems or are the underdog. (Be on guard against attracting too many people with sob stories.) You'll be happiest if you can express your creative imagination in the arts or in the spiritual or healing professions. Because you may tend to escape in fantasies or overreact to the moods of others, you need an emotional anchor to help you keep a firm foothold in reality. Steer clear of too much escapism (especially in alcohol) or reclusiveness. Places near water soothe your moods. Working in a field that gives you emotional variety will also help you be productive.

Celebrity example: Elvis Presley

CHAPTER 5

The Planets: The Power of Ten

If you know a person's sun sign, you can learn some very useful generic information, but when you know the placement of all ten planets (eight planets plus the sun and moon), you've got a much more accurate profile of the person's character. Then the subject of the horoscope becomes a unique individual, as well as a member of a certain sun sign. You'll discover what makes him angry (Mars), pleased (Venus), or fearful (Saturn).

The planets are the doers of the horoscope, each representing a basic force in life. The sign and house where the planet is located indicate how and where its force will operate. For a moment, think of the horoscope as real estate. Prime property is close to the rising sign or at the top of the chart. If two or more planets are grouped together in one sign, they usually operate like a team, playing off each other, rather than expressing their energy singularly. But a loner, a planet that stands far away from the others, is usually outstanding and often calls the shots.

The sign of a planet also has a powerful influence. In some signs, the planet's energies are very much at home and can easily express themselves. In others, the planet has to work harder and is slightly out of sorts. The sign that most corresponds to the planet's energies is said to be ruled by that planet and obviously is the best place for that planet to be. The next best place is a sign where it is exalted, or especially harmonious. On the other hand, there are places in the horoscope where a planet has to stretch itself to play its role, such as the sign opposite a planet's rulership, which embodies the opposite area of life, and the sign opposite its exaltation. However, a planet that must work harder can also be more complete, because it must grow to meet the challenges of living in a more difficult sign. Like world leaders who've had to struggle for greatness, this planet may actually develop strength and character.

Here's a list of the best places for each planet to be. Note that, as new planets were discovered in the last century, they replaced the traditional rulers of signs which best complemented their energies.

ARIES—Mars
TAURUS—Venus, in its most sensual form
GEMINI—Mercury, in its communicative role
CANCER—the moon
LEO—the sun
VIRGO—also Mercury, this time in its more critical capacity
LIBRA—also Venus, in its more aesthetic, judgmental form
SCORPIO—Pluto, co-ruled by Mars
SAGITTARIUS—Jupiter
CAPRICORN—Saturn
AQUARIUS—Uranus, replacing Saturn, its original ruler
PISCES—Neptune, replacing Jupiter, its original ruler

Those who have many planets in exalted signs are lucky indeed, for here is where the planet can accomplish the most and be its most influential and creative.

SUN—exalted in Aries, where its energy creates action
MOON—exalted in Taurus, where instincts and reactions operate on a highly creative level
MERCURY—exalted in Aquarius, where it can reach analytical heights
VENUS—exalted in Pisces, a sign whose sensitivity encourages love and creativity
MARS—exalted in Capricorn, a sign that puts energy to work productively
JUPITER—exalted in Cancer, where it encourages nurturing and growth
SATURN—at home in Libra, where it steadies the scales of justice and promotes balanced, responsible judgment

URANUS—powerful in Scorpio, where it promotes transformation

NEPTUNE—especially favored in Cancer, where it gains the security to transcend to a higher state

PLUTO—exalted in Pisces, where it dissolves the old cycle, to make way for transition to the new

The Personal Planets: Mercury, Venus, and Mars

These planets work in your immediate personal life.

Mercury affects how you communicate and how your mental processes work. Are you a quick study who grasps information rapidly, or do you learn more slowly and thoroughly? How is your concentration? Can you express yourself easily? Are you a good writer? All these questions can be answered by your Mercury placement.

Venus shows what you react to. What turns you on? What appeals to you aesthetically? Are you charming to others? Are you attractive to look at? Your taste, your refinement, your sense of balance and proportion are all Venus-ruled.

Mars is your outgoing energy, your drive and ambition. Do you reach out for new adventures? Are you assertive? Are you motivated? Self-confident? Hot-tempered? How you channel your energy and drive is revealed by your Mars placement.

Mercury Shows How Your Mind Works

Since Mercury never travels far from the sun, read Mercury in your sun sign, and then the signs preceding and following it. Then decide which reflects the way you think.

Mercury in Aries

Your mind is very active and assertive. It approaches a plan aggressively. You never hesitate to say what you think, never shy away from a battle. In fact, you may relish a verbal confrontation. Tact is not your strong point, so you may have to learn not to trip over your tongue.

Mercury in Taurus

This is a much more cautious Mercury. Though you may be a slow learner, you have good concentration and mental stamina. You want to make your ideas really happen. You'll attack a problem methodically and consider every angle thoroughly, never jumping to conclusions. You'll stick with a subject until you master it.

Mercury in Gemini

You are a wonderful communicator with great facility for expressing yourself both verbally and in writing. You love gathering all kinds of information. You probably finish other people's sentences and express yourself with eloquent hand gestures. You can talk to anybody anytime and probably have phone and E-mail bills to prove it. You read anything from sci-fi to Shakespeare and might need an extra room just for your book collection. Though you learn fast, you may lack focus and discipline. Watch a tendency to jump from subject to subject.

Mercury in Cancer

You rely on intuition more than logic. Your mental processes are usually colored by your emotions, so you may seem shy or hesitant to voice your opinions. However, this placement gives you the advantage of great imagination and empathy in the way you communicate with others.

Mercury in Leo

You are enthusiastic and very dramatic in the way you express yourself. You like to hold the attention of groups and could be a great public speaker. Your mind thinks big, so you'd prefer to deal with the overall picture rather than with the details.

Mercury in Virgo

This is one of the best places for Mercury. It should give you critical ability, attention to details, and thorough analysis. Your mind focuses on the practical side of things. This type of thinking is very well suited to being a teacher or editor.

Mercury in Libra

You're either a born diplomat who smoothes over ruffled feathers or a talented debater. Many lawyers have this placement. However, since you're forever weighing the pros and cons of a situation, you may vacillate when making decisions.

Mercury in Scorpio

This is an investigative mind that stops at nothing to get the answers. You may have a sarcastic, stinging wit, a gift for the cutting remark. There's always a grain of truth to your verbal sallies, thanks to your penetrating insight.

Mercury in Sagittarius

You are a super salesman with a tendency to expound. Though you are very broad-minded, you can be dogmatic when it comes to telling others what's good for them. You won't hesitate to tell the truth as you see it, so watch a tendency toward tactlessness. On the plus side, you have a great sense of humor. This position of Mercury is often considered by astrologers to be at a disadvantage because Sagittarius opposes Gemini, the sign Mercury rules, and squares off with Virgo, another Mercury-ruled sign. What often happens is that Mercury in Sagittarius oversteps its bounds and loses sight of the facts in a situation. Do a reality check before making promises that you may not be able to deliver.

Mercury in Capricorn

This placement endows good mental discipline. You have a love of learning and a very orderly approach to your subjects. You will patiently plod through the facts and figures until you have mastered the tasks. You grasp structured situations easily, but may be short on creativity.

Mercury in Aquarius

An independent, original thinker, you'll have more cutting-edge ideas than the average person. You'll be quick to check out any unusual opportunities. Your opinions are so well-researched and grounded that once your mind is made up, it is difficult to change.

Mercury in Pisces

You have the psychic intuitive mind of a natural poet. Learn to make use of your creative imagination. You may think in terms of helping others, but check a tendency to be vague and forgetful of details.

Venus Is the Popularity Planet

Venus tells how you relate to others and to your environment. It shows where you receive pleasure and what you love to do. Find your Venus placement on the chart in this book by looking for the year of your birth in the left-hand column. Then follow the line of that year across the page until you reach the time period of your birthday. The sign heading that column will be your Venus. If you were born on a day when Venus was changing signs, check the signs preceding or following that day to determine if that feels more like your Venus nature.

Venus in Aries

You can't stand to be bored, confined, or ordered around. But a good challenge, maybe even a rousing row, turns you on. Confess—don't you pick a fight now and then just to get someone stirred up? You're attracted by the chase, not the catch, which could cause some problems in your love life, if the object of your affection becomes too attainable. You like to wear red and can spot a trend before anyone else.

Venus in Taurus

All your senses work in high gear. You love to be surrounded by glorious tastes, smells, textures, sounds, and visuals—austerity is not for you. Neither is being rushed. You like time to enjoy your pleasures. Soothing surroundings with plenty of creature comforts are your cup of tea. You like to feel secure in your nest, with no sudden jolts or surprises. You like familiar objects—in fact, you may hate to let anything or anyone go.

Venus in Gemini

You are a lively, sparkling personality who thrives in a situation that affords a constant variety and a frequent change of scenery. A varied social life is important to you, with plenty of mental stimulation and a chance to engage in some light flirtation. Commitment may be difficult, because playing the field is so much fun.

Venus in Cancer

An atmosphere where you feel protected, coddled, and mothered is best for you. You love to be surrounded by children in a cozy, homelike situation. You are attracted to those who are tender and nurturing, who make you feel secure and well provided for. You may be quite secretive about your emotional life or attracted to clandestine relationships.

Venus in Leo

First-class attention in large doses turns you on, and so does the glitter of real gold and the flash of mirrors. You like to feel like a star at all times, surrounded by your admiring audience. The side effect is that you may be attracted to flatterers and tinsel, while the real gold requires some digging.

Venus in Virgo

Everything neatly in its place? On the surface, you are attracted to an atmosphere where everything is in perfect order, but underneath are some basic, earthy urges. You are attracted to those who appeal to your need to teach, be of service, or play out a Pygmalion fantasy. You are at your best when you are busy doing something useful.

Venus in Libra

Elegance and harmony are your key words. You can't abide an atmosphere of contention. Your taste tends toward the classic, with light harmonies of color—nothing clashing, trendy, or outrageous. You love doing things with a partner and should be careful to pick one who is decisive, but patient enough to let you weigh the pros and cons. And steer clear of argumentative types.

Venus in Scorpio

Mysteries intrigue you—in fact, anything that is too open and aboveboard is a bit of a bore. You surely have a stack of whodunits by the bed, along with an erotic magazine or two. You like to solve puzzles. You may also be fascinated with the occult, crime, or scientific research. Intense, all-or-nothing situations add spice to your life, and you love to ferret out the secrets of others. But you could get burned by your flair for living dangerously. The color black, spicy food, dark wood furniture, and heady perfume put you in the right mood.

Venus in Sagittarius

If you are not actually a world traveler, your surroundings are sure to reflect your love of faraway places. You like a casual outdoor atmosphere and a dog or two to pet. There should be plenty of room for athletic equipment and suitcases. You're attracted to kindred souls who love to travel and who share your freedom-loving philosophy of life. Athletics and spiritual or New Age pursuits could be other interests.

Venus in Capricorn

No fly-by-night relationships for you! You want substance in life, and you are attracted to whatever will help you get where you are going. Status objects turn you on. And so do those who have a serious, responsible, businesslike approach, or who remind you of a beloved parent. It is characteristic of this placement to be attracted to someone of a different generation. Antiques, traditional clothing, and dignified behavior are becoming to you.

Venus in Aquarius

This Venus wants to make friends, to be "cool." You like to be in a group, particularly one pushing a worthy cause. You feel quite at home surrounded by people, and could even court fame, yet all the while, you tend to remain detached from intense commitment. Original ideas and unpredictable people fascinate you. You prefer spontaneity and delightful surprises, rather than a well-planned schedule of events.

Venus in Pisces

This Venus loves to give of yourself, and you find plenty of takers. Stray animals and people appeal to your heart and your pocketbook, but be careful to look at their motives realistically once in a while. You are extremely vulnerable to sob stories of all kinds. Fantasy, the arts (especially film, dance, and theater), and psychic or spiritual activities also speak to you.

Mars: The Action Hero

Mars is the mover and shaker in your life. It shows how you pursue your goals, whether you have energy to burn or proceed in a slow, steady pace. It will also show how you get angry. Do you explode, or do a slow burn, or hold everything inside and then get revenge later?

To find your Mars, turn to the chart on pages 82–94. Then find your birth year in the left-hand column and find the line headed by the month of your birth. There you will find an abbreviation of your Mars sign. If the description of your Mars sign doesn't ring true, read the description of the signs preceding and following it. You might have been born on a day when Mars was changing signs, in which case your Mars might fall into the adjacent sign.

Mars in Aries

In the sign it rules, Mars shows its brilliant fiery nature. You have an explosive temper and can be quite impatient. On the other hand, you have tremendous courage, energy, and drive. You'll let nothing stand in your way as you race to be first! Obstacles are met head-on and broken through by force. However, problems that require patience and persistence to solve can have you exploding in rage. You're a great starter, but not necessarily around for the finish.

Mars in Taurus

Slow, steady, concentrated energy gives you the power to last until the finish line. You've great stamina, and you never give up. Your tactic is to wear away obstacles with your persistence. Often you come out a winner because you've had the patience to hang in there. When angered, you do a slow burn.

Mars in Gemini

You can't sit still for long. This Mars craves variety. You often have two or more things going on at once—it's all an amusing game to you. Your life can get very complicated, but that only adds spice and stimulation. What drives you into a nervous, hyper state? Boredom, sameness, routine, and confinement. You can do wonderful things with your hands, and you have a way with words.

Mars in Cancer

You rarely attack head-on. Instead, you'll keep things to yourself, make plans in secret, and always cover your actions. This might be interpreted by some as manipulative, but you are only being self-protective. You get furious when anyone knows too much about you. But you do like to know all about others. Your mothering and feeding instincts can be put to good use, if you work in the food, hotel, or child-care-related businesses. You may have to overcome your fragile sense of security, which prompts you not to take risks and to get physically upset when criticized. Don't take things so personally!

Mars in Leo

You have a very dominant personality that takes center stage—modesty is not one of your traits, nor is taking a back seat. You prefer giving the orders and have been known to make a dramatic scene if they are not obeyed. Properly used, this Mars confers leadership ability, endurance, and courage.

Mars in Virgo

You are the fault-finder of the zodiac, who notices every detail. Mistakes of any kind make you very nervous. You may worry, even if everything is going smoothly. You may not express your anger directly, but you sure can nag. You have definite likes and dislikes, and you are sure you can do the job better than anyone else. You are certainly more industrious and detail-oriented than other signs. Your Mars energy is often most positively expressed in some kind of teaching role.

49

Mars in Libra

This Mars will have a passion for beauty, justice, and art. Generally, you will avoid confrontations at all costs. You prefer to spend your energy finding diplomatic solutions or weighing pros and cons. Your other techniques are passive aggression or exercising your well-known charm to get people to do what you want.

Mars in Scorpio

This is a powerful placement, so intense that it demands careful channeling into worthwhile activities. Otherwise, you could become obsessed with your sexuality or might use your need for power and control to manipulate others. You are strong-willed, shrewd, and very private about your affairs, and you'll usually have a secret agenda behind your actions. Your great stamina, focus, and discipline would be excellent assets for careers in the military or medical fields, especially research or surgery. When angry, you don't get mad—you get even!

Mars in Sagittarius

This expansive Mars often propels people into sales, travel, athletics or philosophy. Your energies function well when you are on the move. You have a hot temper and are inclined to say what you think before you consider the consequences. You shoot for high goals—and talk endlessly about them—but you may be weak on groundwork. This Mars needs a solid foundation. Watch a tendency to take unnecessary risks.

Mars in Capricorn

This is an ambitious Mars with an excellent sense of timing. You have an eye for those who can be of use to you, and you may dismiss people ruthlessly when you're angry. But you drive yourself hard and deliver full value. This is a good placement for an executive. You'll aim for status and a high material position in life, and keep climbing despite the odds. A great Mars to have!

Mars in Aquarius

This is the most rebellious Mars. You seem to have a drive to assert yourself against the status quo. You may enjoy provoking people, shocking them out of traditional views. Or this placement could express itself in an offbeat sex life. Somehow you often find yourself in unconventional situations. You enjoy being a leader of an active group, which pursues forward-looking studies, politics, or goals.

Mars in Pisces

This Mars is a good actor who knows just how to appeal to the sympathies of others. You create and project wonderful fantasies or use your sensitive antennae to crusade for those less fortunate. You get what you want through creating a veil of illusion and glamour. This is a good Mars for someone in the creative and imaginative fields—a dancer, a performer, a photographer, or an actor. Many famous film stars have this placement. Watch a tendency to manipulate by making others feel sorry for you.

Jupiter Is the Optimist

This big, bright, swirling mass of gases is associated with abundance, prosperity, and the kind of windfall you get without too much hard work. You're optimistic under Jupiter's influence, when anything seems possible. You'll travel, expand your mind with higher education, and publish to share your knowledge widely. On the other hand, Jupiter's influence is neither discriminating nor disciplined. It represents the principle of growth without judgment. Therefore, if not kept in check, it could result in extravagance, weight gain, laziness, and carelessness.

Be sure to look up your Jupiter in the tables in this book. When the current position of Jupiter is favorable, you may get that lucky break. This is a great time to try new things, take risks, travel, or get more education. Opportunities seem to open up easily, so take advantage of them.

Once a year, Jupiter changes signs. That means you are due for an expansive time every twelve years, when Jupiter travels through your sun sign. You'll also have periods every four years when Jupiter is in the same element as your sun sign.

Jupiter in Aries

You are the soul of enthusiasm and optimism. Your luckiest times are when you are getting started on an exciting project or selling an ideal that you really believe in. You may have to watch a tendency to be arrogant with those who do not share your enthusiasm. You follow your impulses, often ignoring budget or other commonsense limitations. To produce real, solid benefits, you'll need patience and the will to follow through wherever this Jupiter falls in your horoscope.

Jupiter in Taurus

You'll spend money on beautiful material things, especially those that come from nature—items made of rare woods, natural fabrics, or precious gems, for instance. You can't have too much comfort or too many sensual pleasures. Watch a tendency to overindulge in good food, or to overpamper yourself with nothing but the best. Spartan living is not for you! You may be especially lucky in matters of real estate.

Jupiter in Gemini

You are the great talker of the zodiac, and you may be a great writer too. But restlessness could be your weak point. You jump around and talk too much; you could be a jack-of-all-trades. Keeping a secret is especially difficult, so you'll also have to watch a tendency to spill the beans. Since you love to be at the center of a beehive of activity, you'll have a vibrant social life. Your best opportunities will come through your talent for language: speaking, writing, communicating, and selling.

Jupiter in Cancer

You are luckiest in situations where you can find emotional closeness or deal with basic security needs, such as food, nurturing, or shelter. You may be a great collector, and you may simply love to accumulate things—you are the one who stashes things away for a rainy day. You probably have a very good memory and love children—in fact, you may have many children to care for. The food, hotel, child-care, and shipping businesses hold good opportunities for you.

Jupiter in Leo

You are a natural showman who loves to live in a larger-than-life way. Yours is a personality full of color that always finds its way into the limelight. You can't have too much attention. Showbiz is a natural place for you, and so is any area where you can play to a crowd. Exercising your flair for drama, your natural playfulness, and your romantic nature brings you good fortune. But watch a tendency to be overextravagant or to monopolize center stage.

Jupiter in Virgo

You actually love those minute details others find boring. To you, they make all the difference between the perfect and the ordinary. You are the fine craftsman who spots every flaw. You expand your awareness by finding the most efficient methods and by being of service to others. Many will be drawn to medical or teaching fields. You'll also have luck in publishing, crafts, nutrition, and service professions. Watch out for a tendency to overwork.

Jupiter in Libra

This is an other-directed Jupiter that develops best with a partner, for the stimulation of others helps you grow. You are also most comfortable in harmonious, beautiful situations, and you work well with artistic people. You have a great sense of fair play and an ability to evaluate the pros and cons of a situation. You usually prefer to play the role of diplomat rather than that of adversary.

Jupiter in Scorpio

You love the feeling of power and control, of taking things to their limit. You can't resist a mystery, and your shrewd, penetrating mind sees right through to the heart of most situations and people. You have luck in work that provides for solutions to matters of life and death. You may be drawn to undercover work, behind-the-scenes intrigue, psychotherapy, the occult, and sex-related ventures. Your challenge will be to develop a sense of moderation and tolerance for other beliefs. You may have luck in handling other people's money—insurance, taxes, and inheritance can bring you a windfall.

Jupiter in Sagittarius

Independent, outgoing, and idealistic, you'll shoot for the stars. This Jupiter compels you to travel far and wide, both physically and mentally, via higher education. You may have luck while traveling in an exotic place. You also have luck with outdoor ventures, exercise, and animals, particularly horses. Since you tend to be very open about your opinions, watch a tendency to be tactless and to exaggerate. Instead, use your wonderful sense of humor to make your point.

Jupiter in Capricorn

Jupiter is much more restrained in Capricorn, the sign of rules and authority. Here, Jupiter can make you overwork and heighten any ambition or sense of duty you may have. You'll expand in areas that advance your position, putting you higher up the social or corporate ladder. You are lucky working within the establishment in a very structured situation, where you can show off your ability to organize and reap rewards for your hard work.

Jupiter in Aquarius

This is another freedom-loving Jupiter, with great tolerance and originality. You are at your best when you are working for a humanitarian cause and in the company of many supporters. This is a good Jupiter for a political career. You'll relate to all kinds of people on all social levels. You have an abundance of original ideas, but you are best off away from routine and any situation that imposes rigid rules. You need mental stimulation!

Jupiter in Pisces

You are a giver whose feelings and pocketbook are easily touched by others, so choose your companions with care. You could be the original sucker for a hard-luck story. Better find a worthy hospital or charity to appreciate your selfless support. You have a great creative imagination and may attract good fortune in fields related to oil, perfume, pharmaceuticals, petroleum, dance, footwear, and alcohol. But beware not to overindulge in alcohol—focus on a creative outlet instead.

Saturn Puts on the Brakes

Jupiter speeds you up with lucky breaks, and then along comes Saturn to slow you down with the disciplinary brakes. It is the planet that can help you achieve lasting goals. Saturn has un-fairly been called a malefic planet, one of the bad guys of the zodiac. On the contrary, Saturn is one of our best friends—the kind who tells you what you need to hear, even if it's not good news. Under a Saturn transit, we grow up, take responsibility for our lives, and emerge from whatever test this planet has in store as far wiser, more capable, and mature human beings. After all, it is when we are under pressure that we grow stronger.

When Saturn hits a critical point in your horoscope, you can count on an experience that will make you slow up, pull back, and reexamine your life. It is a call to eliminate what is not working and to shape up. By the end of its twenty-eight-year trip around the zodiac, Saturn will have tested you in all areas of your life. The major tests happen in seven-year cycles, when Saturn passes over the angles of your chart—your rising sign, the top of your chart or midheaven, your descendant, and the nadir or bottom of your chart. This is when the real life-changing experiences happen. But you are also in for a testing period whenever Saturn passes a planet in your chart or stresses that planet from a distance. Therefore, it is useful to check your planetary positions with the timetable of Saturn to prepare in advance, or at least to brace yourself.

When Saturn returns to its location at the time of your birth, at approximately age twenty-eight, you'll have your first Saturn return. At this time, a person usually takes stock or settles down to find his mission in life and assumes full adult duties and responsibilities.

Another way Saturn helps us is to reveal the karmic lessons from previous lives and give us the chance to overcome them. So look at Saturn's challenges as much-needed opportunities for self-improvement. Under a Jupiter influence, you'll have more fun, but Saturn gives you solid, long-lasting results.

Look up your natal Saturn in the tables in this book for clues on where you need work.

Saturn in Aries

Saturn here puts the brakes on Aries's natural drive and enthusiasm. There is often an angry side to this placement. You don't let anyone push you around and you know what's best for yourself. Following orders is not your strong point, nor is diplomacy. You tend to be quick to go on the offensive in relationships, attacking first, before anyone attacks you. Because no one quite lives up to your standards, you often wind up doing everything yourself. You'll have to learn to cooperate and tone down any self-centeredness. Pat Buchanan has this Saturn.

Saturn in Taurus

A big issue is getting control of the cash flow. There will be lean periods that can be frightening, but you have the patience and endurance to stick them out and the methodical drive to prosper in the end. Learn to take a philosophical attitude like Ben Franklin, who also had this placement, and who said, "A penny saved is a penny earned."

Saturn in Gemini

You are a serious student of life, who may have difficulty communicating or sharing your knowledge. You may be shy, speak slowly, or have fears about communicating, like Eleanor Roosevelt. You dwell in the realms of science, theory, or abstract analysis, even when you are dealing with the emotions, like Sigmund Freud, who also had this placement.

Saturn in Cancer

Your tests come with establishing a secure emotional base. In doing so, you may have to deal with some very basic fears centering on your early home environment. Most of your Saturn tests will have emotional roots in those early-childhood experiences. You may have difficulty remaining objective in terms of what you try to achieve, so it will be especially important for you to deal with negative feelings such as guilt, paranoia, jealousy, resentment, and suspicion. Galileo and Michelangelo also navigated these murky waters.

Saturn in Leo

This is an authoritarian Saturn—a strict, demanding parent who may deny the pleasure principle in your zeal to see that rules are followed. Though you may feel guilty about taking the spotlight, you are very ambitious and loyal. You have to watch a tendency toward rigidity, also toward overwork and holding back affection. Joseph Kennedy and Billy Graham share this placement.

Saturn in Virgo

This is a cautious, exacting Saturn, intensely hard on yourself. Most of all, you give yourself the roughest time with your constant worries about every little detail, often making yourself sick. You may have difficulties setting priorities and getting the job done. Your tests will come in learning tolerance and understanding of others. Charles de Gaulle, Mae West, and Nathaniel Hawthorne had this meticulous Saturn.

Saturn in Libra

Saturn is exalted here, which makes this planet an ally. You may choose very serious, older partners in life, perhaps stemming from a fear of dependency. You need to learn to stand solidly on your own before you commit to another. Since you are extremely cautious, you deliberate every involvement—with good reason. It is best that you find an occupation that makes good use of your sense of duty and honor. Steer clear of fly-by-night situations. Both Khrushchev and Mao Tse-tung had this placement.

Saturn in Scorpio

You have great staying power. This Saturn tests you in situations involving the control of others. You may feel drawn to some kind of intrigue or undercover work, like J. Edgar Hoover. Or there may be an air of mystery surrounding your life and death, like Marilyn Monroe and Robert Kennedy, who both had this placement. There are lessons to be learned from your sexual involvements. Often sex is used for manipulation or is somehow out of the ordinary. The Roman emperor Caligula and the transsexual Christine Jorgensen are extreme cases.

Saturn in Sagittarius

Your challenges and lessons will come from tests of your spiritual and philosophical values, as happened to Martin Luther King Jr. and Gandhi. You are high-minded and sincere with this reflective, moral placement. Uncompromising in your ethical standards, you could become a benevolent despot.

Saturn in Capricorn

With the help of Saturn at maximum strength, your judgment will improve with age. And, like Spencer Tracy's screen image, you'll be the gray-haired hero with a strong sense of responsibility. You advance in life slowly but steadily, always with a strong hand at the helm and an eye for the advantageous situation. Like Pat Robertson, you're likely to stand for conservative values. Negatively, you may be a loner, prone to periods of melancholy.

Saturn in Aquarius

Your tests come from relationships with groups. Do you care too much about what others think? Do you feel like an outsider, like Greta Garbo? You may fear being different from others and therefore slight your own unique, forward-looking gifts. Or like Lord Byron and Howard Hughes, you may take the opposite tack and rebel in the extreme. You can apply discipline to accomplish great humanitarian goals, as Albert Schweitzer did.

Saturn in Pisces

Your fear of the unknown and the irrational may lead you to the safety and protection of an institution. You may go on the run like Jesse James to avoid looking too deeply inside. Or you might go in the opposite, more positive direction and develop a disciplined psychoanalytic approach, which puts you more in control of your feelings. Some of you will take refuge in work with hospitals, charities, or religious institutions. Queen Victoria, who had this placement, symbolized an era when institutions of all kinds were sustained. Discipline applied to artistic work, especially poetry and dance, or spiritual work, such as yoga or meditation, might be helpful.

How Uranus, Neptune, and Pluto Influence Your Generation

These three planets remain in signs such a long time that a whole generation bears the imprint of the sign. Mass movements, great sweeping changes, fads that characterize a generation, and even the issues of the conflicts and wars of the time are influenced by these outer three planets. When one of these distant planets changes signs, there is a definite shift in the atmosphere, the feeling of the end of an era.

Since these planets are so far away from the sun—too distant to be seen by the naked eye—they pick up signals from the universe at large. These planetary receivers literally link the sun with distant energies, and then perform a similar function in your horoscope by linking your central character with intuitive, spiritual, transformative forces from the cosmos. Each planet has a special domain and will reflect this in the area of your chart where it falls.

Uranus Is the Surprise Ingredient

Uranus is the surprise ingredient that sets you and your generation apart. There is nothing ordinary about this quirky green planet that seems to be traveling on its side, surrounded by a swarm of moons. Is it any wonder that astrologers assigned it to Aquarius, the most eccentric and gregarious sign? Uranus seems to wend its way around the sun, marching to its own tune.

Significantly, Uranus follows Saturn, the planet of limitations and structures. Often we get caught up in the structures we have created to give ourselves a sense of security. However, if we lose contact with our spiritual roots in the process, Uranus is likely to jolt us out of our comfortable rut and wake us up.

Uranus energy is electrical, happening in sudden flashes. It is not influenced by karma or past events, nor does it regard tradition, sex, or sentiment. Uranus's key words are surprise and awakening. Suddenly, there's that flash of inspiration, that bright idea, or that totally new approach that revolutionizes whatever scheme you were undertaking. A Uranus event takes you by surprise, for better or for worse. The Uranus place in your life is where you awaken and become your own person, leaving the structures of Saturn behind. And it is probably the most unconventional place in your chart.

Look up the sign of Uranus at the time of your birth and see where you follow your own tune.

Uranus in Aries

Birth Dates:
    March 31, 1927–November 4, 1927
    January 13, 1928–June 6, 1934
    October 10, 1934–March 28, 1935
    Your generation is original, creative, and pioneering. It developed the computer, the airplane, and the cyclotron. You let nothing hold you back from exploring the unknown, and you have a powerful mixture of fire and electricity behind you. Women of your generation were among the first to be liberated. You were the unforgettable style setters. You have a surprise in store for everyone. As with Yoko Ono, Grace Kelly, and Jacqueline Onassis, your life may be jolted by sudden and violent changes.

Uranus in Taurus

Birth Dates:
    June 6, 1934–October 10, 1934
    March 28, 1935–August 7, 1941
    October 5, 1941–May 15, 1942
    The great territorial shakeups of World War II began during your generation. You're independent; you're probably self-employed or you would like to be. You have original ideas about making money, and you brace yourself for sudden changes of fortune. This Uranus can cause shake-ups, particularly in finances, but it can also make you a born entrepreneur, like Martha Stewart.

Uranus in Gemini

Birth Dates:
   August 7, 1941–October 5, 1941
   May 15, 1942–August 30, 1948
   November 12, 1948–June 10, 1949

You were the first children to be influenced by television, and in your adult years, your generation stocks up on answering machines, cell phones, computers, and fax machines—any new way you can communicate. You have an inquiring mind, but your interests may be rather short-lived. This Uranus can be easily fragmented if there is no structure and focus.

Uranus in Cancer

Birth Dates:
   August 30–November 12, 1948
   June 10, 1949–August 24, 1955
   January 28, 1956–June 10, 1956

This generation came at a time when divorce was becoming commonplace, so your home image is unconventional. You may have an unusual relationship with your parents, or come from a broken home or an unconventional one. You'll have unorthodox ideas about parenting, intimacy, food, and shelter. You may also be interested in dreams, psychic phenomena, and memory work.

Uranus in Leo

Birth Dates:
   August 24, 1955–January 28, 1956
   June 10, 1956–November 1, 1961
   January 10, 1962–August 10, 1962

This generation understood how to use electronic media. Many of your group are now leaders in the high-tech industries, and you also understand how to use the new media to promote yourself. Like Isadora Duncan, you may have a very eccentric kind of charisma and a life that is sparked by unusual love affairs. Your children may have traits that are out of the ordinary. Where this planet falls in your chart, you'll have a love of freedom, be a bit of an egomaniac, and show the full force of your personality in a unique way, like tennis great Martina Navratilova.

Uranus in Virgo

Birth Dates:
   November 1, 1961–January 10, 1962
   August 10, 1962–September 28, 1968
   May 20, 1969–June 24, 1969
You'll have highly individual work methods, and many will be finding newer, more practical ways to use computers. Like Einstein, who had this placement, you'll break the rules brilliantly. Your generation came at a time of student rebellions, the civil rights movement, and the general acceptance of health foods. Chances are, you're concerned about pollution and cleaning up the environment. You may also be involved with nontraditional healing methods.

Uranus in Libra

Birth Dates:
   September 28, 1968–May 20, 1969
   June 24, 1969–November 21, 1974
   May 1, 1975–September 8, 1975
Your generation will be always changing partners. Born during the era of women's liberation, you may have come from a broken home and may have no clear image of what a marriage entails. There will be many sudden splits and experiments before you settle down. Your generation will be much involved in legal and political reforms and in changing artistic and fashion looks.

Uranus in Scorpio

Birth Dates:
   November 21, 1974–May 1, 1975
   September 8, 1975–February 17, 1981
   March 20, 1981–November 16, 1981
Interest in transformation, meditation, and life after death

signaled the beginning of New Age consciousness. Your generation recognizes no boundaries, no limits, and no external controls. You'll have new attitudes toward death and dying, psychic phenomena, and the occult. Like Mae West and Casanova, you'll shock 'em sexually.

Uranus in Sagittarius

Birth Dates:
   February 17, 1981–March 20, 1981
   November 16, 1981–February 15, 1988
   May 27, 1988–December 2, 1988
   Could this generation be the first to travel in outer space? The new generation with this placement included Charles Lindbergh and a time when the first zeppelins and the Wright Brothers were conquering the skies. Uranus here forecasts great discoveries, mind expansion, and long-distance travel. Like Galileo and Martin Luther, those born in these years will generate new theories about the cosmos and man's relation to it.

Uranus in Capricorn

Birth Dates:
   December 20, 1904–January 30, 1912
   September 4, 1912–November 12, 1912
   February 15, 1988–May 27, 1988
   December 2, 1988–April 1, 1995
   June 9, 1995–January 12, 1996
   This generation, now reaching adulthood, will challenge traditions. In these years, we got organized with the help of technology put to practical use. The Internet was born after the great economic boom of the 1990s. Great leaders who were movers and shakers of history, like Julius Caesar and Henry VIII, were born under this placement.

Uranus in Aquarius

Birth Dates:
   January 30, 1912–September 4, 1912
   November 12, 1912–April 1, 1919

August 16, 1919–January 22, 1920
April 1, 1995–June 9, 1995
January 12, 1996–March 10, 2003
September 15, 2003–December 30, 2003

Uranus in Aquarius is the strongest placement for this planet. Recently, we've had the opportunity to witness the full force of its power of innovation, as well as its sudden wake-up calls and insistence on humanitarian values. This was a time of high-tech development, when home computers became as ubiquitous as television. It was a time of globalization, surprise attacks (9/11), and underdeveloped countries demanding attention. The last generation with this placement produced great innovative minds, such as Leonard Bernstein and Orson Welles. The next will become another radical breakthrough generation, much concerned with global issues that involve all humanity.

Uranus in Pisces

Birth Dates:
April 1, 1919–August 16, 1919
January 22, 1920–March 31, 1927
November 4, 1927–January 12, 1928
March 10, 2003–September 15, 2003
December 30, 2003–May 28, 2010

Uranus is now in Pisces, ushering in a new generation. In the past century, Uranus in Pisces focused attention on the rise of electronic entertainment—radio and the cinema—and the secretiveness of Prohibition. This produced a generation of idealists exemplified by Judy Garland's theme, "Somewhere over the Rainbow." Uranus in Pisces also hints at stealth activities, at hospital and prison reform, at high-tech drugs and medical experiments, at shake-ups in the petroleum industry and new locations for Pisces-ruled off-shore drilling. Issues regarding the water and oil supply, water-related storm damage (Hurricane Katrina), sudden hurricanes, droughts, and floods demand our attention.

Neptune Is the Magic Solvent

Neptune is often maligned as the planet of illusions that dissolves reality, enabling you to escape the material world. Under Neptune's influence, you see what you want to see. But Neptune also encourages you to create. It embodies glamour, subtlety, mystery, and mysticism, and governs anything that takes you beyond the mundane world, including out-of-body experiences.

Neptune breaks through and transcends your ordinary perceptions to take you to another level, where you experience either confusion or ecstasy. Its force can pull you off course only if you allow this to happen. Those who use Neptune wisely can translate their daydreams into poetry, theater, design, or inspired moves in the business world, avoiding the tricky con artist side of this planet.

Find your Neptune listed below:

Neptune in Cancer

Birth Dates:
    July 19, 1901–December 25, 1901
    May 21, 1902–September 23, 1914
    December 14, 1914–July 19, 1915
    March 19, 1916–May 2, 1916
Dreams of the homeland, idealistic patriotism, and glamorization of the nurturing assets of women characterized this time. You who were born here have unusual psychic ability and deep insights into basic needs of others.

Neptune in Leo

Birth Dates:
    September 23, 1914–December 14, 1914
    July 19, 1915–March 19, 1916
    May 2, 1916–September 21, 1928
    February 19, 1929–July 24, 1929
Neptune in Leo brought us the glamour and high living of the 1920s and the big spenders of that time. Neptune temptations of gambling, seduction, theater, and lavish entertaining

distracted from the realities of the age. Those born in that generation also made great advances in the arts.

Neptune in Virgo

Birth Dates:
    September 21, 1928–February 19, 1929
    July 24, 1929–October 3, 1942
    April 17, 1943–August 2, 1943

Neptune in Virgo encompassed the 1930s, the Great Depression, and the beginning of World War II, when a new order was born. This was a time of facing what didn't work. Many were unemployed and found solace at the movies, watching the great Virgo star Greta Garbo or the escapist dance films of Busby Berkeley. New public services were born. Those with Neptune in Virgo later spread the gospel of health and fitness. This generation's devotion to spending hours at the office inspired the word *workaholic*.

Neptune in Libra

Birth Dates:
    October 3, 1942–April 17, 1943
    August 2, 1943–December 24, 1955
    March 12, 1956–October 19, 1956
    June 15, 1957–August 6, 1957

This was the time of World War II, and the immediate postwar period, when the world regained balance and returned to relative stability. Neptune in Libra was the romantic generation who would later be concerned with relating. As this generation matured, there was a new trend toward marriage and commitment. Racial and sexual equality became important issues, as they redesigned traditional roles to suit modern times.

Neptune in Scorpio

Birth Dates:
    December 24, 1955–March 12, 1956
    October 19, 1956–June 15, 1957
    August 6, 1957–January 4, 1970

May 3, 1970–November 6, 1970

Neptune in Scorpio brought in a generation that would become interested in transformative power. Born in an era that glamorized sex, drugs, rock and roll, and Eastern religion, they matured in a more sobering time of AIDS, cocaine abuse, and New Age spirituality. As they evolve, they will become active in healing the planet from the results of the abuse of power.

Neptune in Sagittarius

Birth Dates:
January 4, 1970–May 3, 1970
November 6, 1970–January 19, 1984
June 23, 1984–November 21, 1984

Neptune in Sagittarius was the time when space travel became a reality. The Neptune influence glamorized new approaches to mysticism, religion, and mind expansion. This generation will take a new approach to spiritual life, with emphasis on visions, mysticism, and clairvoyance.

Neptune in Capricorn

Birth Dates:
January 19, 1984–June 23, 1984
November 21, 1984–January 29, 1998

Neptune in Capricorn brought a time when delusions about material power were glamorized in the mideighties and nineties. There was a boom in the stock market, and the Internet era spawned young tycoons who later lost all their wealth. It was also a time when the psychic and occult worlds spawned a new category of business enterprise, and sold services on television.

Neptune in Aquarius

Birth Dates:
January 29, 1998–April 4, 2011

This should continue to be a time of breakthroughs. Here the creative influence of Neptune reaches a universal audience. This is a time of dissolving barriers and globalization—when we truly become one world. During this transit of high-tech Aquarius, new kinds of entertainment media reach across cultural differences. However, the transit of Neptune has also raised boundary issues between cultures, especially in Middle Eastern countries with Neptune-ruled oil fields. As Neptune raises issues of social and political structures not being as solid as they seem, this could continue to produce rebellion and chaos in the environment. However, by using imagination (Neptune) in partnership with a global view (Aquarius), we could reach creative solutions.

Those born with this placement should be true citizens of the world, with a remarkable creative ability to transcend social and cultural barriers.

Pluto Can Transform You

Though Pluto is a tiny, mysterious body in space, its influence is great. When Pluto zaps a strategic point in your horoscope, your life changes dramatically.

Little Pluto is the power behind the scenes; it affects you at deep levels of consciousness, causing events to come to the surface that will transform you and your generation. Nothing escapes, or is sacred, with this probing planet. Its purpose is to wipe out the past so something new can happen.

The Pluto place in your horoscope is where you have invisible power (Mars governs the visible power), where you can transform, heal, and affect the unconscious needs of the masses. Pluto tells lots about how your generation projects power and what makes it seem cool to others. And when Pluto changes signs, there is a whole new concept of what's cool. Pluto's strange elliptical orbit occasionally runs inside the orbit of neighboring Neptune. Because of its eccentric path, the length of time Pluto stays in any given sign can vary from thirteen to thirty-two years. It covered only seven signs in the last century.

Pluto in Gemini

Late 1800s–May 26, 1914

This was a time of mass suggestion and breakthroughs in communications, when many brilliant writers, such as Ernest Hemingway and F. Scott Fitzgerald, were born. Henry Miller, D. H. Lawrence, and James Joyce scandalized society by using explicit sexual images and language in their literature. "Muckraking" journalists exposed corruption. Pluto-ruled Scorpio president Theodore Roosevelt said, "Speak softly, but carry a big stick." This generation had an intense need to communicate and made major breakthroughs in knowledge. A compulsive restlessness and a thirst for a variety of experiences characterize many of this generation.

Pluto in Cancer

Birth Dates:

May 26, 1914–June 14, 1939

Dictators and mass media arose to wield emotional power over the masses. Women's rights were a popular issue. Deep sentimental feelings, acquisitiveness, and possessiveness characterized these times and people. Most of the great stars of the Hollywood era who embodied the American image were born during this period: Grace Kelly, Esther Williams, Frank Sinatra, and Lana Turner, to name a few.

Pluto in Leo

Birth Dates:

June 14, 1939–August 19, 1957

The performing arts played on the emotions of the masses. Mick Jagger, John Lennon, and rock and roll were born at this time. So were baby boomers like Bill and Hillary Clinton. Those born here tend to be self-centered, powerful, and boisterous. This generation does its own thing, for better or for worse. They are quick to embrace self-transformation in the form of antiaging and plastic surgery techniques, to stay forever young and stay relevant in society.

Pluto in Virgo

Birth Dates:
August 19, 1957–October 5, 1971
April 17, 1972–July 30, 1972

This is the yuppie generation that sparked a mass movement toward fitness, health, and career. It is a much more sober, serious, and driven generation than the fun-loving Pluto in Leo. During this time, machines were invented to process detail work efficiently. Inventions took a practical turn with answering machines, fax machines, car phones, and home-office equipment—all making the workplace far more efficient.

Pluto in Libra

Birth Dates:
October 5, 1971–April 17, 1972
July 30, 1972–November 5, 1983
May 18, 1984–August 27, 1984

A mellower generation, people born at this time are concerned with partnerships, working together, and finding diplomatic solutions to problems. Marriage is important to this generation, and they will define it by combining traditional values with equal partnership. This was a time of women's liberation, gay rights, the ERA, and legal battles over abortion—all of which transformed our ideas about relationships.

Pluto in Scorpio

Birth Dates:
November 5, 1983–May 18, 1984
August 27, 1984–January 17, 1995

Pluto was in its ruling sign for a comparatively short period of time. However, this was a time of record achievements, destructive sexually transmitted diseases, nuclear power controversies, and explosive political issues. Pluto destroys in order to create new understanding—the phoenix rising from the ashes—which should be some consolation for those of you who felt Pluto's force before 1995. Sexual shockers were par for the course during these intense years, when black clothing, transvestites, body piercing, tattoos, and sexually explicit advertising pushed the boundaries of good taste.

Pluto in Sagittarius

Birth Dates:
> January 17, 1995–April 20, 1995
> November 10, 1995–January 27, 2008
> June 13, 2008–November 26, 2008

During the most recent Pluto transit, we were pushed to expand our horizons and find deeper spiritual meaning in life.

Pluto's opposition with Saturn in 2001 brought an enormous conflict between traditional societies and the forces of change. It signaled a time when religious convictions exerted power in our political life as well.

Since Sagittarius is associated with travel, Pluto, the planet of extremes, made space travel a reality for wealthy adventurers, who paid for the privilege of travel on space shuttles. Globalization transformed business and traditional societies as outsourcing became the norm.

New dimensions in electronic publishing, concern with animal rights and the environment, and an increasing emphasis on extreme forms of religion were other signs of Pluto in Sagittarius. Charismatic religious leaders asserted themselves and questions of the boundaries between church and state arose. There were also sexual scandals associated with the church, which transformed the religious power structure.

Pluto in Capricorn

Birth Dates:
> January 25, 2008–June 13, 2008
> November 26, 2008–January 20, 2024

As Pluto in Jupiter-ruled Sagittarius signaled a time of expansion and globalization, Pluto's entry into Saturn-ruled Capricorn in 2008 signaled a time of adjustment, of facing reality and limitations, then finding pragmatic solutions. It will be a time when a new structure is imposed, when we become concerned with what actually works.

As Capricorn is associated with corporations and also with

responsibility and duty, look for dramatic changes in business practices, hopefully with more attention paid to ethical and social responsibility as well as the bottom line. Big business will have enormous power during this transit, perhaps handling what governments have been unable to accomplish. There will be an emphasis on trimming down, perhaps a new belt-tightening regime. And, since Capricorn is the sign of Father Time, there will be a new emphasis on the aging of the population. The generation born now is sure to be a more practical and realistic one than that of their older Pluto in Sagittarius siblings.

VENUS SIGNS 1901–2010

	Aries	Taurus	Gemini	Cancer	Leo	Virgo
1901	3/29–4/22	4/22–5/17	5/17–6/10	6/10–7/5	7/5–7/29	7/29–8/23
1902	5/7–6/3	6/3–6/30	6/30–7/25	7/25–8/19	8/19–9/13	9/13–10/7
1903	2/28–3/24	3/24–4/18	4/18–5/13	5/13–6/9	6/9–7/7	7/7–8/17 9/6–11/8
1904	3/13–5/7	5/7–6/1	6/1–6/25	6/25–7/19	7/19–8/13	8/13–9/6
1905	2/3–3/6 4/9–5/28	3/6–4/9 5/28–7/8	7/8–8/6	8/6–9/1	9/1–9/27	9/27–10/21
1906	3/1–4/7	4/7–5/2	5/2–5/26	5/26–6/20	6/20–7/16	7/16–8/11
1907	4/27–5/22	5/22–6/16	6/16–7/11	7/11–8/4	8/4–8/29	8/29–9/22
1908	2/14–3/10	3/10–4/5	4/5–5/5	5/5–9/8	9/8–10/8	10/8–11/3
1909	3/29–4/22	4/22–5/16	5/16–6/10	6/10–7/4	7/4–7/29	7/29–8/23
1910	5/7–6/3	6/4–6/29	6/30–7/24	7/25–8/18	8/19–9/12	9/13–10/6
1911	2/28–3/23	3/24–4/17	4/18–5/12	5/13–6/8	6/9–7/7	7/8–11/18
1912	4/13–5/6	5/7–5/31	6/1–6/24	6/24–7/18	7/19–8/12	8/13–9/5
1913	2/3–3/6 5/2–5/30	3/7–5/1 5/31–7/7	7/8–8/5	8/6–8/31	9/1–9/26	9/27–10/20
1914	3/14–4/6	4/7–5/1	5/2–5/25	5/26–6/19	6/20–7/15	7/16–8/10
1915	4/27–5/21	5/22–6/15	6/16–7/10	7/11–8/3	8/4–8/28	8/29–9/21
1916	2/14–3/9	3/10–4/5	4/6–5/5	5/6–9/8	9/9–10/7	10/8–11/2
1917	3/29–4/21	4/22–5/15	5/16–6/9	6/10–7/3	7/4–7/28	7/29–8/21
1918	5/7–6/2	6/3–6/28	6/29–7/24	7/25–8/18	8/19–9/11	9/12–10/5
1919	2/27–3/22	3/23–4/16	4/17–5/12	5/13–6/7	6/8–7/7	7/8–11/8
1920	4/12–5/6	5/7–5/30	5/31–6/23	6/24–7/18	7/19–8/11	8/12–9/4
1921	2/3–3/6 4/26–6/1	3/7–4/25 6/2–7/7	7/8–8/5	8/6–8/31	9/1–9/25	9/26–10/20
1922	3/13–4/6	4/7–4/30	5/1–5/25	5/26–6/19	6/20–7/14	7/15–8/9
1923	4/27–5/21	5/22–6/14	6/15–7/9	7/10–8/3	8/4–8/27	8/28–9/20
1924	2/13–3/8	3/9–4/4	4/5–5/5	5/6–9/8	9/9–10/7	10/8–11/12
1925	3/28–4/20	4/21–5/15	5/16–6/8	6/9–7/3	7/4–7/27	7/28–8/21
1926	5/7–6/2	6/3–6/28	6/29–7/23	7/24–8/17	8/18–9/11	9/12–10/5
1927	2/27–3/22	3/23–4/16	4/17–5/11	5/12–6/7	6/8–7/7	7/8–11/9

Libra	Scorpio	Sagittarius	Capricorn	Aquarius	Pisces
8/23–9/17	9/17–10/12	10/12–1/16	1/16–2/9	2/9–3/5	3/5–3/29
			11/7–12/5	12/5–1/11	
10/7–10/31	10/31–11/24	11/24–12/18	12/18–1/11	2/6–4/4	1/11–2/6
					4/4–5/7
8/17–9/6	12/9–1/5			1/11–2/4	2/4–2/28
11/8–12/9					
9/6–9/30	9/30–10/25	1/5–1/30	1/30–2/24	2/24–3/19	3/19–4/13
		10/25–11/18	11/18–12/13	12/13–1/7	
10/21–11/14	11/14–12/8	12/8–1/1/06			1/7–2/3
8/11–9/7	9/7–10/9	10/9–12/15	1/1–1/25	1/25–2/18	2/18–3/14
	12/15–12/25	12/25–2/6			
9/22–10/16	10/16–11/9	11/9–12/3	2/6–3/6	3/6–4/2	4/2–4/27
			12/3–12/27	12/27–1/20	
11/3–11/28	11/28–12/22	12/22–1/15			1/20–2/4
8/23–9/17	9/17–10/12	10/12–11/17	1/15–2/9	2/9–3/5	3/5–3/29
			11/17–12/5	12/5–1/15	
10/7–10/30	10/31–11/23	11/24–12/17	12/18–12/31	1/1–1/15	1/16–1/28
				1/29–4/4	4/5–5/6
11/19–12/8	12/9–12/31		1/1–1/10	1/11–2/2	2/3–2/27
9/6–9/30	1/1–1/4	1/5–1/29	1/30–2/23	2/24–3/18	3/19–4/12
	10/1–10/24	10/25–11/17	11/18–12/12	12/13–12/31	
10/21–11/13	11/14–12/7	12/8–12/31		1/1–1/6	1/7–2/2
8/11–9/6	9/7–10/9	10/10–12/5	1/1–1/24	1/25–2/17	2/18–3/13
	12/6–12/30	12/31			
9/22–10/15	10/16–11/8	1/1–2/6	2/7–3/6	3/7–4/1	4/2–4/26
		11/9–12/2	12/3–12/26	12/27–12/31	
11/3–11/27	11/28–12/21	12/22–12/31		1/1–1/19	1/20–2/13
8/22–9/16	9/17–10/11	1/1–1/14	1/15–2/7	2/8–3/4	3/5–3/28
		10/12–11/6	11/7–12/5	12/6–12/31	
10/6–10/29	10/30–11/22	11/23–12/16	12/17–12/31	1/1–4/5	4/6–5/6
11/9–12/8	12/9–12/31		1/1–1/9	1/10–2/2	2/3–2/26
9/5–9/30	1/1–1/3	1/4–1/28	1/29–2/22	2/23–3/18	3/19–4/11
	9/31–10/23	10/24–11/17	11/18–12/11	12/12–12/31	
10/21–11/13	11/14–12/7	12/8–12/31		1/1–1/6	1/7–2/2
8/10–9/6	9/7–10/10	10/11–11/28	1/1–1/24	1/25–2/16	2/17–3/12
	11/29–12/31				
9/21–10/14	1/1	1/2–2/6	2/7–3/5	3/6–3/31	4/1–4/26
	10/15–11/7	11/8–12/1	12/2–12/25	12/26–12/31	
11/13–11/26	11/27–12/21	12/22–12/31		1/1–1/19	1/20–2/12
8/22–9/15	9/16–10/11	1/1–1/14	1/15–2/7	2/8–3/3	3/4–3/27
		10/12–11/6	11/7–12/5	12/6–12/31	
10/6–10/29	10/30–11/22	11/23–12/16	12/17–12/31	1/1–4/5	4/6–5/6
11/10–12/8	12/9–12/31	1/1–1/7	1/8	1/9–2/1	2/2–2/26

VENUS SIGNS 1901–2010

	Aries	Taurus	Gemini	Cancer	Leo	Virgo
1928	4/12–5/5	5/6–5/29	5/30–6/23	6/24–7/17	7/18–8/11	8/12–9/4
1929	2/3–3/7 4/20–6/2	3/8–4/19 6/3–7/7	7/8–8/4	8/5–8/30	8/31–9/25	9/26–10/19
1930	3/13–4/5	4/6–4/30	5/1–5/24	5/25–6/18	6/19–7/14	7/15–8/9
1931	4/26–5/20	5/21–6/13	6/14–7/8	7/9–8/2	8/3–8/26	8/27–9/19
1932	2/12–3/8	3/9–4/3	4/4–5/5 7/13–7/27	5/6–7/12 7/28–9/8	9/9–10/6	10/7–11/1
1933	3/27–4/19	4/20–5/28	5/29–6/8	6/9–7/2	7/3–7/26	7/27–8/20
1934	5/6–6/1	6/2–6/27	6/28–7/22	7/23–8/16	8/17–9/10	9/11–10/4
1935	2/26–3/21	3/22–4/15	4/16–5/10	5/11–6/6	6/7–7/6	7/7–11/8
1936	4/11–5/4	5/5–5/28	5/29–6/22	6/23–7/16	7/17–8/10	8/11–9/4
1937	2/2–3/8 4/14–6/3	3/9–4/13 6/4–7/6	7/7–8/3	8/4–8/29	8/30–9/24	9/25–10/18
1938	3/12–4/4	4/5–4/28	4/29–5/23	5/24–6/18	6/19–7/13	7/14–8/8
1939	4/25–5/19	5/20–6/13	6/14–7/8	7/9–8/1	8/2–8/25	8/26–9/19
1940	2/12–3/7	3/8–4/3	4/4–5/5 7/5–7/31	5/6–7/4 8/1–9/8	9/9–10/5	10/6–10/31
1941	3/27–4/19	4/20–5/13	5/14–6/6	6/7–7/1	7/2–7/26	7/27–8/20
1942	5/6–6/1	6/2–6/26	6/27–7/22	7/23–8/16	8/17–9/9	9/10–10/3
1943	2/25–3/20	3/21–4/14	4/15–5/10	5/11–6/6	6/7–7/6	7/7–11/8
1944	4/10–5/3	5/4–5/28	5/29–6/21	6/22–7/16	7/17–8/9	8/10–9/2
1945	2/2–3/10 4/7–6/3	3/11–4/6 6/4–7/6	7/7–8/3	8/4–8/29	8/30–9/23	9/24–10/18
1946	3/11–4/4	4/5–4/28	4/29–5/23	5/24–6/17	6/18–7/12	7/13–8/8
1947	4/25–5/19	5/20–6/12	6/13–7/7	7/8–8/1	8/2–8/25	8/26–9/18
1948	2/11–3/7	3/8–4/3	4/4–5/6 6/29–8/2	5/7–6/28 8/3–9/7	9/8–10/5	10/6–10/31
1949	3/26–4/19	4/20–5/13	5/14–6/6	6/7–6/30	7/1–7/25	7/26–8/19
1950	5/5–5/31	6/1–6/26	6/27–7/21	7/22–8/15	8/16–9/9	9/10–10/3
1951	2/25–3/21	3/22–4/15	4/16–5/10	5/11–6/6	6/7–7/7	7/8–11/9
1952	4/10–5/4	5/5–5/28	5/29–6/21	6/22–7/16	7/17–8/9	8/10–9/3
1953	2/2–3/3 4/1–6/5	3/4–3/31 6/6–7/7	7/8–8/3	8/4–8/29	8/30–9/24	9/25–10/18

Libra	Scorpio	Sagittarius	Capricorn	Aquarius	Pisces
9/5–9/28	1/1–1/3	1/4–1/28	1/29–2/22	2/23–3/17	3/18–4/11
	9/29–10/23	10/24–11/16	11/17–12/11	12/12–12/31	
10/20–11/12	11/13–12/6	12/7–12/30	12/31	1/1–1/5	1/6–2/2
8/10–9/6	9/7–10/11	10/12–11/21	1/1–1/23	1/24–2/16	2/17–3/12
	11/22–12/31				
9/20–10/13	1/1–1/3	1/4–2/6	2/7–3/4	3/5–3/31	4/1–4/25
	10/14–11/6	11/7–11/30	12/1–12/24	12/25–12/31	
11/2–11/25	11/26–12/20	12/21–12/31		1/1–1/18	1/19–2/11
8/21–9/14	9/15–10/10	1/1–1/13	1/14–2/6	2/7–3/2	3/3–3/26
		10/11–11/5	11/6–12/4	12/5–12/31	
10/5–10/28	10/29–11/21	11/22–12/15	12/16–12/31	1/1–4/5	4/6–5/5
11/9–12/7	12/8–12/31		1/1–1/7	1/8–1/31	2/1–2/25
9/5–9/27	1/1–1/2	1/3–1/27	1/28–2/21	2/22–3/16	3/17–4/10
	9/28–10/22	10/23–11/15	11/16–12/10	12/11–12/31	
10/19–11/11	11/12–12/5	12/6–12/29	12/30–12/31	1/1–1/5	1/6–2/1
8/9–9/6	9/7–10/13	10/14–11/14	1/1–1/22	1/23–2/15	2/16–3/11
	11/15–12/31				
9/20–10/13	1/1–1/3	1/4–2/5	2/6–3/4	3/5–3/30	3/31–4/24
	10/14–11/6	11/7–11/30	12/1–12/24	12/25–12/31	
11/1–11/25	11/26–12/19	12/20–12/31		1/1–1/18	1/19–2/11
8/21–9/14	9/15–10/9	1/1–1/12	1/13–2/5	2/6–3/1	3/2–3/26
		10/10–11/5	11/6–12/4	12/5–12/31	
10/4–10/27	10/28–11/20	11/21–12/14	12/15–12/31	1/1–4/5	4/6–5/5
11/9–12/7	12/8–12/31		1/1–1/7	1/8–1/31	2/1–2/24
9/3–9/27	1/1–1/2	1/3–1/27	1/28–2/20	2/21–3/16	3/17–4/9
	9/28–10/21	10/22–11/15	11/16–12/10	12/11–12/31	
10/19–11/11	11/12–12/5	12/6–12/29	12/30–12/31	1/1–1/4	1/5–2/1
8/9–9/6	9/7–10/15	10/16–11/7	1/1–1/21	1/22–2/14	2/15–3/10
	11/8–12/31				
9/19–10/12	1/1–1/4	1/5–2/5	2/6–3/4	3/5–3/29	3/30–4/24
	10/13–11/5	11/6–11/29	11/30–12/23	12/24–12/31	
11/1–11/25	11/26–12/19	12/20–12/31		1/1–1/17	1/18–2/10
8/20–9/14	9/15–10/9	1/1–1/12	1/13–2/5	2/6–3/1	3/2–3/25
		10/10–11/5	11/6–12/5	12/6–12/31	
10/4–10/27	10/28–11/20	11/21–12/13	12/14–12/31	1/1–4/5	4/6–5/4
11/10–12/7	12/8–12/31		1/1–1/7	1/8–1/31	2/1–2/24
9/4–9/27	1/1–1/2	1/3–1/27	1/28–2/20	2/21–3/16	3/17–4/9
	9/28–10/21	10/22–11/15	11/16–12/10	12/11–12/31	
10/19–11/11	11/12–12/5	12/6–12/29	12/30–12/31	1/1–1/5	1/6–2/1

VENUS SIGNS 1901–2010

	Aries	Taurus	Gemini	Cancer	Leo	Virgo
1954	3/12–4/4	4/5–4/28	4/29–5/23	5/24–6/17	6/18–7/13	7/14–8/8
1955	4/25–5/19	5/20–6/13	6/14–7/7	7/8–8/1	8/2–8/25	8/26–9/18
1956	2/12–3/7	3/8–4/4	4/5–5/7 6/24–8/4	5/8–6/23 8/5–9/8	9/9–10/5	10/6–10/31
1957	3/26–4/19	4/20–5/13	5/14–6/6	6/7–7/1	7/2–7/26	7/27–8/19
1958	5/6–5/31	6/1–6/26	6/27–7/22	7/23–8/15	8/16–9/9	9/10–10/3
1959	2/25–3/20	3/21–4/14	4/15–5/10	5/11–6/6	6/7–7/8 9/21–9/24	7/9–9/20 9/25–11/9
1960	4/10–5/3	5/4–5/28	5/29–6/21	6/22–7/15	7/16–8/9	8/10–9/2
1961	2/3–6/5	6/6–7/7	7/8–8/3	8/4–8/29	8/30–9/23	9/24–10/17
1962	3/11–4/3	4/4–4/28	4/29–5/22	5/23–6/17	6/18–7/12	7/13–8/8
1963	4/24–5/18	5/19–6/12	6/13–7/7	7/8–7/31	8/1–8/25	8/26–9/18
1964	2/11–3/7	3/8–4/4	4/5–5/9 6/18–8/5	5/10–6/17 8/6–9/8	9/9–10/5	10/6–10/31
1965	3/26–4/18	4/19–5/12	5/13–6/6	6/7–6/30	7/1–7/25	7/26–8/19
1966	5/6–5/31	6/1–6/26	6/27–7/21	7/22–8/15	8/16–9/8	9/9–10/2
1967	2/24–3/20	3/21–4/14	4/15–5/10	5/11–6/6	6/7–7/8 9/10–10/1	7/9–9/9 10/2–11/9
1968	4/9–5/3	5/4–5/27	5/28–6/20	6/21–7/15	7/16–8/8	8/9–9/2
1969	2/3–6/6	6/7–7/6	7/7–8/3	8/4–8/28	8/29–9/22	9/23–10/17
1970	3/11–4/3	4/4–4/27	4/28–5/22	5/23–6/16	6/17–7/12	7/13–8/8
1971	4/24–5/18	5/19–6/12	6/13–7/6	7/7–7/31	8/1–8/24	8/25–9/17
1972	2/11–3/7	3/8–4/3	4/4–5/10 6/12–8/6	5/11–6/11 8/7–9/8	9/9–10/5	10/6–10/30
1973	3/25–4/18	4/18–5/12	5/13–6/5	6/6–6/29	7/1–7/25	7/26–8/19
1974	5/5–5/31	6/1–6/25	6/26–7/21	7/22–8/14	8/15–9/8	9/9–10/2
1975	2/24–3/20	3/21–4/13	4/14–5/9	5/10–6/6	6/7–7/9 9/3–10/4	7/10–9/2 10/5–11/9
1976	4/8–5/2	5/2–5/27	5/27–6/20	6/20–7/14	7/14–8/8	8/8–9/1
1977	2/2–6/6	6/6–7/6	7/6–8/2	8/2–8/28	8/28–9/22	9/22–10/17
1978	3/9–4/2	4/2–4/27	4/27–5/22	5/22–6/16	6/16–7/12	7/12–8/6
1979	4/23–5/18	5/18–6/11	6/11–7/6	7/6–7/30	7/30–8/24	8/24–9/17
1980	2/9–3/6	3/6–4/3	4/3–5/12 6/5–8/6	5/12–6/5 8/6–9/7	9/7–10/4	10/4–10/30
1981	3/24–4/17	4/17–5/11	5/11–6/5	6/5–6/29	6/29–7/24	7/24–8/18

Libra	Scorpio	Sagittarius	Capricorn	Aquarius	Pisces
8/9–9/6	9/7–10/22	10/23–10/27	1/1–1/22	1/23–2/15	2/16–3/11
	10/28–12/31				
9/19–10/13	1/1–1/6	1/7–2/5	2/6–3/4	3/5–3/30	3/31–4/24
	10/14–11/5	11/6–11/30	12/1–12/24	12/25–12/31	
11/1–11/25	11/26–12/19	12/20–12/31		1/1–1/17	1/18–2/11
8/20–9/14	9/15–10/9	1/1–1/12	1/13–2/5	2/6–3/1	3/2–3/25
		10/10–11/5	11/6–12/6	12/7–12/31	
10/4–10/27	10/28–11/20	11/21–12/14	12/15–12/31	1/1–4/6	4/7–5/5
11/10–12/7	12/8–12/31		1/1–1/7	1/8–1/31	2/1–2/24
9/3–9/26	1/1–1/2	1/3–1/27	1/28–2/20	2/21–3/15	3/16–4/9
	9/27–10/21	10/22–11/15	11/16–12/10	12/11–12/31	
10/18–11/11	11/12–12/4	12/5–12/28	12/29–12/31	1/1–1/5	1/6–2/2
8/9–9/6	9/7–12/31		1/1–1/21	1/22–2/14	2/15–3/10
9/19–10/12	1/1–1/6	1/7–2/5	2/6–3/4	3/5–3/29	3/30–4/23
	10/13–11/5	11/6–11/29	11/30–12/23	12/24–12/31	
11/1–11/24	11/25–12/19	12/20–12/31		1/1–1/16	1/17–2/10
8/20–9/13	9/14–10/9	1/1–1/12	1/13–2/5	2/6–3/1	3/2–3/25
		10/10–11/5	11/6–12/7	12/8–12/31	
10/3–10/26	10/27–11/19	11/20–12/13	2/7–2/25	1/1–2/6	4/7–5/5
			12/14–12/31	2/26–4/6	
11/10–12/7	12/8–12/31		1/1–1/6	1/7–1/30	1/31–2/23
9/3–9/26	1/1	1/2–1/26	1/27–2/20	2/21–3/15	3/16–4/8
	9/27–10/21	10/22–11/14	11/15–12/9	12/10–12/31	
10/18–11/10	11/11–12/4	12/5–12/28	12/29–12/31	1/1–1/4	1/5–2/2
8/9–9/7	9/8–12/31		1/1–1/21	1/22–2/14	2/15–3/10
9/18–10/11	1/1–1/7	1/8–2/5	2/6–3/4	3/5–3/29	3/30–4/23
	10/12–11/5	11/6–11/29	11/30–12/23	12/24–12/31	
10/31–11/24	11/25–12/18	12/19–12/31		1/1–1/16	1/17–2/10
8/20–9/13	9/14–10/8	1/1–1/12	1/13–2/4	2/5–2/28	3/1–3/24
		10/9–11/5	11/6–12/7	12/8–12/31	
10/3–10/26	10/27–11/19	11/20–12/13	12/14–12/31	3/1–4/6	4/7–5/4
			1/30–2/28	1/1–1/29	
11/10–12/7	12/8–12/31		1/1–1/6	1/7–1/30	1/31–2/23
9/1–9/26	9/26–10/20	1/1–1/26	1/26–2/19	2/19–3/15	3/15–4/8
10/17–11/10	11/10–12/4	12/4–12/27	12/27–1/20/78		1/4–2/2
8/6–9/7	9/7–1/7			1/20–2/13	2/13–3/9
9/17–10/11	10/11–11/4	1/7–2/5	2/5–3/3	3/3–3/29	3/29–4/23
		11/4–11/28	11/28–12/22	12/22–1/16/80	
10/30–11/24	11/24–12/18	12/18–1/11/81			1/16–2/9
8/18–9/12	9/12–10/9	10/9–11/5	1/11–2/4	2/4–2/28	2/28–3/24
			11/5–12/8	12/8–1/23/82	

VENUS SIGNS 1901–2010

	Aries	Taurus	Gemini	Cancer	Leo	Virgo
1982	5/4–5/30	5/30–6/25	6/25–7/20	7/20–8/14	8/14–9/7	9/7–10/2
1983	2/22–3/19	3/19–4/13	4/13–5/9	5/9–6/6	6/6–7/10 8/27–10/5	7/10–8/27 10/5–11/9
1984	4/7–5/2	5/2–5/26	5/26–6/20	6/20–7/14	7/14–8/7	8/7–9/1
1985	2/2–6/6	6/7–7/6	7/6–8/2	8/2–8/28	8/28–9/22	9/22–10/16
1986	3/9–4/2	4/2–4/26	4/26–5/21	5/21–6/15	6/15–7/11	7/11–8/7
1987	4/22–5/17	5/17–6/11	6/11–7/5	7/5–7/30	7/30–8/23	8/23–9/16
1988	2/9–3/6	3/6–4/3	4/3–5/17 5/27–8/6	5/17–5/27 8/28–9/22	9/7–10/4 9/22–10/16	10/4–10/29
1989	3/23–4/16	4/16–5/11	5/11–6/4	6/4–6/29	6/29–7/24	7/24–8/18
1990	5/4–5/30	5/30–6/25	6/25–7/20	7/20–8/13	8/13–9/7	9/7–10/1
1991	2/22–3/18	3/18–4/13	4/13–5/9	5/9–6/6	6/6–7/11 8/21–10/6	7/11–8/21 10/6–11/9
1992	4/7–5/1	5/1–5/26	5/26–6/19	6/19–7/13	7/13–8/7	8/7–8/31
1993	2/2–6/6	6/6–7/6	7/6–8/1	8/1–8/27	8/27–9/21	9/21–10/16
1994	3/8–4/1	4/1–4/26	4/26–5/21	5/21–6/15	6/15–7/11	7/11–8/7
1995	4/22–5/16	5/16–6/10	6/10–7/5	7/5–7/29	7/29–8/23	8/23–9/16
1996	2/9–3/6	3/6–4/3	4/3–8/7	8/7–9/7	9/7–10/4	10/4–10/29
1997	3/23–4/16	4/16–5/10	5/10–6/4	6/4–6/28	6/28–7/23	7/23–8/17
1998	5/3–5/29	5/29–6/24	6/24–7/19	7/19–8/13	8/13–9/6	9/6–9/30
1999	2/21–3/18	3/18–4/12	4/12–5/8	5/8–6/5	6/5–7/12 8/15–10/7	7/12–8/15 10/7–11/9
2000	4/6–5/1	5/1–5/25	5/25–6/13	6/13–7/13	7/13–8/6	8/6–8/31
2001	2/2–6/6	6/6–7/5	7/5–8/1	8/1–8/26	8/26–9/20	9/20–10/15
2002	3/7–4/1	4/1–4/25	4/25–5/20	5/20–6/14	6/14–7/10	7/10–8/7
2003	4/21–5/16	5/16–6/9	6/9–7/4	7/4–7/29	7/29–8/22	8/22–9/15
2004	2/8–3/5	3/5–4/3	4/3–8/7	8/7–9/6	9/6–10/3	10/3–10/28
2005	3/22–4/15	4/15–5/10	5/10–6/3	6/3–6/28	6/28–7/23	7/23–8/17
2006	5/3–5/29	5/29–6/24	6/24–7/19	7/19–8/12	8/12–9/6	9/6–9/30
2007	2/21–3/16	3/17–4/10	4/11–5/7	5/8–6/4	6/5–7/13 8/8–10/6	7/14–8/7 10/7–11/7
2008	4/6–4/30	5/1–5/24	5/25–6/17	6/18–7/11	7/12–8/4	8/5–8/29
2009	2/2–4/11 4/24–6/6	6/6–7/5	7/5–7/31	731/–8/26	8/26–9/20	9/20–10/14
2010	3/7–3/31	3/31–4/25	4/25–5/20	5/20–6/14	6/14–7/10	7/10–8/7

Libra	Scorpio	Sagittarius	Capricorn	Aquarius	Pisces
10/2–10/26	10/26–11/18	11/18–12/12	1/23–3/2 12/12–1/5/83	3/2–4/6	4/6–5/4
11/9–12/6	12/6–1/1/84			1/5–1/29	1/29–2/22
9/1–9/25	9/25–10/20	1/1–1/25 10/20–11/13	1/25–2/19 11/13–12/9	2/19–3/14 12/10–1/4	3/14–4/7
10/16–11/9	11/9–12/3	12/3–12/27	12/28–1/19		1/4–2/2
8/7–9/7	9/7–1/7			1/20–2/13	2/13–3/9
9/16–10/10	10/10–11/3	1/7–2/5 11/3–11/28	2/5–3/3 11/28–12/22	3/3–3/28 12/22–1/15	3/28–4/22
10/29–11/23	11/23–12/17	12/17–1/10			1/15–2/9
8/18–9/12	9/12–10/8	10/8–11/5	1/10–2/3 11/5–12/10	2/3–2/27 12/10–1/16/90	2/27–3/23
10/1–10/25	10/25–11/18	11/18–12/12	1/16–3/3 12/12–1/5	3/3–4/6	4/6–5/4
11/9–12/6	12/6–12/31	12/31–1/25/92		1/5–1/29	1/29–2/22
8/31–9/25	9/25–10/19	10/19–11/13	1/25–2/18 11/13–12/8	2/18–3/13 12/8–1/3/93	3/13–4/7
10/16–11/9	11/9–12/2	12/2–12/26	12/26–1/19		1/3–2/2
8/7–9/7	9/7–1/7			1/19–2/12	2/12–3/8
9/16–10/10	10/10–11/13	1/7–2/4 11/3–11/27	2/4–3/2 11/27–12/21	3/2–3/28 12/21–1/15	3/28–4/22
10/29–11/23	11/23–12/17	12/17–1/10/97			1/15–2/9
8/17–9/12	9/12–10/8	10/8–11/5	1/10–2/3 11/5–12/12	2/3–2/27 12/12–1/9	2/27–3/23
9/30–10/24	10/24–11/17	11/17–12/11	1/9–3/4	3/4–4/6	4/6–5/3
11/9–12/5	12/5–12/31	12/31–1/24		1/4–1/28	1/28–2/21
8/31–9/24	9/24–10/19	10/19–11/13	1/24–2/18 11/13–12/8	2/18–3/12 12/8	3/13–4/6
10/15–11/8	11/8–12/2	12/2–12/26	12/26/01– 1/18/02	12/8/00–1/3/01	1/3–2/2
8/7–9/7	9/7–1/7/03		12/26/01–1/18	1/18–2/11	2/11–3/7
9/15–10/9	10/9–11/2	1/7–2/4 11/2–11/26	2/4–3/2 11/26–12/21	3/2–3/27 12/21–1/14/04	3/27–4/21
10/28–11/22	11/22–12/16	12/16–1/9/05		1/1–1/14	1/14–2/8
8/17–9/11	9/11–10/8	10/8–11/15	1/9–2/2 11/5–12/15	2/2–2/26 12/15–1/1/06	2/26–3/22
9/30–10/24	10/24–11/17	11/17–12/11	1/1–3/5	3/5–4/6	4/6–5/3
11/8–12/4	12/5–12/29	12/30–1/24/08		1/3–1/26	1/27–2/20
8/6–9/7	9/7–1/7			1/20–2/13	2/13–3/9
8/30–9/22	9/23–10/17	10/18–11/11	1/24–2/16 11/12–12/6	2/17–3/11 12/7–1/2/09	3/12–4/5
10/14–11/7	11/7–12/1	12/1–12/25	12/25–1/18/10	12/7/08– 1/31/09	1/3–2/2 4/11–4/24
8/7–9/8	9/8–11/8			1/18/10– 2/11/10	2/11–3/7
11/8–11/30	11/30–1/7/11				

81

How to Use the Mars, Jupiter, and Saturn Tables

Find the year of your birth on the left side of each column. The dates when the planet entered each sign are listed on the right side of each column. (Signs are abbreviated to three letters.) Your birthday should fall on or between each date listed, and your planetary placement should correspond to the earlier sign of that period.

All planet changes are calculated for the Greenwich Mean Time zone.

MARS SIGNS 1901–2010

1901	MAR	1	Leo
	MAY	11	Vir
	JUL	13	Lib
	AUG	31	Scp
	OCT	14	Sag
	NOV	24	Cap
1902	JAN	1	Aqu
	FEB	8	Pic
	MAR	19	Ari
	APR	27	Tau
	JUN	7	Gem
	JUL	20	Can
	SEP	4	Leo
	OCT	23	Vir
	DEC	20	Lib
1903	APR	19	Vir
	MAY	30	Lib
	AUG	6	Scp
	SEP	22	Sag
	NOV	3	Cap
	DEC	12	Aqu
1904	JAN	19	Pic
	FEB	27	Ari
	APR	6	Tau
	MAY	18	Gem
	JUN	30	Can
	AUG	15	Leo

	OCT	1	Vir
	NOV	20	Lib
1905	JAN	13	Scp
	AUG	21	Sag
	OCT	8	Cap
	NOV	18	Aqu
	DEC	27	Pic
1906	FEB	4	Ari
	MAR	17	Tau
	APR	28	Gem
	JUN	11	Can
	JUL	27	Leo
	SEP	12	Vir
	OCT	30	Lib
	DEC	17	Scp
1907	FEB	5	Sag
	APR	1	Cap
	OCT	13	Aqu
	NOV	29	Pic
1908	JAN	11	Ari
	FEB	23	Tau
	APR	7	Gem
	MAY	22	Can
	JUL	8	Leo
	AUG	24	Vir
	OCT	10	Lib
	NOV	25	Scp

1909	JAN	10	Sag		MAR	9	Pic
	FEB	24	Cap		APR	16	Ari
	APR	9	Aqu		MAY	26	Tau
	MAY	25	Pic		JUL	6	Gem
	JUL	21	Ari		AUG	19	Can
	SEP	26	Pic		OCT	7	Leo
	NOV	20	Ari	1916	MAY	28	Vir
1910	JAN	23	Tau		JUL	23	Lib
	MAR	14	Gem		SEP	8	Scp
	MAY	1	Can		OCT	22	Sag
	JUN	19	Leo		DEC	1	Cap
	AUG	6	Vir	1917	JAN	9	Aqu
	SEP	22	Lib		FEB	16	Pic
	NOV	6	Scp		MAR	26	Ari
	DEC	20	Sag		MAY	4	Tau
1911	JAN	31	Cap		JUN	14	Gem
	MAR	14	Aqu		JUL	28	Can
	APR	23	Pic		SEP	12	Leo
	JUN	2	Ari		NOV	2	Vir
	JUL	15	Tau	1918	JAN	11	Lib
	SEP	5	Gem		FEB	25	Vir
	NOV	30	Tau		JUN	23	Lib
1912	JAN	30	Gem		AUG	17	Scp
	APR	5	Can		OCT	1	Sag
	MAY	28	Leo		NOV	11	Cap
	JUL	17	Vir		DEC	20	Aqu
	SEP	2	Lib	1919	JAN	27	Pic
	OCT	18	Scp		MAR	6	Ari
	NOV	30	Sag		APR	15	Tau
1913	JAN	10	Cap		MAY	26	Gem
	FEB	19	Aqu		JUL	8	Can
	MAR	30	Pic		AUG	23	Leo
	MAY	8	Ari		OCT	10	Vir
	JUN	17	Tau		NOV	30	Lib
	JUL	29	Gem	1920	JAN	31	Scp
	SEP	15	Can		APR	23	Lib
1914	MAY	1	Leo		JUL	10	Scp
	JUN	26	Vir		SEP	4	Sag
	AUG	14	Lib		OCT	18	Cap
	SEP	29	Scp		NOV	27	Aqu
	NOV	11	Sag	1921	JAN	5	Pic
	DEC	22	Cap		FEB	13	Ari
1915	JAN	30	Aqu		MAR	25	Tau

	MAY	6	Gem		OCT	26	Scp
	JUN	18	Can		DEC	8	Sag
	AUG	3	Leo	1928	JAN	19	Cap
	SEP	19	Vir		FEB	28	Aqu
	NOV	6	Lib		APR	7	Pic
	DEC	26	Scp		MAY	16	Ari
1922	FEB	18	Sag		JUN	26	Tau
	SEP	13	Cap		AUG	9	Gem
	OCT	30	Aqu		OCT	3	Can
	DEC	11	Pic		DEC	20	Gem
1923	JAN	21	Ari	1929	MAR	10	Can
	MAR	4	Tau		MAY	13	Leo
	APR	16	Gem		JUL	4	Vir
	MAY	30	Can		AUG	21	Lib
	JUL	16	Leo		OCT	6	Scp
	SEP	1	Vir		NOV	18	Sag
	OCT	18	Lib		DEC	29	Cap
	DEC	4	Scp	1930	FEB	6	Aqu
1924	JAN	19	Sag		MAR	17	Pic
	MAR	6	Cap		APR	24	Ari
	APR	24	Aqu		JUN	3	Tau
	JUN	24	Pic		JUL	14	Gem
	AUG	24	Aqu		AUG	28	Can
	OCT	19	Pic		OCT	20	Leo
	DEC	19	Ari	1931	FEB	16	Can
1925	FEB	5	Tau		MAR	30	Leo
	MAR	24	Gem		JUN	10	Vir
	MAY	9	Can		AUG	1	Lib
	JUN	26	Leo		SEP	17	Scp
	AUG	12	Vir		OCT	30	Sag
	SEP	28	Lib		DEC	10	Cap
	NOV	13	Scp	1932	JAN	18	Aqu
	DEC	28	Sag		FEB	25	Pic
1926	FEB	9	Cap		APR	3	Ari
	MAR	23	Aqu		MAY	12	Tau
	MAY	3	Pic		JUN	22	Gem
	JUN	15	Ari		AUG	4	Can
	AUG	1	Tau		SEP	20	Leo
1927	FEB	22	Gem		NOV	13	Vir
	APR	17	Can	1933	JUL	6	Lib
	JUN	6	Leo		AUG	26	Scp
	JUL	25	Vir		OCT	9	Sag
	SEP	10	Lib		NOV	19	Cap

	DEC	28	Aqu		FEB	17	Tau
1934	FEB	4	Pic		APR	1	Gem
	MAR	14	Ari		MAY	17	Can
	APR	22	Tau		JUL	3	Leo
	JUN	2	Gem		AUG	19	Vir
	JUL	15	Can		OCT	5	Lib
	AUG	30	Leo		NOV	20	Scp
	OCT	18	Vir	1941	JAN	4	Sag
	DEC	11	Lib		FEB	17	Cap
1935	JUL	29	Scp		APR	2	Aqu
	SEP	16	Sag		MAY	16	Pic
	OCT	28	Cap		JUL	2	Ari
	DEC	7	Aqu	1942	JAN	11	Tau
1936	JAN	14	Pic		MAR	7	Gem
	FEB	22	Ari		APR	26	Can
	APR	1	Tau		JUN	14	Leo
	MAY	13	Gem		AUG	1	Vir
	JUN	25	Can		SEP	17	Lib
	AUG	10	Leo		NOV	1	Scp
	SEP	26	Vir		DEC	15	Sag
	NOV	14	Lib	1943	JAN	26	Cap
1937	JAN	5	Scp		MAR	8	Aqu
	MAR	13	Sag		APR	17	Pic
	MAY	14	Scp		MAY	27	Ari
	AUG	8	Sag		JUL	7	Tau
	SEP	30	Cap		AUG	23	Gem
	NOV	11	Aqu	1944	MAR	28	Can
	DEC	21	Pic		MAY	22	Leo
1938	JAN	30	Ari		JUL	12	Vir
	MAR	12	Tau		AUG	29	Lib
	APR	23	Gem		OCT	13	Scp
	JUN	7	Can		NOV	25	Sag
	JUL	22	Leo	1945	JAN	5	Cap
	SEP	7	Vir		FEB	14	Aqu
	OCT	25	Lib		MAR	25	Pic
	DEC	11	Scp		MAY	2	Ari
1939	JAN	29	Sag		JUN	11	Tau
	MAR	21	Cap		JUL	23	Gem
	MAY	25	Aqu		SEP	7	Can
	JUL	21	Cap		NOV	11	Leo
	SEP	24	Aqu		DEC	26	Can
	NOV	19	Pic	1946	APR	22	Leo
1940	JAN	4	Ari		JUN	20	Vir

	AUG	9	Lib		OCT	12	Cap
	SEP	24	Scp		NOV	21	Aqu
	NOV	6	Sag		DEC	30	Pic
	DEC	17	Cap	1953	FEB	8	Ari
1947	JAN	25	Aqu		MAR	20	Tau
	MAR	4	Pic		MAY	1	Gem
	APR	11	Ari		JUN	14	Can
	MAY	21	Tau		JUL	29	Leo
	JUL	1	Gem		SEP	14	Vir
	AUG	13	Can		NOV	1	Lib
	OCT	1	Leo		DEC	20	Scp
	DEC	1	Vir	1954	FEB	9	Sag
1948	FEB	12	Leo		APR	12	Cap
	MAY	18	Vir		JUL	3	Sag
	JUL	17	Lib		AUG	24	Cap
	SEP	3	Scp		OCT	21	Aqu
	OCT	17	Sag		DEC	4	Pic
	NOV	26	Cap	1955	JAN	15	Ari
1949	JAN	4	Aqu		FEB	26	Tau
	FEB	11	Pic		APR	10	Gem
	MAR	21	Ari		MAY	26	Can
	APR	30	Tau		JUL	11	Leo
	JUN	10	Gem		AUG	27	Vir
	JUL	23	Can		OCT	13	Lib
	SEP	7	Leo		NOV	29	Scp
	OCT	27	Vir	1956	JAN	14	Sag
	DEC	26	Lib		FEB	28	Cap
1950	MAR	28	Vir		APR	14	Aqu
	JUN	11	Lib		JUN	3	Pic
	AUG	10	Scp		DEC	6	Ari
	SEP	25	Sag	1957	JAN	28	Tau
	NOV	6	Cap		MAR	17	Gem
	DEC	15	Aqu		MAY	4	Can
1951	JAN	22	Pic		JUN	21	Leo
	MAR	1	Ari		AUG	8	Vir
	APR	10	Tau		SEP	24	Lib
	MAY	21	Gem		NOV	8	Scp
	JUL	3	Can		DEC	23	Sag
	AUG	18	Leo	1958	FEB	3	Cap
	OCT	5	Vir		MAR	17	Aqu
	NOV	24	Lib		APR	27	Pic
1952	JAN	20	Scp		JUN	7	Ari
	AUG	27	Sag		JUL	21	Tau

	SEP	21	Gem		NOV	6	Vir
	OCT	29	Tau	1965	JUN	29	Lib
1959	FEB	10	Gem		AUG	20	Scp
	APR	10	Can		OCT	4	Sag
	JUN	1	Leo		NOV	14	Cap
	JUL	20	Vir		DEC	23	Aqu
	SEP	5	Lib	1966	JAN	30	Pic
	OCT	21	Scp		MAR	9	Ari
	DEC	3	Sag		APR	17	Tau
1960	JAN	14	Cap		MAY	28	Gem
	FEB	23	Aqu		JUL	11	Can
	APR	2	Pic		AUG	25	Leo
	MAY	11	Ari		OCT	12	Vir
	JUN	20	Tau		DEC	4	Lib
	AUG	2	Gem	1967	FEB	12	Scp
	SEP	21	Can		MAR	31	Lib
1961	FEB	5	Gem		JUL	19	Scp
	FEB	7	Can		SEP	10	Sag
	MAY	6	Leo		OCT	23	Cap
	JUN	28	Vir		DEC	1	Aqu
	AUG	17	Lib	1968	JAN	9	Pic
	OCT	1	Scp		FEB	17	Ari
	NOV	13	Sag		MAR	27	Tau
	DEC	24	Cap		MAY	8	Gem
1962	FEB	1	Aqu		JUN	21	Can
	MAR	12	Pic		AUG	5	Leo
	APR	19	Ari		SEP	21	Vir
	MAY	28	Tau		NOV	9	Lib
	JUL	9	Gem		DEC	29	Scp
	AUG	22	Can	1969	FEB	25	Sag
	OCT	11	Leo		SEP	21	Cap
1963	JUN	3	Vir		NOV	4	Aqu
	JUL	27	Lib		DEC	15	Pic
	SEP	12	Scp	1970	JAN	24	Ari
	OCT	25	Sag		MAR	7	Tau
	DEC	5	Cap		APR	18	Gem
1964	JAN	13	Aqu		JUN	2	Can
	FEB	20	Pic		JUL	18	Leo
	MAR	29	Ari		SEP	3	Vir
	MAY	7	Tau		OCT	20	Lib
	JUN	17	Gem		DEC	6	Scp
	JUL	30	Can	1971	JAN	23	Sag
	SEP	15	Leo		MAR	12	Cap

	MAY	3	Aqu		JUN	6	Tau
	NOV	6	Pic		JUL	17	Gem
	DEC	26	Ari		SEP	1	Can
1972	FEB	10	Tau		OCT	26	Leo
	MAR	27	Gem	1978	JAN	26	Can
	MAY	12	Can		APR	10	Leo
	JUN	28	Leo		JUN	14	Vir
	AUG	15	Vir		AUG	4	Lib
	SEP	30	Lib		SEP	19	Scp
	NOV	15	Scp		NOV	2	Sag
	DEC	30	Sag		DEC	12	Cap
1973	FEB	12	Cap	1979	JAN	20	Aqu
	MAR	26	Aqu		FEB	27	Pic
	MAY	8	Pic		APR	7	Ari
	JUN	20	Ari		MAY	16	Tau
	AUG	12	Tau		JUN	26	Gem
	OCT	29	Ari		AUG	8	Can
	DEC	24	Tau		SEP	24	Leo
1974	FEB	27	Gem		NOV	19	Vir
	APR	20	Can	1980	MAR	11	Leo
	JUN	9	Leo		MAY	4	Vir
	JUL	27	Vir		JUL	10	Lib
	SEP	12	Lib		AUG	29	Scp
	OCT	28	Scp		OCT	12	Sag
	DEC	10	Sag		NOV	22	Cap
1975	JAN	21	Cap		DEC	30	Aqu
	MAR	3	Aqu	1981	FEB	6	Pic
	APR	11	Pic		MAR	17	Ari
	MAY	21	Ari		APR	25	Tau
	JUL	1	Tau		JUN	5	Gem
	AUG	14	Gem		JUL	18	Can
	OCT	17	Can		SEP	2	Leo
	NOV	25	Gem		OCT	21	Vir
1976	MAR	18	Can		DEC	16	Lib
	MAY	16	Leo	1982	AUG	3	Scp
	JUL	6	Vir		SEP	20	Sag
	AUG	24	Lib		OCT	31	Cap
	OCT	8	Scp		DEC	10	Aqu
	NOV	20	Sag	1983	JAN	17	Pic
1977	JAN	1	Cap		FEB	25	Ari
	FEB	9	Aqu		APR	5	Tau
	MAR	20	Pic		MAY	16	Gem
	APR	27	Ari		JUN	29	Can

	AUG	13	Leo	1990	JAN	29	Cap
	SEP	30	Vir		MAR	11	Aqu
	NOV	18	Lib		APR	20	Pic
1984	JAN	11	Scp		MAY	31	Ari
	AUG	17	Sag		JUL	12	Tau
	OCT	5	Cap		AUG	31	Gem
	NOV	15	Aqu		DEC	14	Tau
	DEC	25	Pic	1991	JAN	21	Gem
1985	FEB	2	Ari		APR	3	Can
	MAR	15	Tau		MAY	26	Leo
	APR	26	Gem		JUL	15	Vir
	JUN	9	Can		SEP	1	Lib
	JUL	25	Leo		OCT	16	Scp
	SEP	10	Vir		NOV	29	Sag
	OCT	27	Lib	1992	JAN	9	Cap
	DEC	14	Scp		FEB	18	Aqu
1986	FEB	2	Sag		MAR	28	Pic
	MAR	28	Cap		MAY	5	Ari
	OCT	9	Aqu		JUN	14	Tau
	NOV	26	Pic		JUL	26	Gem
1987	JAN	8	Ari		SEP	12	Can
	FEB	20	Tau	1993	APR	27	Leo
	APR	5	Gem		JUN	23	Vir
	MAY	21	Can		AUG	12	Lib
	JUL	6	Leo		SEP	27	Scp
	AUG	22	Vir		NOV	9	Sag
	OCT	8	Lib		DEC	20	Cap
	NOV	24	Scp	1994	JAN	28	Aqu
1988	JAN	8	Sag		MAR	7	Pic
	FEB	22	Cap		APR	14	Ari
	APR	6	Aqu		MAY	23	Tau
	MAY	22	Pic		JUL	3	Gem
	JUL	13	Ari		AUG	16	Can
	OCT	23	Pic		OCT	4	Leo
	NOV	1	Ari		DEC	12	Vir
1989	JAN	19	Tau	1995	JAN	22	Leo
	MAR	11	Gem		MAY	25	Vir
	APR	29	Can		JUL	21	Lib
	JUN	16	Leo		SEP	7	Scp
	AUG	3	Vir		OCT	20	Sag
	SEP	19	Lib		NOV	30	Cap
	NOV	4	Scp	1996	JAN	8	Aqu
	DEC	18	Sag		FEB	15	Pic

	MAR	24	Ari	MAY	28	Can
	MAY	2	Tau	JUL	13	Leo
	JUN	12	Gem	AUG	29	Vir
	JUL	25	Can	OCT	15	Lib
	SEP	9	Leo	DEC	1	Scp
	OCT	30	Vir	2003 JAN	17	Sag
1997	JAN	3	Lib	MAR	4	Cap
	MAR	8	Vir	APR	21	Aqu
	JUN	19	Lib	JUN	17	Pic
	AUG	14	Scp	DEC	16	Ari
	SEP	28	Sag	2004 FEB	3	Tau
	NOV	9	Cap	MAR	21	Gem
	DEC	18	Aqu	MAY	7	Can
1998	JAN	25	Pic	JUN	23	Leo
	MAR	4	Ari	AUG	10	Vir
	APR	13	Tau	SEP	26	Lib
	MAY	24	Gem	NOV	11	Sep
	JUL	6	Can	DEC	25	Sag
	AUG	20	Leo	2005 FEB	6	Cap
	OCT	7	Vir	MAR	20	Aqu
	NOV	27	Lib	MAY	1	Pic
1999	JAN	26	Scp	JUN	12	Ari
	MAY	5	Lib	JUL	28	Tau
	JUL	5	Scp	2006 FEB	17	Gem
	SEP	2	Sag	APR	14	Can
	OCT	17	Cap	JUN	3	Leo
	NOV	26	Aqu	JUL	22	Vir
2000	JAN	4	Pic	SEP	8	Lib
	FEB	12	Ari	OCT	23	Scp
	MAR	23	Tau	DEC	6	Sag
	MAY	3	Gem	2007 JAN	16	Cap
	JUN	16	Can	FEB	25	Aqu
	AUG	1	Leo	APR	6	Pic
	SEP	17	Vir	MAY	15	Ari
	NOV	4	Lib	JUNE	24	Tau
	DEC	23	Scp	AUG	7	Gem
2001	FEB	14	Sag	SEP	28	Can
	SEP	8	Cap	DEC	31	Gem*
	OCT	27	Aqu	2008 MAR	4	Can
	DEC	8	Pic	MAY	9	Leo
2002	JAN	18	Ari	JUL	1	Vir
	MAR	1	Tau	AUG	19	Lib
	APR	13	Gem	OCT	3	Scp

	NOV	16	Sag		AUG	25	Can
	DEC	27	Cap		OCT	16	Leo
2009	FEB	4	Aqu	2010	JUN	7	Vir
	MAR	14	Pic		JUL	29	Lib
	APR	22	Ari		SEP	14	Scp
	MAY	31	Tau		OCT	28	Sag
	JUL	11	Gem		DEC	7	Cap

JUPITER SIGNS 1901–2010

Year	Mon	Day	Sign	Year	Mon	Day	Sign
1901	JAN	19	Cap	1927	JAN	18	Pic
1902	FEB	6	Aqu		JUN	6	Ari
1903	FEB	20	Pic		SEP	11	Pic
1904	MAR	1	Ari	1928	JAN	23	Ari
	AUG	8	Tau		JUN	4	Tau
	AUG	31	Ari	1929	JUN	12	Gem
1905	MAR	7	Tau	1930	JUN	26	Can
	JUL	21	Gem	1931	JUL	17	Leo
	DEC	4	Tau	1932	AUG	11	Vir
1906	MAR	9	Gem	1933	SEP	10	Lib
	JUL	30	Can	1934	OCT	11	Scp
1907	AUG	18	Leo	1935	NOV	9	Sag
1908	SEP	12	Vir	1936	DEC	2	Cap
1909	OCT	11	Lib	1937	DEC	20	Aqu
1910	NOV	11	Scp	1938	MAY	14	Pic
1911	DEC	10	Sag		JUL	30	Aqu
1913	JAN	2	Cap		DEC	29	Pic
1914	JAN	21	Aqu	1939	MAY	11	Ari
1915	FEB	4	Pic		OCT	30	Pic
1916	FEB	12	Ari		DEC	20	Ari
	JUN	26	Tau	1940	MAY	16	Tau
	OCT	26	Ari	1941	MAY	26	Gem
1917	FEB	12	Tau	1942	JUN	10	Can
	JUN	29	Gem	1943	JUN	30	Leo
1918	JUL	13	Can	1944	JUL	26	Vir
1919	AUG	2	Leo	1945	AUG	25	Lib
1920	AUG	27	Vir	1946	SEP	25	Scp
1921	SEP	25	Lib	1947	OCT	24	Sag
1922	OCT	26	Scp	1948	NOV	15	Cap
1923	NOV	24	Sag	1949	APR	12	Aqu
1924	DEC	18	Cap		JUN	27	Cap
1926	JAN	6	Aqu		NOV	30	Aqu

1950	APR	15	Pic
	SEP	15	Aqu
	DEC	1	Pic
1951	APR	21	Ari
1952	APR	28	Tau
1953	MAY	9	Gem
1954	MAY	24	Can
1955	JUN	13	Leo
	NOV	17	Vir
1956	JAN	18	Leo
	JUL	7	Vir
	DEC	13	Lib
1957	FEB	19	Vir
	AUG	7	Lib
1958	JAN	13	Scp
	MAR	20	Lib
	SEP	7	Scp
1959	FEB	10	Sag
	APR	24	Scp
	OCT	5	Sag
1960	MAR	1	Cap
	JUN	10	Sag
	OCT	26	Cap
1961	MAR	15	Aqu
	AUG	12	Cap
	NOV	4	Aqu
1962	MAR	25	Pic
1963	APR	4	Ari
1964	APR	12	Tau
1965	APR	22	Gem
	SEP	21	Can
	NOV	17	Gem
1966	MAY	5	Can
	SEP	27	Leo
1967	JAN	16	Can
	MAY	23	Leo
	OCT	19	Vir
1968	FEB	27	Leo
	JUN	15	Vir
	NOV	15	Lib
1969	MAR	30	Vir
	JUL	15	Lib
	DEC	16	Scp

1970	APR	30	Lib
	AUG	15	Scp
1971	JAN	14	Sag
	JUN	5	Scp
	SEP	11	Sag
1972	FEB	6	Cap
	JUL	24	Sag
	SEP	25	Cap
1973	FEB	23	Aqu
1974	MAR	8	Pic
1975	MAR	18	Ari
1976	MAR	26	Tau
	AUG	23	Gem
	OCT	16	Tau
1977	APR	3	Gem
	AUG	20	Can
	DEC	30	Gem
1978	APR	12	Can
	SEP	5	Leo
1979	FEB	28	Can
	APR	20	Leo
	SEP	29	Vir
1980	OCT	27	Lib
1981	NOV	27	Scp
1982	DEC	26	Sag
1984	JAN	19	Cap
1985	FEB	6	Aqu
1986	FEB	20	Pic
1987	MAR	2	Ari
1988	MAR	8	Tau
	JUL	22	Gem
	NOV	30	Tau
1989	MAR	11	Gem
	JUL	30	Can
1990	AUG	18	Leo
1991	SEP	12	Vir
1992	OCT	10	Lib
1993	NOV	10	Scp
1994	DEC	9	Sag
1996	JAN	3	Cap
1997	JAN	21	Aqu
1998	FEB	4	Pic
1999	FEB	13	Ari

	JUN	28	Tau	2005	OCT	26	Scp
	OCT	23	Ari	2006	NOV	24	Sag
2000	FEB	14	Tau	2007	DEC	17	Cap
	JUN	30	Gem	2009	JAN	5	Aqu
2001	JUL	14	Can	2010	JAN	18	Pis
2002	AUG	1	Leo		JUN	6	Ari
2003	AUG	27	Vir		SEP	9	Pis
2004	SEP	24	Lib				

SATURN SIGNS 1903–2010

1903	JAN	19	Aqu		OCT	18	Pic
1905	APR	13	Pic	1938	JAN	14	Ari
	AUG	17	Aqu	1939	JUL	6	Tau
1906	JAN	8	Pic		SEP	22	Ari
1908	MAR	19	Ari	1940	MAR	20	Tau
1910	MAY	17	Tau	1942	MAY	8	Gem
	DEC	14	Ari	1944	JUN	20	Can
1911	JAN	20	Tau	1946	AUG	2	Leo
1912	JUL	7	Gem	1948	SEP	19	Vir
	NOV	30	Tau	1949	APR	3	Leo
1913	MAR	26	Gem		MAY	29	Vir
1914	AUG	24	Can	1950	NOV	20	Lib
	DEC	7	Gem	1951	MAR	7	Vir
1915	MAY	11	Can		AUG	13	Lib
1916	OCT	17	Leo	1953	OCT	22	Scp
	DEC	7	Can	1956	JAN	12	Sag
1917	JUN	24	Leo		MAY	14	Scp
1919	AUG	12	Vir		OCT	10	Sag
1921	OCT	7	Lib	1959	JAN	5	Cap
1923	DEC	20	Scp	1962	JAN	3	Aqu
1924	APR	6	Lib	1964	MAR	24	Pic
	SEP	13	Scp		SEP	16	Aqu
1926	DEC	2	Sag		DEC	16	Pic
1929	MAR	15	Cap	1967	MAR	3	Ari
	MAY	5	Sag	1969	APR	29	Tau
	NOV	30	Cap	1971	JUN	18	Gem
1932	FEB	24	Aqu	1972	JAN	10	Tau
	AUG	13	Cap		FEB	21	Gem
	NOV	20	Aqu	1973	AUG	1	Can
1935	FEB	14	Pic	1974	JAN	7	Gem
1937	APR	25	Ari		APR	18	Can

93

1975	SEP	17	Leo		JUN	30	Aqu
1976	JAN	14	Can	1994	JAN	28	Pic
	JUN	5	Leo	1996	APR	7	Ari
1977	NOV	17	Vir	1998	JUN	9	Tau
1978	JAN	5	Leo		OCT	25	Ari
	JUL	26	Vir	1999	MAR	1	Tau
1980	SEP	21	Lib	2000	AUG	10	Gem
1982	NOV	29	Scp		OCT	16	Tau
1983	MAY	6	Lib	2001	APR	21	Gem
	AUG	24	Scp	2003	JUN	3	Can
1985	NOV	17	Sag	2005	JUL	16	Leo
1988	FEB	13	Cap	2007	SEP	2	Vir
	JUN	10	Sag	2009	OCT	29	Lib
	NOV	12	Cap	2010	APR	7	Vir
1991	FEB	6	Aqu		JUL	21	Lib
1993	MAY	21	Pic				

CHAPTER 6

Where It All Happens:
Your Rising Sign

To find out what's happening in a horoscope, you first have to look east. The degree of the zodiac ascending over the eastern horizon at the time you were born, which is called the rising sign or ascendant, marks the beginning of the first house, one of twelve divisions of the horoscope, each of which represents a different area of life. These "houses" contain the planets, the doers in a chart. After the rising sign, the other houses parade around the chart in sequence, with the following sign on the next house cusp. Therefore, the setup of the chart—*what* happens *where*—depends on the rising sign.

Though you can learn much about a person by the signs and interactions of the sun, moon, and planets in the horoscope, without a valid rising sign, the collection of planets has no "homes." One would have no idea which area of life could be influenced by a particular planet. For example, you might know that a person has Mars in Aries, which will describe that person's dynamic fiery energy. But if you also know that the person has a Capricorn rising sign, this Mars will fall in the fourth house of home and family, so you know where that energy will operate.

Due to the earth's rotation, the rising sign changes every two hours, which means that babies born later or earlier on the same day in the same hospital will have most planets in the same signs, but may not have the same rising sign. Therefore, their planets may fall in different houses in the chart. For instance, if Mars is in Gemini and your rising sign is Taurus,

Mars will most likely be active in the second or financial house of your chart. Someone born later in the same day when the rising sign is Virgo would have Mars positioned at the top of the chart, energizing the tenth house of career.

Most astrologers insist on knowing the exact time of a client's birth before they analyze a chart. The more accurate your birth time, the more accurately an astrologer can position the planets in your chart by determining the correct rising sign.

How Your Rising Sign Can Influence Your Sun Sign

Your rising sign has an important relationship with your sun sign. Some will complement the sun sign; others hide it under a totally different mask, as if playing an entirely different role, making it difficult to guess the person's sun sign from outer appearances. This may be the reason why you might not look or act like your sun sign's archetype. For example, a Leo with a conservative Capricorn ascendant would come across as much more serious than a Leo with a fiery Aries or Sagittarius ascendant.

Though the rising sign usually creates the first impression you make, there are exceptions. When the sun sign is reinforced by other planets in the same sign, this might overpower the impression of the rising sign. For instance, a Leo sun plus a Leo Venus and Leo Jupiter would counteract the more conservative image that would otherwise be conveyed by the person's Capricorn ascendant.

Those born early in the morning when the sun was on the horizon will be most likely to project the image of their sun sign. These people are often called a "double Aries" or a "double Virgo" because the same sun sign and ascendant reinforce each other.

Find Your Rising Sign

Look up your rising sign on the chart at the end of this chapter. Since rising signs change every two hours, it is important to know your birth time as close to the minute as possible. Even a few minutes' difference could change the rising sign and therefore the setup of your chart. If you are unsure about the exact time, but know within a few hours, check the following descriptions to see which is most like the personality you project.

Aries Rising: Alpha Energy

You are the most aggressive version of your sun sign, with boundless energy that can be used productively if it's channeled in the right direction. Watch a tendency to overreact emotionally and blow your top. You come across as openly competitive, a positive asset in business or sports. Be on guard against impatience, which could lead to head injuries. Your walk and bearing could have the telltale head-forward Aries posture. You may wear more bright colors, especially red, than others of your sign, or be a redhead. You may also have a tendency to drive your car faster.

Can you see the alpha Aries tendency in Barbra Streisand (a sun sign Taurus) and Bette Midler (a sun sign Sagittarius)?

Taurus Rising: Down-to-Earth

You're slow-moving, with a beautiful (or distinctive) speaking or singing voice. You probably surround yourself with comfort, good food, luxurious surroundings, and other sensual pleasures. You prefer welcoming others into your home to gadding about. You may have a talent for business, especially in trading, appraising, and real estate. A Taurus ascendant gives a well-padded physique that gains weight easily, like Liza Minnelli. This ascendant can also endow females with a curvaceous beauty.

Gemini Rising: A Way with Words

You're naturally sociable, with lighter, more ethereal mannerisms than others of your sign, especially if you're female. You love to communicate with people, and express your ideas easily, like former British prime minister Tony Blair. You may have a talent for writing or public speaking. You thrive on variety, a constantly changing scene, and a lively social life. However, you may relate to others at a deeper level than might be suspected. And you will be far more sympathetic and caring than you project. You will probably travel widely, changing partners and jobs several times (or juggle two at once). Physically, your nerves are quite sensitive. Occasionally, you would benefit from a calm, tranquil atmosphere away from your usual social scene.

Cancer Rising: Nurturing Instincts

You are naturally acquisitive, possessive, private, a money-maker like Bill Gates or Michael Bloomberg. You easily pick up others' needs and feelings—a great gift in business, the arts, and personal relationships. But you must guard against overreacting or taking things too personally, especially during full-moon periods. Find creative outlets for your natural nurturing gifts, such as helping the less fortunate, particularly children. Your insights would be helpful in psychology. Your desire to feed and care for others would be useful in the restaurant, hotel, or child-care industries. You may be especially fond of wearing romantic old clothes, collecting antiques, and dining on exquisite food. Since your body may retain fluids, pay attention to your diet. To relax, escape to places near water.

Leo Rising: Diva Dazzle

You may come across as more poised than you really feel. However, you play it to the hilt, projecting a proud royal presence. A Leo ascendant gives you a natural flair for drama, like Marilyn Monroe, and you might be accused of stealing the spotlight. You'll also project a much more outgoing, optimistic, and sunny personality than others of your sign. You take care to please your public by always projecting star quality, probably tossing a luxuriant mane of hair, sporting a striking hairstyle, or dressing to impress. Females often dazzle with colorful clothing or spectacular jewelry. Since you may have a strong parental nature, you could well become a family matriarch or patriarch, like George H. W. Bush.

Virgo Rising: High Standards

Virgo rising endows you with a practical, analytical outer image. You seem neat, orderly, and more particular than others of your sign. Others in your life may feel they must live up to your high standards. Though at times you may be openly critical, this masks a well-meaning desire to have only the best for loved ones. Your sharp eye for details could be used in the financial world, or your literary skills could draw you to teaching or publishing. The healing arts, health care, and service-oriented professions attract many with a Virgo ascendant. You're likely to take good care of yourself, with great attention to health, diet, and exercise, like Madonna. You might even show some hypochondriac tendencies, like Woody Allen. Physically, you may have a very sensitive digestive system.

Libra Rising: The Charmer

Libra rising gives you a charming, social, and public persona, like John F. Kennedy and Bill Clinton. You tend to avoid confrontations in relationships, preferring to smooth the way or negotiate diplomatically rather than give in to an emotional reaction. Because you are interested in all aspects of a situation, you may be slow to reach decisions. Physically, you'll have good proportions and physical symmetry. You will move with natural grace and balance. You're likely to have pleasing, if not beautiful, facial features, with a winning smile, like Cary Grant. You'll show natural good taste and harmony in your clothes and home decor. Legal, diplomatic, or public relations professions could draw your interest.

Scorpio Rising: Air of Mystery

You project an intriguing air of mystery with this ascendant, as the Scorpio secretiveness and sense of underlying power combine with your sun sign. Like Jacqueline Kennedy Onassis, you convey that there's more to you than meets the eye. You seem like someone who is always in control and who can move comfortably in the world of power. Your physical look comes across as intense. Many of you have remarkable eyes, with a direct, penetrating gaze. But you'll never reveal your private agenda, and you tend to keep your true feelings under wraps (watch a tendency toward paranoia). You may have an interesting romantic history with secret love affairs, like Grace Kelly. Many of you heighten your air of mystery by wearing black. You're happiest near water; you should provide yourself with a seaside retreat.

Sagittarius Rising: The Explorer

You travel with this ascendant. You may also be a more outdoor, sportive type, with an athletic, casual, and outgoing air. Your moods are camouflaged with cheerful optimism or a philosophical attitude. Though you don't hesitate to speak your mind—like Ted Turner, who was called the Mouth of the South—you can also laugh at your troubles or crack a joke more easily than others of your sign. A Sagittarius ascendant can also draw you to the field of higher education or to spiritual life. You'll seem to have less attachment to things and people, and you may explore the globe. Your strong, fast legs are a physical bonus.

Capricorn Rising: Serious Business

This rising sign makes you come across as serious, goal-oriented, disciplined, and careful with cash. You are not one of the zodiac's big spenders, though you might splurge occasionally on items with good investment value. You're the conservative type in dress and environment, and you might come across as quite formal and businesslike, like Rupert Murdoch. You'll function well in a structured or corporate environment where you can climb to the top. (You are always aware of who's the boss.) In your personal life, you could be a loner or a single parent who is father and mother to your children.

Aquarius Rising: One of a Kind

You come across as less concerned about what others think and could even be a bit eccentric. Your appearance is sure to be unique and memorable. You're more at ease with groups of people than others in your sign, and you may be attracted to public life, like Jay Leno. Your appearance may be unique, either unconventional or unimportant to you. Those of you whose sun is in a water sign (Cancer, Scorpio, or Pisces) may exercise your nurturing qualities with a large group, an extended family, or a day-care or community center.

Pisces Rising: Romantic Roles

Your creative, nurturing talents are heightened and so is your ability to project emotional drama. And, like Antonio Banderas, your dreamy eyes and poetic air bring out the protective instinct in others. You could be attracted to the arts, especially theater, dance, film, and photography, or to psychology, spiritual practice, and charity work. You are happiest when you are using your creative ability to help others. Since you are vulnerable to mood swings, it is important for you to find interesting, creative work where you can express your talents and heighten your self-esteem. Accentuate the positive. Be wary of escapist tendencies, particularly involving alcohol or drugs to which you are supersensitive, like Whitney Houston.

RISING SIGNS—A.M. BIRTHS

	1 AM	2 AM	3 AM	4 AM	5 AM	6 AM	7 AM	8 AM	9 AM	10 AM	11 AM	12 NOON
Jan 1	Lib	Sc	Sc	Sc	Sag	Sag	Cap	Cap	Aq	Aq	Pis	Ar
Jan 9	Lib	Sc	Sc	Sag	Sag	Sag	Cap	Cap	Aq	Pis	Ar	Tau
Jan 17	Sc	Sc	Sc	Sag	Sag	Sag	Cap	Cap	Aq	Aq	Pis	Ar
Jan 25	Sc	Sc	Sag	Sag	Sag	Cap	Cap	Aq	Pis	Ar	Tau	Tau
Feb 2	Sc	Sc	Sag	Sag	Cap	Cap	Aq	Pis	Pis	Ar	Tau	Gem
Feb 10	Sc	Sag	Sag	Sag	Cap	Cap	Aq	Pis	Ar	Tau	Tau	Gem
Feb 18	Sc	Sag	Sag	Cap	Cap	Aq	Pis	Pis	Ar	Tau	Gem	Gem
Feb 26	Sag	Sag	Sag	Cap	Aq	Aq	Pis	Ar	Tau	Tau	Gem	Gem
Mar 6	Sag	Sag	Cap	Cap	Aq	Pis	Pis	Ar	Tau	Gem	Gem	Can
Mar 14	Sag	Cap	Cap	Aq	Aq	Pis	Ar	Tau	Tau	Gem	Gem	Can
Mar 22	Sag	Cap	Cap	Aq	Pis	Ar	Ar	Tau	Gem	Gem	Can	Can
Mar 30	Cap	Cap	Aq	Pis	Pis	Ar	Tau	Tau	Gem	Can	Can	Can
Apr 7	Cap	Cap	Aq	Pis	Ar	Ar	Tau	Gem	Gem	Can	Can	Leo
Apr 14	Cap	Aq	Aq	Pis	Ar	Tau	Tau	Gem	Gem	Can	Can	Leo
Apr 22	Cap	Aq	Pis	Ar	Ar	Tau	Gem	Gem	Can	Can	Leo	Leo
Apr 30	Aq	Aq	Pis	Ar	Tau	Tau	Gem	Can	Can	Can	Leo	Leo
May 8	Aq	Pis	Ar	Ar	Tau	Gem	Gem	Can	Can	Leo	Leo	Leo
May 16	Aq	Pis	Ar	Tau	Gem	Gem	Can	Can	Can	Leo	Leo	Vir
May 24	Pis	Ar	Ar	Tau	Gem	Gem	Can	Can	Leo	Leo	Leo	Vir
June 1	Pis	Ar	Tau	Gem	Gem	Can	Can	Can	Leo	Leo	Vir	Vir
June 9	Ar	Ar	Tau	Gem	Gem	Can	Can	Leo	Leo	Leo	Vir	Vir
June 17	Ar	Tau	Gem	Gem	Can	Can	Can	Leo	Leo	Vir	Vir	Vir
June 25	Tau	Tau	Gem	Gem	Can	Can	Leo	Leo	Leo	Vir	Vir	Lib
July 3	Tau	Gem	Gem	Can	Can	Can	Leo	Leo	Vir	Vir	Vir	Lib
July 11	Tau	Gem	Gem	Can	Can	Leo	Leo	Leo	Vir	Vir	Lib	Lib
July 18	Gem	Gem	Can	Can	Can	Leo	Leo	Vir	Vir	Vir	Lib	Lib
July 26	Gem	Gem	Can	Can	Leo	Leo	Vir	Vir	Vir	Lib	Lib	Lib
Aug 3	Gem	Can	Can	Can	Leo	Leo	Vir	Vir	Vir	Lib	Lib	Sc
Aug 11	Gem	Can	Can	Leo	Leo	Leo	Vir	Vir	Lib	Lib	Lib	Sc
Aug 18	Can	Can	Can	Leo	Leo	Vir	Vir	Vir	Lib	Lib	Sc	Sc
Aug 27	Can	Can	Leo	Leo	Leo	Vir	Vir	Lib	Lib	Lib	Sc	Sc
Sept 4	Can	Can	Leo	Leo	Leo	Vir	Vir	Vir	Lib	Lib	Sc	Sc
Sept 12	Can	Leo	Leo	Leo	Vir	Vir	Lib	Lib	Lib	Sc	Sc	Sag
Sept 20	Leo	Leo	Leo	Vir	Vir	Vir	Lib	Lib	Sc	Sc	Sc	Sag
Sept 28	Leo	Leo	Leo	Vir	Vir	Lib	Lib	Lib	Sc	Sc	Sag	Sag
Oct 6	Leo	Leo	Vir	Vir	Vir	Lib	Lib	Sc	Sc	Sc	Sag	Sag
Oct 14	Leo	Vir	Vir	Vir	Lib	Lib	Lib	Sc	Sc	Sag	Sag	Cap
Oct 22	Leo	Vir	Vir	Lib	Lib	Lib	Sc	Sc	Sc	Sag	Sag	Cap
Oct 30	Vir	Vir	Vir	Lib	Lib	Sc	Sc	Sc	Sag	Sag	Cap	Cap
Nov 7	Vir	Vir	Lib	Lib	Lib	Sc	Sc	Sc	Sag	Sag	Cap	Cap
Nov 15	Vir	Vir	Lib	Lib	Sc	Sc	Sc	Sag	Sag	Cap	Cap	Aq
Nov 23	Vir	Lib	Lib	Lib	Sc	Sc	Sag	Sag	Sag	Cap	Cap	Aq
Dec 1	Vir	Lib	Lib	Sc	Sc	Sc	Sag	Sag	Cap	Cap	Aq	Aq
Dec 9	Lib	Lib	Lib	Sc	Sc	Sag	Sag	Sag	Cap	Cap	Aq	Pis
Dec 18	Lib	Lib	Sc	Sc	Sc	Sag	Sag	Cap	Cap	Aq	Aq	Pis
Dec 28	Lib	Lib	Sc	Sc	Sag	Sag	Sag	Cap	Aq	Aq	Pis	Ar

RISING SIGNS—P.M. BIRTHS

	1 PM	2 PM	3 PM	4 PM	5 PM	6 PM	7 PM	8 PM	9 PM	10 PM	11 PM	12 MID-NIGHT
Jan 1	Tau	Gem	Gem	Can	Can	Can	Leo	Leo	Vir	Vir	Vir	Lib
Jan 9	Tau	Gem	Gem	Can	Can	Leo	Leo	Leo	Vir	Vir	Vir	Lib
Jan 17	Gem	Gem	Can	Can	Can	Leo	Leo	Vir	Vir	Vir	Lib	Lib
Jan 25	Gem	Gem	Can	Can	Leo	Leo	Leo	Vir	Vir	Lib	Lib	Lib
Feb 2	Gem	Can	Can	Can	Leo	Leo	Vir	Vir	Vir	Lib	Lib	Sc
Feb 10	Gem	Can	Can	Leo	Leo	Leo	Vir	Vir	Lib	Lib	Lib	Sc
Feb 18	Can	Can	Can	Leo	Leo	Vir	Vir	Vir	Lib	Lib	Sc	Sc
Feb 26	Can	Can	Leo	Leo	Leo	Vir	Vir	Lib	Lib	Lib	Sc	Sc
Mar 6	Can	Leo	Leo	Leo	Vir	Vir	Vir	Lib	Lib	Sc	Sc	Sc
Mar 14	Can	Leo	Leo	Vir	Vir	Vir	Lib	Lib	Lib	Sc	Sc	Sag
Mar 22	Leo	Leo	Leo	Vir	Vir	Lib	Lib	Lib	Sc	Sc	Sc	Sag
Mar 30	Leo	Leo	Vir	Vir	Vir	Lib	Lib	Sc	Sc	Sc	Sag	Sag
Apr 7	Leo	Leo	Vir	Vir	Lib	Lib	Lib	Sc	Sc	Sc	Sag	Sag
Apr 14	Leo	Vir	Vir	Vir	Lib	Lib	Sc	Sc	Sc	Sag	Sag	Cap
Apr 22	Leo	Vir	Vir	Lib	Lib	Lib	Sc	Sc	Sc	Sag	Sag	Cap
Apr 30	Vir	Vir	Vir	Lib	Lib	Sc	Sc	Sc	Sag	Sag	Cap	Cap
May 8	Vir	Vir	Lib	Lib	Lib	Sc	Sc	Sc	Sag	Sag	Cap	Cap
May 16	Vir	Vir	Lib	Lib	Sc	Sc	Sc	Sag	Sag	Cap	Cap	Aq
May 24	Vir	Lib	Lib	Lib	Sc	Sc	Sag	Sag	Sag	Cap	Cap	Aq
June 1	Vir	Lib	Lib	Sc	Sc	Sc	Sag	Sag	Cap	Cap	Aq	Aq
June 9	Lib	Lib	Lib	Sc	Sc	Sag	Sag	Sag	Cap	Cap	Aq	Pis
June 17	Lib	Lib	Sc	Sc	Sc	Sag	Sag	Cap	Cap	Aq	Aq	Pis
June 25	Lib	Lib	Sc	Sc	Sag	Sag	Sag	Cap	Cap	Aq	Pis	Ar
July 3	Lib	Sc	Sc	Sc	Sag	Sag	Cap	Cap	Aq	Aq	Pis	Ar
July 11	Lib	Sc	Sc	Sag	Sag	Sag	Cap	Cap	Aq	Pis	Ar	Tau
July 18	Sc	Sc	Sc	Sag	Sag	Cap	Cap	Aq	Aq	Pis	Ar	Tau
July 26	Sc	Sc	Sag	Sag	Sag	Cap	Cap	Aq	Pis	Ar	Tau	Tau
Aug 3	Sc	Sc	Sag	Sag	Cap	Cap	Aq	Aq	Pis	Ar	Tau	Gem
Aug 11	Sc	Sag	Sag	Sag	Cap	Cap	Aq	Pis	Ar	Tau	Tau	Gem
Aug 18	Sc	Sag	Sag	Cap	Cap	Aq	Pis	Pis	Ar	Tau	Gem	Gem
Aug 27	Sag	Sag	Sag	Cap	Cap	Aq	Pis	Ar	Tau	Tau	Gem	Gem
Sept 4	Sag	Sag	Cap	Cap	Aq	Pis	Pis	Ar	Tau	Gem	Gem	Can
Sept 12	Sag	Sag	Cap	Aq	Aq	Pis	Ar	Tau	Tau	Gem	Gem	Can
Sept 20	Sag	Cap	Cap	Aq	Pis	Pis	Ar	Tau	Gem	Gem	Can	Can
Sept 28	Cap	Cap	Aq	Aq	Pis	Ar	Tau	Tau	Gem	Can	Can	Can
Oct 6	Cap	Cap	Aq	Pis	Ar	Ar	Tau	Gem	Gem	Can	Can	Leo
Oct 14	Cap	Aq	Aq	Pis	Ar	Tau	Tau	Gem	Gem	Can	Can	Leo
Oct 22	Cap	Aq	Pis	Ar	Ar	Tau	Gem	Gem	Can	Can	Leo	Leo
Oct 30	Aq	Aq	Pis	Ar	Tau	Tau	Gem	Can	Can	Can	Leo	Leo
Nov 7	Aq	Aq	Pis	Ar	Tau	Tau	Gem	Can	Can	Can	Leo	Leo
Nov 15	Aq	Pis	Ar	Tau	Gem	Gem	Can	Can	Can	Leo	Leo	Vir
Nov 23	Pis	Ar	Ar	Tau	Gem	Gem	Can	Can	Leo	Leo	Leo	Vir
Dec 1	Pis	Ar	Tau	Gem	Gem	Can	Can	Leo	Leo	Leo	Vir	Vir
Dec 9	Ar	Tau	Tau	Gem	Gem	Can	Can	Leo	Leo	Leo	Vir	Vir
Dec 18	Ar	Tau	Gem	Gem	Can	Can	Can	Leo	Leo	Vir	Vir	Vir
Dec 28	Tau	Tau	Gem	Gem	Can	Can	Leo	Leo	Vir	Vir	Vir	Lib

CHAPTER 7

The Keys to Reading Your Horoscope: The Glyphs

Are you ready to take your astrology knowledge to the next level and read your first horoscope chart? If so, you'll encounter a new language of symbols, because horoscope charts are written in glyphs, a centuries-old pictographic language. These little "pictures" are a type of shorthand used by astrologers around the world to indicate the planets and the signs.

There's no way to avoid learning the glyphs, if you want to get deeper into astrology. Whether you download your chart from one of the many Internet sites that offer free charts or you buy one of the many interesting astrology programs, you'll find charts are always written in glyph language. Some software makes it easier for beginners by listing the planets and their signs in English alongside the chart and other programs will pop up an English interpretation as your roll your mouse over the glyph. However, in the long run, it's much easier—and more fun—to learn the glyphs yourself.

There's an extra bonus to learning the glyphs: They contain a kind of visual code, with built-in clues that will tell you not only which sign or planet each represents, but what the symbol means in a deeper, more esoteric sense. Actually the physical act of writing the symbol is a mystical experience in itself, a way to invoke the deeper meaning of the sign or planet through age-old visual elements that have been with us since time began.

Since there are only twelve signs and ten planets (not counting a few asteroids and other space objects some astrologers use), it's a lot easier than learning to read a foreign language. Here's a code cracker for the glyphs, beginning with the glyphs for the planets. To those who already know their glyphs, don't just skim over the chapter. These familiar graphics have hidden meanings you will discover!

The Glyphs for the Planets

The glyphs for the planets are easy to learn. They're simple combinations of the most basic visual elements: the circle, the semicircle or arc, and the cross. However, each component of a glyph has a special meaning in relation to the other parts of the symbol.

The circle, which has no beginning or end, is one of the oldest symbols of spirit or spiritual forces. Early diagrams of the heavens—spiritual territory—are shown in circular form. The never-ending line of the circle is the perfect symbol for eternity. The semicircle or arc is an incomplete circle, symbolizing the receptive, finite soul, which contains spiritual potential in the curving line.

The vertical line of the cross symbolizes movement from heaven to earth. The horizontal line describes temporal movement, here and now, in time and space. Combined in a cross, the vertical and horizontal planes symbolize manifestation in the material world.

The Sun Glyph ⊙

The sun is always shown by this powerful solar symbol, a circle with a point in the center. The center point is you, your spiritual center, and the symbol represents your infinite personality incarnating (the point) into the finite cycles of birth and death.

The sun has been represented by a circle or disk since ancient Egyptian times when the solar disk represented the sun god, Ra. Some archaeologists believe the great stone circles found in England were centers of sun worship. This particular version of the symbol was brought into common use in the sixteenth century after German occultist and scholar Cornelius Agrippa (1486–1535) wrote a book called *Die Occulta Philosophia,* which became accepted as the authority in the field. Agrippa collected many of the medieval astrological and magical symbols in this book, which have been used by astrologers since then.

The Moon Glyph ☽

The moon glyph is the most recognizable symbol on a chart, a left-facing arc stylized into the crescent moon. As part of a circle, the arc symbolizes the potential fulfillment of the entire circle, the life force that is still incomplete. Therefore, it is the ideal representation of the reactive, receptive, emotional nature of the moon.

The Mercury Glyph ☿

Mercury contains all three elemental symbols: the crescent, the circle, and the cross in vertical order. This is the "Venus with a hat" glyph (compare with the symbol of Venus). With another stretch of the imagination, can't you see the winged cap of Mercury the messenger? Think of the upturned crescent as antennae that tune in and transmit messages from the sun, reminding you that Mercury is the way you communicate, the way your mind works. The upturned arc is receiving energy into the spirit or solar circle, which will later be translated into action on the material plane, symbolized by the cross. All the elements are equally sized because Mercury is neutral; it doesn't play favorites! This planet symbolizes objective, detached, unemotional thinking.

The Venus Glyph ♀

Here the relationship is between two components: the circle of spirit and the cross of matter. Spirit is elevated over matter, pulling it upward. Venus asks, "What is beautiful? What do you like best? What do you love to have done to you?" Consequently, Venus determines both your ideal of beauty and what feels good sensually. It governs your own allure and power to attract, as well as what attracts and pleases you.

The Mars Glyph ♂

In this glyph, the cross of matter is stylized into an arrowhead pointed up and outward, propelled by the circle of spirit. With a little imagination, you can visualize it as the shield and spear of Mars, the ancient god of war. You can deduce that Mars embodies your spiritual energy projected into the outer world. It's your assertiveness, your initiative, your aggressive drive, what you like to do to others, your temper. If you know someone's Mars, you know whether they'll blow up when angry or do a slow burn. Your task is to use your outgoing Mars energy wisely and well.

The Jupiter Glyph ♃

Jupiter is the basic cross of matter, with a large stylized crescent perched on the left side of the horizontal, temporal plane. You might think of the crescent as an open hand, because one meaning of Jupiter is "luck," what's handed to you. You don't have to work for what you get from Jupiter; it comes to you, if you're open to it.

The Jupiter glyph might also remind you of a jumbo jet plane, with a huge tail fin, about to take off. This is the planet of travel, mental and spiritual, of expanding your horizons via new ideas, new spiritual dimensions, and new places. Jupiter embodies the optimism and enthusiasm of the traveler about to embark on an exciting adventure.

The Saturn Glyph ♄

Flip Jupiter over, and you've got Saturn. This might not be immediately apparent because Saturn is usually stylized into an "h" form like the one shown here. The principle it expresses is the opposite of Jupiter's expansive tendencies. Saturn pulls you back to earth: the receptive arc is pushed down underneath the cross of matter. Before there are any rewards or expansion, the duties and obligations of the material world must be considered. Saturn says, "Stop, wait, finish your chores before you take off!"

Saturn's glyph also resembles the sickle of old "Father Time."

Saturn was first known as Chronos, the Greek god of time, for time brings all matter to an end. When it was the most distant planet (before the discovery of Uranus), Saturn was believed to be the place where time stopped. After the soul departed from earth, it journeyed back to the outer reaches of the universe and finally stopped at Saturn, or at "the end of time."

The Uranus Glyph ♅

The glyph for Uranus is often stylized to form a capital *H* after Sir William Herschel, who discovered the planet. But the more esoteric version curves the two pillars of the H into crescent antennae, or "ears," like satellite disks receiving signals from space. These are perched on the horizontal material line of the cross of matter and pushed from below by the circle of the spirit. To many sci-fi fans, Uranus looks like an orbiting satellite.

Uranus channels the highest energy of all, the white electrical light of the universal spiritual force that holds the cosmos together. This pure electrical energy is gathered from all over the universe. Because Uranus energy doesn't follow any ordinary celestial drumbeat, it can't be controlled or predicted (which is also true of those who are strongly influenced by this eccentric planet). In the symbol, this energy is manifested through the balance of polarities (the two opposite arms of the glyph) like the two polarized wires of a lightbulb.

The Neptune Glyph ♆

Neptune's glyph is usually stylized to look like a trident, the weapon of the Roman god Neptune. However, on a more esoteric level, it shows the large upturned crescent of the soul pierced through by the cross of matter. Neptune nails down, or materializes, soul energy, bringing impulses from the soul level into manifestation. That is why Neptune is associated with imagination or "imagining in," making an image of the soul. Neptune works through feelings, sensitivity, and the mystical capacity to bring the divine into the earthly realm.

The Pluto Glyph ♀

Pluto is written two ways. One is a composite of the letters *PL,* the first two letters of the word Pluto and coincidentally the initials of Percival Lowell, one of the planet's discoverers. The other, more esoteric symbol is a small circle above a large open crescent that surmounts the cross of matter. This depicts Pluto's power to regenerate. Imagine a new little spirit emerging from the sheltering cup of the soul. Pluto rules the forces of life and death. After this planet has passed a sensitive point in your chart, you are transformed, reborn in some way.

Sci-fi fans might visualize this glyph as a small satellite (the circle) being launched. It was shortly after Pluto's discovery that we learned how to harness the nuclear forces that made space exploration possible. Pluto rules the transformative power of atomic energy, which totally changed our lives and from which there is no turning back.

The Glyphs for the Signs

On an astrology chart, the glyph for the sign will appear after that of the planet. For example, when you see the moon glyph followed first by a number and then by another glyph representing the sign, this means that the moon was passing over a certain degree of that astrological sign at the time of the chart. On the dividing lines between the houses on your chart, you'll find the symbol for the sign that rules the house.

Because sun sign symbols do not contain the same basic geometric components of the planetary glyphs, we must look elsewhere for clues to their meanings. Many have been passed down from ancient Egyptian and Chaldean civilizations with few modifications. Others have been adapted over the centuries.

In deciphering many of the glyphs, you'll often find that the symbols reveal a dual nature of the sign, which is not always apparent in the usual sun sign descriptions. For instance, the Gemini glyph is similar to the Roman numeral for two, and reveals this sign's longing to discover a twin soul. The Cancer glyph may be interpreted as resembling either the nurturing breasts or the self-protective claws of a crab, both symbols associated with the contrasting qualities of this sign. Libra's glyph embodies the duality of the spirit balanced with material reality. The Sagittarius glyph shows that the aspirant must also carry along the earthly animal nature in his quest. The Capricorn sea goat is another symbol with dual emphasis. The goat climbs high, yet is always pulled back by the deep waters of the unconscious. Aquarius embodies the double waves of mental detachment, balanced by the desire for connection with others, in a friendly way. Finally, the two fishes of Pisces, which are forever tied together, show the duality of the soul and the spirit that must be reconciled.

The Aries Glyph ♈

Since the symbol for Aries is the Ram, this glyph is obviously associated with a ram's horns, which characterize one aspect of the Aries personality—an aggressive, me-first, leaping-headfirst attitude. But the symbol can be interpreted in other ways as well. Some astrologers liken it to a fountain of energy, which Aries people also embody. The first sign of the zodiac bursts on the scene eagerly, ready to go. Another analogy is to the eyebrows and nose of the human head, which Aries rules, and the thinking power that is initiated by the brain.

One theory of this symbol links it to the Egyptian god Amun, represented by a ram in ancient times. As Amun-Ra, this god was believed to embody the creator of the universe, the leader of all the other gods. This relates easily to the position of Aries as the leader (or first sign) of the zodiac, which begins at the spring equinox, a time of the year when nature is renewed.

The Taurus Glyph ♉

This is another easy glyph to draw and identify. It takes little imagination to decipher the bull's head with long curving horns. Like its symbol the Bull, the archetypal Taurus is slow to anger but ferocious when provoked, as well as stubborn, steady, and sensual. Another association is the larynx (and thyroid) of the throat area (ruled by Taurus) and the eustachian tubes running up to the ears, which coincides with the relationship of Taurus to the voice, song, and music. Many famous singers, musicians, and composers have prominent Taurus influences.

Many ancient religions involved a bull as the central figure in fertility rites or initiations, usually symbolizing the victory of man over his animal nature. Another possible origin is in the sacred bull of Egypt, who embodied the incarnate form of Osiris, god of death and resurrection. In early Christian imagery, the Taurus Bull represented St. Luke.

The Gemini Glyph ♊

The standard glyph immediately calls to mind the Roman numeral for two (II) and the Twins symbol, as it is called, for Gemini. In almost all drawings and images used for this sign, the relationship between two persons is emphasized. Usually one twin will be touching the other, which signifies communication, human contact, the desire to share.

The top line of the Gemini glyph indicates mental communication, while the bottom line indicates shared physical space.

The most famous Gemini legend is that of the twin sons Castor and Pollux, one of whom had a mortal father while the other was the son of Zeus, king of the gods. When it came time for the mortal twin to die, his grief-stricken brother pleaded with Zeus, who agreed to let them spend half the year on earth in mortal form and half in immortal life, with the gods on Mount Olympus. This reflects a basic duality of humankind, which possesses an immortal soul yet is also subject to the limits of mortality.

The Cancer Glyph ♋

Two convenient images relate to the Cancer glyph. It is easiest to decode the curving claws of the Cancer symbol, the Crab. Like the crab's, Cancer's element is water. This sensitive sign also has a hard protective shell to protect its tender interior. The crab must be wily to escape predators, scampering sideways and hiding under rocks. The crab also responds to the cycles of the moon, as do all shellfish. The other image is that of two female breasts, which Cancer rules, showing that this is a sign that nurtures and protects others as well as itself.

In ancient Egypt, Cancer was also represented by the scarab beetle, a symbol of regeneration and eternal life.

The Leo Glyph ♌

Notice that the Leo glyph seems to be an extension of Cancer's glyph, with a significant difference. In the Cancer glyph, the lines curve inward protectively. The Leo glyph expresses energy outwardly. And there is no duality in the symbol, the Lion, or in Leo, the sign.

Lions have belonged to the sign of Leo since earliest times. It is not difficult to imagine the king of beasts with his sweeping mane and curling tail from this glyph. The upward sweep of the glyph easily describes the positive energy of Leo: the flourishing tail, the flamboyant qualities. Another analogy, perhaps a stretch of the imagination, is that of a heart leaping up with joy and enthusiasm, also very typical of Leo, which also rules the heart. In early Christian imagery, the Leo Lion represented St. Mark.

The Virgo Glyph ♍

You can read much into this mysterious glyph. For instance, it could represent the initials of "Mary Virgin," or a young woman holding a staff of wheat, or stylized female genitalia, all common interpretations. The M shape might also remind you that Virgo is ruled by Mercury. The cross beneath the symbol reveals the grounded, practical nature of this earth sign.

The earliest zodiacs link Virgo with the Egyptian goddess Isis, who gave birth to the god Horus after her husband Osiris had been killed, in the archetype of a miraculous conception. There are many ancient statues of Isis nursing her baby son, which are reminiscent of medieval Virgin and Child motifs. This sign has also been associated with the image of the Holy Grail, when the Virgo symbol was substituted with a chalice.

The Libra Glyph ♎

It is not difficult to read the standard image for Libra, the Scales, into this glyph. There is another meaning, however, that is equally relevant: the setting sun as it descends over the horizon. Libra's natural position on the zodiac wheel is the descendant, or sunset position (as the Aries natural position is the ascendant, or rising sign). Both images relate to Libra's personality. Libra is always weighing pros and cons for a balanced decision. In the sunset image, the sun (male) hovers over the horizontal earth (female) before setting. Libra is the space between these lines, harmonizing yin and yang, spiritual and material, male and female, ideal and real worlds. The glyph has also been linked to the kidneys, which are associated with Libra.

The Scorpio Glyph ♏

With its barbed tail, this glyph is easy to identify as the Scorpion for the sign of Scorpio. It also represents the male sexual parts, over which the sign rules. From the arrowhead, you can draw the conclusion that Mars was once its ruler. Some earlier Egyptian glyphs for Scorpio represent it as an erect serpent, so the Serpent is an alternate symbol.

Another symbol for Scorpio, which is not identifiable in this glyph, is the Eagle. Scorpios can go to extremes, either in soaring like the eagle or self-destructing like the scorpion. In early Christian imagery, which often used zodiacal symbols, the Scorpio Eagle was chosen to symbolize the intense apostle St. John the Evangelist.

The Sagittarius Glyph ♐

This is one of the easiest to spot and draw: an upward pointing arrow lifting up a cross. The arrow is pointing skyward, while the cross represents the four elements of the material world, which the arrow must convey. Elevating materiality into spirituality is an important Sagittarius quality, which explains why this sign is associated with higher learning, religion, philosophy, travel—the aspiring professions. Sagittarius can also send barbed arrows of frankness in the pursuit of truth, so the Archer symbol for Sagittarius is apt. (Sagittarius is also the sign of the supersalesman.)

Sagittarius is symbolically represented by the centaur, a mythological creature who is half man, half horse, aiming his arrow toward the skies. Though Sagittarius is motivated by spiritual aspiration, it also must balance the powerful appetites of the animal nature. The centaur Chiron, a figure in Greek mythology, became a wise teacher who, after many adventures and world travels, was killed by a poisoned arrow.

The Capricorn Glyph ♑

One of the most difficult symbols to draw, this glyph may take some practice. It is a representation of the sea goat: a mythical animal that is a goat with a curving fish's tail. The goat part of Capricorn wants to leave the waters of the emotions and climb to the elevated areas of life. But the fish tail is the unconscious, the deep chaotic psychic level that draws the goat back. Capricorn is often trying to escape the deep, feeling part of life by submerging himself in work, steadily ascending to the top. To some people, the glyph represents a seated figure with a bent knee, a reminder that Capricorn governs the knee area of the body.

An interesting aspect of this glyph is the contrast of the sharp pointed horns—which represent the penetrating, shrewd, conscious side of Capricorn—with the swishing tail—which represents its serpentine, unconscious, emotional force. One Capricorn legend, which dates from Roman times, tells of the earthy fertility god, Pan, who tried to save himself from uncontrollable sexual desires by jumping into the Nile. His upper body then turned into a goat, while the lower part became a fish. Later, Jupiter gave him a safe haven as a constellation in the skies.

The Aquarius Glyph ♒

This ancient water symbol can be traced back to an Egyptian hieroglyph representing streams of life force. Symbolized by the Water Bearer, Aquarius is distributor of the waters of life—the magic liquid of regeneration. The two waves can also be linked to the positive and negative charges of the electrical energy that Aquarius rules, a sort of universal wavelength. Aquarius is tuned in intuitively to higher forces via this electrical force. The duality of the glyph could also refer to the dual nature of Aquarius, a sign that runs hot and cold and that is friendly but also detached in the mental world of air signs.

In Greek legends, Aquarius is represented by Ganymede, who was carried to heaven by an eagle in order to become the cupbearer of Zeus and to supervise the annual flooding of the Nile. The sign later became associated with aviation and notions of flight. Like the other fixed signs (Taurus, Scorpio, and Leo), Aquarius is associated with an apostle, in this case St. Matthew.

The Pisces Glyph ♓

Here is an abstraction of the familiar image of Pisces, two Fishes swimming in opposite directions yet bound together by a cord. The Fishes represent the spirit—which yearns for the freedom of heaven—and the soul—which remains attached to the desires of the temporal world. During life on earth, the spirit and the soul are bound together. When they complement each other, instead of pulling in opposite directions, they facilitate the Pisces creativity. The ancient version of this glyph, taken from the Egyptians, had no connecting line, which was added in the fourteenth century.

In another interpretation, it is said that the left fish indicates the direction of involution or the beginning of a cycle, while the right fish signifies the direction of evolution, the way to completion of a cycle. It's an appropriate grand finale for Pisces, the last sign of the zodiac.

CHAPTER 8

Join the Astrology Community

Astrology fans love to share their knowledge and socialize. So why not join the community of astrologers online or at a conference? You might be surprised to find an astrology club in your local area. Connecting with other astrology fans and learning more about this fascinating subject has never been easier. In fact the many options available with just a click of your computer are mind-boggling.

You need only type the word *astrology* into any Internet search engine and watch hundreds of listings of astrology-related sites pop up. There are local meetings and international conferences where you can meet and study with other astrologers, and books and tapes to help you learn at home. You could even combine your vacation with an astrological workshop in an exotic locale, such as Bali or Mexico.

To help you sort out the variety of options available, here are our top picks of the Internet and the astrological community at large.

National Council for Geocosmic Research (NCGR)

Whether you'd like to know more about such specialties as financial astrology or techniques for timing events, or if you'd prefer the psychological or mythological approach, you'll meet the top astrologers at conferences sponsored by the National Council for Geocosmic Research. NCGR is dedicated to providing quality education, bringing astrologers and astrology fans together at conferences, and promoting fellowship. Their course structure provides a systematized study of the many facets of astrology. The organization sponsors educational workshops, taped lectures, conferences, and a directory of professional astrologers.

For an annual membership fee, you get their excellent publications and newsletters, plus the opportunity to network with other astrology buffs at local chapter events. At this writing there are chapters in twenty-six states and four countries.

To join NCGR and for the latest information on upcoming events and chapters in your city, consult their Web site: www. geocosmic.org.

American Federation of Astrologers (AFA)

Established in 1938, this is one of the oldest astrological organizations in the United States. AFA offers conferences, conventions, and a correspondence course. If you are looking for a reading, their interesting Web site will refer you to an accredited AFA astrologer.

6535 South Rural Road
Tempe, AZ 85283
Phone: (888) 301-7630 or (480) 838-1751
Fax: (480) 838-8293
Web site: www.astrologers.com

Association for Astrological Networking (AFAN)

Did you know that astrologers are still being harassed for practicing astrology? AFAN provides support and legal information, and works toward improving the public image of astrology. AFAN's network of local astrologers links with the international astrological community. Here are the people who will go to bat for astrology when it is attacked in the media. Everyone who cares about astrology should join!

8306 Wilshire Boulevard
PMB 537
Beverly Hills, CA 90211
Phone: (800) 578-2326
E-mail: info@afan.org
Web site: www.afan.org

International Society for Astrology Research (ISAR)

An international organization of professional astrologers dedicated to encouraging the highest standards of quality in the field of astrology with an emphasis on research. Among ISAR's benefits are quarterly journals, a weekly e-mail newsletter, and a free membership directory.

P.O. Box 38613
Los Angeles, CA 90038
Fax: (805) 933-0301
Web site: www.isarastrology.com

Astrology Magazines

In addition to articles by top astrologers, most have listings of astrology conferences, events, and local happenings.

Horoscope Guide
Kappa Publishing Group
6198 Butler Pike
Suite 200
Blue Bell, PA 19422-2600
Web site: www.kappapublishing.com/astrology

Dell Horoscope
Their Web site features a listing of local astrological meetings.

Customer Service
6 Prowitt Street
Norwalk, CT 06855
Phone: (800) 220-7443
Web site: www.dellhoroscope.com

The Mountain Astrologer
A favorite magazine of astrology fans,*The Mountain Astrologer* also has an interesting Web site featuring the latest news from an astrological point of view, plus feature articles from the magazine.

P.O. Box 970
Cedar Ridge, CA 95924
Web site: www.mountainastrologer.com

Astrology College

Kepler College of Astrological Arts and Sciences

A degree-granting college, which is also a center of astrology, has long been the dream of the astrological community and is a giant step forward in providing credibility to the profession. Therefore, the opening of Kepler College in 2000 was a historical event for astrology. It is the only college in the United States authorized to issue BA and MA degrees in astrological studies. Here is where to study with the best scholars, teachers, and communicators in the field. A long-distance study program is available for those interested.

Kepler College also offers online noncredit courses that anyone can take via the Kepler Community Learning Center. Classes range from two days to ten weeks in length, and the cost will vary depending upon the class taken. Students can access an online Web site to enroll in specific classes and interact with other students and instructors.

For more information, contact:

4630 200th Street SW
Suite P
Lynnwood, WA 98036
Phone: (425) 673-4292
Fax: (425) 673-4983
Web site: www.kepler.edu

Our Favorite Web sites

Of the thousands of astrological Web sites that come and go on the Internet, these have stood the test of time and are likely to still be operating when this book is published.

Astrodienst (www.astro.com)

Don't miss this fabulous international site, which has long been one of the best astrology resources on the Internet. It's a great place to view your own astrology chart. The world atlas on this site will give you the accurate longitude and latitude of your birthplace for setting up your horoscope. Then you can print out your free chart in a range of easy-to-read formats. Other attractions: a list of famous people born on your birth date, a feature that helps you choose the best vacation spot, and articles by world-famous astrologers.

AstroDatabank (www.astrodatabank.com)

When the news is breaking, you can bet this site will be the first to get accurate birthdays of the headliners. The late astrologer Lois Rodden was a stickler for factual information and her meticulous research is being continued, much to the benefit of the astrological community. The Web site specializes in charts of current newsmakers, political figures, and international celebrities. You can also participate in discussions and analysis of the charts and see what some of the world's best astrologers have to say about them. Their AstroDatabank program, which you can purchase at the site, provides thousands of birthdays sorted into categories. It's an excellent research tool.

StarIQ (www.stariq.com)

Find out how top astrologers view the latest headlines at the must-see StarIQ site. Many of the best minds in astrology comment on the latest news, stock market ups and downs, and political contenders. You can sign up to receive e-mail forecasts at the most important times keyed to your individual chart. (This is one of the best of the online forecasts.)

Astro-Noetics (www.astro-noetics.com)

For those who are ready to explore astrology's interface with politics, popular culture, and current events, here is a sophisticated site with in-depth articles and personality profiles. Lots of depth and content here for the astrology-savvy surfer.

Astrology Books (www.astroamerica.com)

The Astrology Center of America sells a wide selection of books on all aspects of astrology, from the basics to the most advanced, at this online bookstore. Also available are many hard-to-find and used books.

Astrology Scholars' Sites

See what Robert Hand, one of astrology's great teachers, has to offer on his site at www.robhand.com. A leading expert on the history of astrology, he's on the cutting edge of the latest research.

The Project Hindsight group of astrologers is devoted to restoring the astrology of the Hellenistic period, the primary source for all later Western astrology. There are fascinating articles for astrology fans on this site at www.projecthindsight. com.

Financial Astrology Sites

Financial astrology is a hot specialty, with many tipsters, players, and theorists. There are online columns, newsletters, specialized financial astrology software, and mutual funds run by astrology seers. One of the more respected financial astrologers is Ray Merriman, whose market comments on www. mmacycles.com are a must for those following the bulls and bears.

Explore Your Relationships (www.topsynergy.com)

Ever wondered how you'd get along with Brad Pitt, Halle Berry, or another famous hottie? TopSynergy offers a clever tool called a relationship analyst that will help you use astrology to analyze past, present, or possible future relationships. There's a database of celebrity horoscopes for you to partner with your own as well. It's free for unlimited use.

How to Zoom Around the Sky

If you haven't already discovered the wonders of Google Earth (www.earth.google.com), then you've been missing close-up aerial views of anyplace on the planet from your old hometown to the beaches of Hawaii. Even more fascinating for astrology buffs is the newest feature called Google Sky, a marvel of computer technology that lets you view the sky overhead from anyplace you choose. Want to see the stars over Paris at the moment? A few clicks of your mouse will take you there. Then you can follow the tracks of the sun, moon, and planets or check astronomical information and beautiful Hubble images. Go to the Google Web site to download this free program. Then get ready to take a cosmic tour around the earth and sky.

Listen to the Sounds of Your Sign

Astrology Weekly (www.astrologyweekly.com) is a Web site from Romania, with lots to offer astro surfers. Here you can check all the planetary placements for the week, get free charts, join an international discussion group, and check out charts for countries and world leaders. Of special interest is the chart generator, an easy-to-use feature that will create a natal chart. Just click on *new chart* and enter the year, month, day, time, longitude, and latitude of your birth place. Select the Placidus or Koch house system and click on *show it*. Your chart should come right up on the screen. You can then copy the link to your astrology chart, store it, and later share your chart with friends. If you don't have astrology software, this is a good way to view charts instantly. This site also has some fun ways to pass the time, such as listening to music especially chosen for your sun sign.

Stellar Gifts

If you've ever wondered what to give your astrology buddies, here's the place to find foolproof gifts. How about a mug, mouse pad, or plaque decorated with someone's chart? Would a special person like a pendant personalized with their planets? Check out www.milestonegifts.co.uk for some great ideas for putting those astrology charts to decorative use.

CHAPTER 9

The Best Astrology Software: Take Your Knowledge to the Next Level

Are you ready to begin looking at charts of friends and family? Would you like to call up your favorite celebrity's chart or check the aspects every day on your BlackBerry? Perhaps you'd like to study astrology in depth and would prefer a more comprehensive program that adapts to your needs as you learn. If you haven't discovered the wonders of astrology software, you're missing out!

Astrology technology has advanced to the point where even a computerphobe can call up a Web site on a BlackBerry browser and put a chart on the screen in seconds. It does help to have some basic knowledge of the signs, houses, planets, and especially the glyphs for the planets and the signs. Then you can practice reading charts and relating the planets to the lives of friends, relatives, and daily events, the ideal way to get more involved with astrology.

There's a program for every level of interest at all price points—starting with free. For the dabbler, there are the affordable Winstar Express, Know, and Time Passages. For the serious student, there are Astrology (free), Solar Fire, Kepler, Winstar Plus—software that does every technique on the planet and gives you beautiful chart printouts. If you're a MAC user, you'll be satisfied with the wonderful IO and Time Passages software.

However, since all the programs use the astrology symbols, or glyphs, for planets and signs, rather than written words, you should learn the glyphs before you purchase your software. Chapter 7 will help you do just that. Here are some software options for you to explore.

Easy for Beginners

Time Passages

Designed for either a Macintosh or Windows computer, Time Passages is straightforward and easy to use. It allows you to generate charts and interpretation reports for yourself or friends and loved ones at the touch of a button. If you haven't yet learned the astrology symbols, this might be the program for you. Just roll your mouse over any symbols of the planets, signs, or house cusps, and you'll be shown a description in plain English below the chart. Then click on the planet, sign, or house cusp and up pops a detailed interpretation. Couldn't be easier. A new Basic Edition, under fifty dollars at this writing, is bargain priced and ideal for beginners.

Time Passages
(866) 772-7876 (866-77-ASTRO)
Web site: www.astrograph.com

The "Know Thru Astrology" Series

This new series is designed especially for the nonastrologer. There are four programs in the series: KNOW Your Self, KNOW Your Future, KNOW Your Lover, and KNOW Your Child, each priced at an affordable $49.95 (at this writing). Though it is billed as beginner software, the KNOW series offers many sophisticated options, such as a calendar to let you navigate future or past influences, detailed chart interpretations, built-in pop-ups to show you what everything means. You'll need a PC running current Windows versions starting with Windows 98 SE, with 512 Mb RAM, and a hard drive with 170–300 Mb free space.

Matrix Software
126 South Michigan Avenue
Big Rapids, MI 49307
(800) 752-6387
Web site: www.astrologysoftware.com

Growth Opportunities

Astrolabe

Astrolabe is one of the top astrology software resources. Check out the latest version of their powerful Solar Fire software for Windows. It's a breeze to use and will grow with your increasing knowledge of astrology to the most sophisticated levels. This company also markets a variety of programs for all levels of expertise and a wide selection of computer-generated astrology readings. This is a good resource for innovative software as well as applications for older computers.

The Astrolabe Web site is a great place to start your astrology tour of the Internet. Visitors to the site are greeted with a chart of the time you log on. And you can get your chart calculated, also free, with a mini interpretation e-mailed to you.

Astrolabe
Box 1750-R
Brewster, MA 02631
Phone: (800) 843-6682
Web site: www.alabe.com

Matrix Software

You'll find a wide variety of software at student and advanced levels in all price ranges, demo disks, lots of interesting readings. Check out Winstar Express, a powerful but reasonably priced program suitable for all skill levels. The Matrix Web site offers lots of fun activities for Web surfers, such as free readings from the I Ching, the runes, and the tarot. There are many free desktop backgrounds with astrology themes.

Matrix Software
126 South Michigan Avenue
Big Rapids, MI 49307
Phone: (800) 752-6387
Web site: www.astrologysoftware.com

Astro Computing Services (ACS)

Books, software, individual charts, and telephone readings
are offered by this company. Their freebies include astrology
greeting cards and new moon reports. Find technical astrology materials here such as *The American Ephemeris* and PC
atlases. ACS will calculate and send charts to you, a valuable
service if you do not have a computer.

Starcrafts Publishing
334 Calef Hwy.
Epping, NH 03042
Phone: (866) 953-8458
Web site: www.astrocom.com

Air Software

Here you'll find powerful, creative astrology software, plus
current stock market analysis. Financial astrology programs
for stock market traders are a specialty. There are some interesting freebees at this site. Check out the maps of eclipse
paths for any year and a free astrology clock program.

Air Software
115 Caya Avenue
West Hartford, CT 06110
Phone: (800) 659-1247
Web site: www.alphee.com

Kepler: State of the Art

Here's a program that's got everything. Gorgeous graphic images, audio-visual effects, and myriad sophisticated chart options are built into this fascinating software. It's even got an

astrological encyclopedia, plus diagrams and images to help you understand advanced concepts. This program is pricey, but if you're serious about learning astrology, it's an investment that will grow with you! Check out its features at www.astrosoftware.com.

Timecycles Research: For Mac Users

Here's where Mac users can find astrology software that's as sophisticated as it gets. If you have a Mac, you'll love their beautiful graphic IO Series programs.

Time Cycles Research
P.O. Box 797
Waterford, CT 06385
(800) 827-2240
Web site: www.timecycles.com

Shareware and Freeware: The Price Is Right!

Halloran Software: A Super Shareware Program

Check out Halloran Software's Web site, which offers several levels of Windows astrology software. Beginners should consider their Astrology for Windows shareware program, which is available in unregistered demo form as a free download and in registered form for a very reasonable price.

Halloran Software
P.O. Box 75713
Los Angeles, CA 90075
(800) 732-4628
Web site: www.halloran.com

ASTROLOG

If you're computer-savvy, you can't go wrong with Walter Pullen's amazingly complete Astrology program, which is offered absolutely free at the site. The Web address is www.astrolog.org/astrolog.htm.

Astrolog is an ultrasophisticated program with all the features of much more expensive programs. It comes in versions for all formats: DOS, Windows, Mac, and UNIX. It has some cool features, such as a revolving globe and a constellation map. If you are looking for astrology software with all the bells and whistles that doesn't cost big bucks, this program has it all!

Buying a Computer with Astrology in Mind?

The good news is that astrology software is becoming more sophisticated and fun to use. However, if you've inherited an old computer, don't despair. You don't need the fastest processor and all the newest bells and whistles to run perfectly adequate astrology software. It is still possible to find programs for elder systems, including many new exciting programs.

To take full advantage of all the options, it is best to have a system that runs versions of Windows starting with Windows 98 SE. If you're buying a new computer, invest in one with as much RAM as possible, at least 1 GB. A CD drive will be necessary to load programs or an Internet connection, if you prefer to download programs online.

Mac fans who want to run Windows astrology software should invest in dual boot computers that will operate both the Mac and the Windows XP and Vista platforms.

CHAPTER 10

Ask the Expert: A Personal Reading Could Help

In these changing times, preparing ourselves for challenges ahead becomes a top priority as new issues surface in our lives. This could be the ideal time to add an astrologer to your dream team of advisers. Horoscopes can offer general advice to all members of your sign, but a personal reading can deal with what matters most to you. It can help you sort out a problem, find and use the strengths in your horoscope, set you on a more fulfilling career path, give you insight into your romantic life, or help you decide where to relocate. Many people consult astrologers to find the optimum time to schedule an important event, such as a wedding or business meeting.

Another good reason for a reading is to refine your knowledge of astrology by consulting with someone who has years of experience analyzing charts. You might choose an astrologer with a specialty that intrigues you. Armed with the knowledge of your chart that you have acquired so far, you can then learn to interpret subtle nuances or gain insight into your talents and abilities.

How do you choose when there are so many different kinds of readings available, especially since the Internet has brought astrology into the mainstream? Besides individual one-on-one readings with a professional astrologer, there are personal readings by mail, telephone, Internet, and tape. Well-advertised computer-generated reports and celebrity-sponsored readings are sure to attract your attention on commercial Web sites and in magazines. You can even purchase a reading that is incorporated into an expensive handmade fine art book. Then there are astrologers who specialize in specific areas such as finance or medical astrology. And unfortunately, there are many questionable practitioners who range from streetwise Gypsy fortune-tellers to unscrupulous scam artists.

The following basic guidelines can help you sort out your options to find the reading that's right for you.

One-on-One Consultations with a Professional Astrologer

Nothing compares to a one-on-one consultation with a professional astrologer who has analyzed thousands of charts and can pinpoint the potential in yours. During your reading, you can get your specific questions answered and discuss possible paths you might take. There are many astrologers who now combine their skills with training in psychology and are well-suited to help you examine your alternatives.

To give you an accurate reading, an astrologer needs certain information from you: the date, time, and place where you were born. (A horoscope can be cast about anyone or anything that has a specific time and place.) Most astrologers will then enter this information into a computer, which will calculate a chart in seconds, and interpret the resulting chart.

If you don't know your exact birth time, you can usually locate it at the Bureau of Vital Statistics at the city hall of the town or the county seat in the state where you were born. If you still have no success in getting your time of birth, some astrologers can estimate an approximate birth time by using past events in your life to determine the chart. This technique is called rectification.

How to Find an Astrologer

Choose your astrologer with the same care as you would any trusted adviser, such as a doctor, lawyer, or banker. Unfortunately, anyone can claim to be an astrologer—to date, there is no licensing of astrologers or universally established professional criteria. However, there are nationwide organizations of serious, committed astrologers that can help you in your search.

Good places to start your investigation are organizations such as the American Federation of Astrologers (AFA) or the National Council for Geocosmic Research (NCGR), which offer a program of study and certification. If you live near a major city, there is sure to be an active NCGR chapter or astrology club in your area; many are listed in astrology magazines available at your local newsstand. In response to many requests for referrals, both the AFA and the NCGR have directories of professional astrologers listed on their Web sites; these directories include a glossary of terms and an explanation of specialties within the astrological field. Contact the NCGR and AFA headquarters for information. (See also Chapter 8.)

What Happens in a Reading

As a potentially lucrative freelance business, astrology has always attracted self-styled experts who may not have the knowledge or the counseling experience to give a helpful reading. These astrologers can range from the well-meaning amateur to the charlatan or street-corner Gypsy who has for many years given astrology a bad name. Be very wary of astrologers who claim to have occult powers or who make pretentious claims of celebrated clients or miraculous achievements. You can often tell from the initial phone conversation if the astrologer is legitimate. He or she should ask for your birthday time and place and then conduct the conversation in a professional manner. Any astrologer who gives a reading based only on your sun sign is highly suspect.

When you arrive at the reading, the astrologer should be prepared. The consultation should be conducted in a private, quiet place. The astrologer should be interested in your problems of the moment. A good reading is interactive and involves feedback on your part, so if the reading is not relating to your concerns, you should let the astrologer know. You should feel free to ask questions and get clarifications of any technical terms. The more you actively participate, rather than expecting the astrologer to carry the reading or come forth with oracular predictions, the more meaningful your experience will be. An astrologer should help you validate your current experience and be frank about possible negative happenings, but also suggest a positive course of action.

In their approach to a reading, some astrologers may be more literal and others more intuitive. Those who have had counseling training may take a more psychological approach. Though some astrologers may seem to have an almost psychic ability, extrasensory perception or any other parapsychological talent is not essential. A very accurate picture can be drawn from the data in your horoscope chart.

An astrologer may do several charts for each client, including one for the time of birth and a progressed chart, showing the evolution from birth to the present time. According to your individual needs, there are many other possibilities, such as a chart for a different location if you are contemplating a change of place. Relationships between any two people, things, or events can be interpreted with a chart that compares one partner's horoscope with the other's. A composite chart, which uses the midpoint between planets in two individual charts to describe the relationship, is another commonly used device.

An astrologer will be particularly interested in transits, those times when cycling planets activate the planets or sensitive points in your birth chart. These indicate important events in your life.

Many astrologers offer readings recorded on tape or CD, which is another option to consider, especially if the astrologer you choose lives at a distance from you. In this case, you'll be mailed a recorded reading based on your birth chart. This type of reading is more personal than a computer printout and can give you valuable insights, though it is not equivalent to a live dialogue with the astrologer when you can discuss your specific interest and issues of the moment.

The Telephone Reading

Telephone readings come in two varieties: a dial-in taped reading, usually recorded in advance by an astrologer, or a live consultation with an "astrologer" on the other end of the line. The recorded readings are general daily or weekly forecasts, applied to all members of your sign and charged by the minute. The quality depends on the astrologer. Be aware that these readings can run up quite a telephone bill, especially if you get into the habit of calling every day. Be sure that you are aware of the per-minute cost of each call beforehand.

Live telephone readings also vary with the expertise of the astrologer. Ideally, the astrologer at the other end of the line enters your birth data into a computer, which then quickly calculates your chart. This chart will be referred to during the consultation. The advantage of a live telephone reading is that your individual chart is used and you can ask about a specific problem. However, before you invest in any reading, be sure that your astrologer is qualified and that you fully understand in advance how much you will be charged. There should be no unpleasant financial surprises later. The best astrologer is one who is recommended to you by a friend or family member.

Computer-Generated Reports

Companies that offer computer programs (such as ACS, Matrix, and Astrolabe) also offer a variety of computer-generated horoscope readings. These can be quite comprehensive, offering a beautiful printout of the chart plus many pages of detailed information about each planet and aspect of the chart. You can then study it at your convenience. Of course, the interpretations will be general, since there is no personal input from you, and might not cover your immediate concerns. Since computer-generated horoscopes are much lower in cost than live consultations, you might consider them as either a supplement or a preparation for an eventual live reading. You'll then be more familiar with your chart and able to plan specific questions in advance. They also make a terrific gift for astrology fans. In chapter 9, there are listed several companies that offer computerized readings prepared by reputable astrologers.

Whichever option you decide to pursue, may your reading be an empowering one!

CHAPTER 11

Loving Every Sign in the Zodiac

In times of change, we crave the comfort of a loving partner more than ever. If we don't have love, we want to know how and where to find it; and if we already have a loving relationship, we want to know how to make it last forever. You can use astrology to find a lover, understand the one you have, or add excitement to your current relationship. Here are sun-sign seduction tips for romancing every sign in the zodiac.

Aries: Play Hard to Get

This highly physical sign is walking dynamite with a brief attention span. Don't be too easy to get, ladies. A little challenge, a lively debate, and a merry chase only heat them up. They want to see what you're made of. Once you've lured them into your lair, be a challenge and a bit of a daredevil. Pull out your X-rated tricks. Don't give your all—let them know there's more where that came from. Make it exciting; show you're up for adventure. Wear bright red somewhere interesting. Since Aries rules the head and face, be sure to focus on these areas in your lovemaking. Use your lips, tongue, breath, and even your eyelashes to the max. Practice scalp massages and deep kissing techniques. Aries won't wait, so when you make your move, be sure you're ready to follow through. No head games or teasing!

To keep you happy, you've got to voice your *own* needs, because this lover will be focused on *his*. Teach him how to please, or this could be a one-sided adventure.

Taurus: Appeal to All Their Senses

Taurus wins as the most sensual sign, with the most sexual stamina. This man is earthy and lusty in bed; he can go on all night. This is not a sign to tease. Like a bull, he'll see red, not bed. So make him comfortable, and then bombard all his senses. Good food gets Taurus in the mood. So do the right music, fragrance, revealing clothes, and luxurious bedlinens. Give him a massage with delicious-smelling and -tasting oils; focus on the neck area.

Don't forget to turn off the phone! Taurus hates interruptions. Since they can be very vocal lovers, choose a setting where you won't be disturbed. And don't ever rush; enjoy a long, slow, delicious encounter.

Gemini: Be a Playmate

Playful Gemini loves games, so make your seduction fun. Be their lost twin soul or confidante. Good communication is essential, so share deep secrets and live out fantasies. This sign adores variety. Nothing bores Gemini more than making love the same way all the time, or bringing on the heavy emotions. So trot out all the roles you've been longing to play. Here's the perfect partner. But remember to keep it light and fun. Gemini's turn-on zone is the hands, and this sign gives the best massages. Gadgets that can be activated with a touch amuse Gemini. This sign is great at doing two things at once, like making love while watching an erotic film. Turn the cell phone off unless you want company. On the other hand, Gemini is your sign for superhot phone sex.

Gemini loves a change of scene. So experiment on the floor, in the shower, or on the kitchen table. Borrow a friend's apartment or rent a hotel room for variety.

Cancer: Use the Moon

The key to Cancer is to get this moon child in the mood. Consult the moon—a full moon is best. Wining, dining, old-fashioned courtship, and breakfast in bed are turn-ons. Whatever makes your Cancer feel secure will promote shedding inhibitions in the sack. (Don't try any of your Aries daredevil techniques here!) Cancer prefers familiar, comfortable, homey surroundings. Cancer's turn-on zone is the breasts. Cancer women often have naturally inflated chests. Cancer men may fantasize about a well-endowed playmate. If your breasts are enhanced, show them off. Cancer will want to know all your deepest secrets, so invent a few good ones. But lots of luck delving into *their* innermost thoughts!

Take your Cancer near water. The sight and sound of the sea can be their aphrodisiac. A moonlit beach, a deserted swimming pool, a Jacuzzi, or a bubble bath are good seduction spots. Listen to the rain patter on the roof in a mountain cabin.

Leo: Offer the Royal Treatment

Leo must be the best and hear it from you often. In return, they'll perform for you, telling you just what you want to hear (true or not). They like a lover with style and endurance, and to be swept off their feet and into bed. Leos like to go first-class all the way, so build them up with lots of attention, wining and dining, and special gifts.

Never mention other lovers or make them feel second-best. A sure signal for Leo to look elsewhere is a competitive spouse. Leos take great pride in their bodies, so you should pour on the admiration. A few well-placed mirrors could inspire them. So would a striptease with beautiful lingerie, expensive fragrance on the sheets, and, if female, an occasional luxury hotel room, with champagne and caviar delivered by room service. Leo's erogenous zone is the lower back, so a massage with expensive oils would make your lion purr with pleasure.

Virgo: Let Them Be the Teacher

Virgo's standards are so sky-high that you may feel intimidated at first. The key to pleasing fussy Virgo lovers is to look for the hot fantasy beneath their cool surface. They're really looking for someone to make over. So let Virgo play teacher, and you play the willing student; the doctor-patient routine works as well. Be Eliza Doolittle to his Henry Higgins.

Let Virgo help you improve your life, quit smoking, learn French, and diet. Read an erotic book together, and then practice the techniques. Or study esoteric, erotic exercises from the Far East.

The Virgo erogenous zone is the tummy area, which should be your base of operations. Virgo likes things pristine and clean. Fall onto crisp, immaculate white sheets. Wear a sheer virginal white nightie. Smell shower-fresh with no heavy perfume. Be sure your surroundings pass the hospital test. A shower together afterward (with great-smelling soap) could get the ball rolling again.

Libra: Look Your Best

Libra must be turned on aesthetically. Make sure you look as beautiful as possible, and wear something stylishly seductive but never vulgar. Have a mental affair first, as you flirt and flatter this sign. Then proceed to the physical. Approach Libra like a dance partner, ready to waltz or tango.

Libra must be in the mood for love; otherwise, forget it. Any kind of ugliness is a turnoff. Provide an elegant and harmonious atmosphere, with no loud noise, clashing colors, or uncomfortable beds. Libra is not an especially spontaneous lover, so it is best to spend time warming them up. Libra's back is his erogenous zone, your cue to provide back rubs with scented potions. Once in bed, you can be a bit aggressive sexually. Libra loves strong, decisive moves. Set the scene, know what you want, and let Libra be happy to provide it.

Scorpio: Be an All-or-Nothing Lover

Scorpio is legendary in bed, often called the sex sign of the zodiac. But seducing them is often a power game. Scorpio likes to be in control, even the quiet, unassuming ones. Scorpio loves a mystery, so don't tell all. Keep them guessing about you, offering tantalizing hints along the way. The hint of danger often turns Scorpio on, so you'll find members of this sign experimenting with the exotic and highly erotic forms of sex. Sadomasochism, bondage, or anything that tests the limits of power could be a turn-on for Scorpio.

Invest in some sexy black leather and some powerful music. Clothes that lace, buckle, or zip tempt Scorpio to untie you. Present yourself as a mysterious package just waiting to be unwrapped.

Once in bed, there are no holds barred with Scorpio. They'll find your most pleasurable pressure points, and touch you as you've never been touched before. They are quickly aroused (the genital area belongs to this sign) and are willing to try anything. But they can be possessive. Don't expect your Scorpio to share you with anyone. It's all or nothing for them.

Sagittarius: Be a Happy Wanderer

Sagittarius men are the Don Juans of the zodiac—love-'em-and-leave-'em types who are difficult to pin down. Your seduction strategy is to join them in their many pursuits, and then hook them with love on the road. Sagittarius enjoys sex in venues that suggest movement; planes, SUVs, or boats. But a favorite turn-on place is outdoors, in nature. A deserted hiking path, a field of tall grass, or a remote woodland glade—all give the centaur sexy ideas. Athletic Sagittarius might go for some personal training in an empty gym. Join your Sagittarius for amorous aerobics, meditate together, and explore the tantric forms of sex. Lovemaking after hiking and skiing would be healthy fun.

Sagittarius enjoys lovers from exotic ethnic backgrounds, or lovers met in spiritual pursuits or on college campuses. Sagittarius are great cheerleaders and motivators, and will enjoy feeling that they have inspired you to be all that you can be.

There may be a canine or feline companion sharing your Sagittarius lover's bed with you, so check your allergies. And bring Fido or Felix a toy to keep them occupied.

Capricorn: Take Their Mind off Business

The great news about Capricorn lovers is that they improve with age. They are probably the sexiest seniors. So stick around, if you have a young one. They're lusty in bed (it's not the sign of the goat for nothing), and can be quite raunchy and turned on by X-rated words and deeds. If this is not your thing, let them know. The Capricorn erogenous zone is the knees. Some discreet fondling in public places could be your opener. Capricorn tends to think of sex as part of a game plan for the future. They are well-organized, and might regard lovemaking as relaxation after a long day's work. This sign often combines business with pleasure. So look for a Capricorn where there's a convention, trade show, or work-related conference.

Getting Capricorn's mind off his agenda and onto yours could take some doing. Separate him from his buddies by whispering sexy secrets in his ear. Then convince him you're an asset to his image and a boon to his health. Though he may seem uptight at first, you'll soon discover he's a love animal who makes a wonderful and permanent pet.

Aquarius: Give Them Enough Space

This sign really does not want an all-consuming passion or an all-or-nothing relationship. Aquarius needs space. But once they feel free to experiment with a spontaneous and exciting partner, Aquarius can give you a far-out sexual adventure.

Passion begins in the mind, so a good mental buildup is key. Aquarius is an inventive sign who believes love is a playground without rules. Plan surprise, unpredictable encounters in unusual places. Find ways to make love transcendental, an extraordinary and unique experience. Be ready to try anything Aquarius suggests, if only once. Calves and ankles are the special Aquarius erogenous zone, so perfect your legwork.

Be careful not to be too possessive. Your Aquarius needs lots of space and tolerance for friends (including old lovers) and their many outside interests.

Pisces: Live Their Fantasies

Pisces is the sign of fantasy and imagination. This sign has great theatrical talent. Pisces looks for lovers who will take care of them. Pisces will return the favor! Here is someone who can psych out your deepest desires without mentioning them. Pisces falls for sob stories and is always ready to empathize. It wouldn't hurt to have a small problem for Pisces to help you overcome. It might help if you cry on his shoulder, for this sign needs to be needed. Use your imagination when setting the scene for love. A dramatic setting brings out Pisces theatrical talents. Or creatively use the element of water. Rain on the roof, waterfalls, showers, beach houses, water beds, and Jacuzzis could turn up the heat. Experiment with pulsating jets of water. Take midnight skinny-dips in deserted pools.

The Pisces erogenous zone is the feet. This is your cue to give a sensuous foot massage using scented lotions. Let him paint your toes. Beautiful toenails in sexy sandals are a special turn-on.

Your Hottest Love Match

Here's a tip for finding your hottest love match. If your lover's Mars sign makes favorable aspects to your Venus, is in the same element (earth, air, fire, water), or is in the same sign, your lover will do what you want done! Mars influences how we act when we make love, while Venus shows what we like done to us. Sometimes fighting and making up is the sexiest fun of all. If you're the type who needs a spark to keep lust alive (you know who you are!), then look for Mars and Venus in different signs of the same quality (fixed or cardinal or mutable). For instance, a fixed sign (Taurus, Leo, Scorpio, Aquarius) paired with another fixed sign can have a sexy tug-of-war before you finally surrender. Two cardinal signs (Aries, Cancer, Libra, Capricorn) set off passionate fireworks when they clash. Mutable signs (Gemini, Virgo, Sagittarius, Pisces) play a fascinating game of cat and mouse, never quite catching each other.

Your Most Seductive Time

The best time for love is when Venus is in your sign, making you the most desirable sign in the zodiac. This only lasts about three weeks (unless Venus is retrograde) so don't waste time! And find out the time this year when Venus is in your sign by consulting the Venus chart at the end of chapter 5.

What's the Sexiest Sign?

It depends on what sign you are. Astrology has traditionally given this honor to Scorpio, the sign associated with the sex organs. However, we are all a combination of different signs (and turn-ons). Gemini's communicating ability and manual dexterity could deliver the magic touch. Cancer's tenderness and understanding could bring out your passion more than regal Leo.

Which Is the Most Faithful Sign?

The earth signs of Capricorn, Taurus, and Virgo are usually the most faithful. They tend to be more home- and family-oriented, and they are usually choosy about their mates. It's impractical, inconvenient, and probably expensive to play around, or so they think.

Who'll Play Around?

The mutable signs of Gemini, Pisces, and Sagittarius win the playboy or playgirl sweepstakes. These signs tend to be changeable, fickle, and easily bored. But they're so much fun!

CHAPTER 12

Financial Tips from the Stars

Getting the most bang from our buck will be our personal challenge this year, as we continue to learn to live within our means and balance our budgets. One of the advantages of astrology is that we can know the natural direction of the cosmic forces in advance and make financial plans accordingly.

Over the past few years, we've experienced a dramatic shift from the expansive risk taking of Pluto in Sagittarius to the conservative, thrift-promoting Pluto in Capricorn. This influence should continue for several years. Financially savvy astrologers also look to the movement of Jupiter, the planet of luck and expansion, for growth opportunities. Jupiter gives an extra boost to the sign it is passing through. Jupiter moves through Pisces, a sign that Jupiter especially favors, so Pisces and fellow water signs, Cancer and Scorpio, receive extra-lucky rays. Most of us could benefit from using some Pisces-inspired creativity, insight, and imagination especially in the area of our horoscope where Jupiter will be giving us growth opportunities. Pisces will give us the imaginative ideas; then Jupiter enters Aries briefly over the summer and for a lengthy stay next year, which should give us the courage and pioneering spirit to pursue them.

Aries

You've got a taste for fast money, quick turnover, and edgy investments, with no patience for gradual, long-term gains.

You're an impulse buyer with the nerve for risky tactics that could backfire. On the other hand, you're a pioneer who can see into the future, who dares to take a gamble on a new idea or product that could change the world ... like Sam Walton of the Wal-Mart stores, who changed the way we shop. You need a backup plan in case one of your big ideas burns out. To protect your money, get a backup plan you can follow without thinking about it. Have a percentage of your income automatically put into a savings or retirement account. Then give yourself some extra funds to play with. Your weak point is your impatience; so you're not one to wait out a slow market or watch savings slowly accumulate. When Jupiter moves into Aries temporarily this summer, you'll want to move full steam ahead. However, you may have to reevaluate your goals in the fall. Save your big moves for next year, when Jupiter reenters Aries and you can make real progress.

Taurus

You're a saver who loves to see your cash, as well as your possessions, accumulate. You have no qualms about steadily increasing your fortune. You're a savvy trader and a shrewd investor, in there for long-term gains. You have low toleration for risk; you hate to lose anything. But you do enjoy luxuries, and may need to reward yourself frequently. You might pass up an opportunity because it seems too risky, but you should take a chance once in a while. Since you're inspired by Jupiter in Pisces and Aries this year, it's time to support your long-range goals and ideals by exploring socially conscious investments, especially in the clean-energy field and the creative arts. You're especially lucky in real estate or any occupation that requires appraising and trading, as well as earth-centered businesses like organic farming and conservation.

Gemini

With Gemini, the cash can flow in and then out just as quickly. You naturally multi-task, and you are sure to have several projects going at once, as well as several credit cards, which can easily get out of hand. Saving is not one of your strong points—too boring. You fall in and out of love with different ideas; you have probably tried a round of savings techniques. Diversification is your best strategy. Have several different kinds of investments—at least one should be a long-term plan. Set savings goals and then regularly deposit small amounts into your accounts. Follow the lead of Gemini financial adviser Suze Orman and get a good relationship going with your money! With lucky Jupiter accenting your public image, there should be new career opportunities this year. Investigate careers in communications and the media.

Cancer

You can be a natural moneymaker with your peerless intuition. You can spot a winner that everyone else misses. Consider Cancer success stories like those of cosmetics queen Estee Lauder and Roxanne Quimby, of Burt's Bees, who turned her friend's stash of beeswax into a thriving cosmetics business. Who knew? So trust your intuition. You are a saver who always has a backup plan, just in case. Remember to treat and nurture yourself as well as others. Investments in the food industry, restaurants, hotels, shipping, and water-related industries are Cancer territory. You're one of the luckiest signs this year, so keep your antennae tuned for new investment opportunities.

Leo

You love the first-class lifestyle, but may not always have the resources to support it. Finding a way to fund your extravagant tastes is the Leo challenge. Some courses in money management or an expert financial coach could set you on the right track. However, you're also a terrific salesperson, and you're fabulous in high-profile jobs that pay a lot. You're the community tastemaker; you satisfy your appetite for "the best" by working for a quality company that sells luxury goods, splendid real estate, dream vacations, and first-class travel—that way you'll have access to the lifestyle without having to pay for it. This year, Jupiter brings luck through fortunate partnerships and travel.

Virgo

Your sign is a stickler for details, which includes your money management. You like to follow your spending and saving closely; you enjoy planning, budgeting, and price comparison. Your sign usually has no problem sticking to a savings or investment plan. You have a critical eye for quality, and you like to bargain and to shop to get the best value. In fact, Warren Buffet, a Virgo billionaire, is known for value investing. You buy cheap and sell at a profit. Investing in health care, organic products, and food could be profitable for you. With Jupiter in Pisces accenting partnerships, you might want to team up for investing purposes this year.

Libra

Oh, do you ever love to shop! And you often have an irresistible urge to acquire an exquisite object or a designer dress you can't really afford or to splurge on the perfect antique armoire. You don't like to settle for second-rate or bargain buys. Learning to prioritize your spending is especially difficult for your sign, so try to find a good money manager to do it for you. Following a strictly balanced budget is your key to financial success. With Libra's keen eye for quality and good taste, you are a savvy picker at auctions and antiques fairs, so you might be able to turn around your purchase for a profit. With Jupiter accenting the care and maintenance part of your life, this is an excellent year to put your finances in order and balance the budget.

Scorpio

Scorpios prefer to stay in control of their finances at all times. You're sure to have a financial-tracking program on your computer. You're not an impulse buyer, unless you see something that immediately turns you on. Rely on your instincts! Scorpio is the sign of credit cards, taxes, and loans, so you are able to use these tools cleverly. Investing for Scorpio is rarely casual. You'll do extensive research and track your investments by reading the financial pages, annual reports, and profit-loss statements. Investigate the arts, media, and oil and water projects for Jupiter-favored investments this year.

Sagittarius

Sagittarius is a natural gambler, with a high tolerance for risk. It's important for you to learn when to hold 'em, and when to fold 'em, as the song goes, by setting limits on your risk taking and covering your assets. You enjoy the thrill of playing the stock market, where you could win big and lose big. Money itself is rarely the object for Sagittarius—it's the game that counts. Since your sign rarely saves for a rainy day, your best strategy might be a savings plan that transfers a certain amount into a savings account. Regular bill-paying plans are another strategy to keep you on track. Jupiter favors invest-

ing in home improvements and family-related businesses this
year.

Capricorn

You're one of the strongest money managers in the zodiac,
which should serve you well this year when Jupiter, the planet
of luck and expansion, is blessing your house of finance. You're
a born bargain hunter and clever negotiator—a saver rather
than a spender. You are the sign of self-discipline, which works
well when it comes to sticking with a budget and living fru-
gally while waiting for resources to accumulate. You are likely
to plan carefully for your elder years, profiting from long-term
investments. You have a keen sense of value, and you will pick
up a bargain and then turn it around at a nice profit. Jupiter
favors the communications industry and opportunities in your
local area this year.

Aquarius

There should be many chances to speculate on forward-looking
ventures this year. The Aquarius trait of unpredictability extends to your financial life, where you surprise us all with your
ability to turn something totally unique into a money spinner.
Consider your wealthy sign mates Oprah Winfrey and Michael
Bloomberg, who have been able to intuit what the public will
buy at a given moment. Some of your ideas might sound far-
out, but they turn out to be right on the money. Investing in
high-tech companies that are on the cutting edge of their field
is good for Aquarius. You'll probably intuit which ones will
stay the course. You'll feel good about investing in companies
that improve the environment, such as new types of fuel, or
ones that are related to your favorite cause.

Pisces

Luck is with you this year! The typical Pisces is probably the sign least interested in money management. However, there are many billionaires born under your sign, such as Michael Dell, David Geffen, and Steve Jobs. Generally they have made money from innovative ideas and left the details to others. That might work for you. Find a Scorpio, Capricorn, or Virgo to help you set a profitable course and systematically save (which is not in your nature). Sign up for automatic bill paying so you won't have to think about it. If you keep in mind how much less stressful life will be and how much more you can do when you're not worried about paying bills, you might be motivated enough to stick to a sensible budget. Investment-wise, consider anything to do with water—off-shore drilling, water conservation and purifying, shipping, and seafood. Petroleum is also ruled by your sign, as are institutions related to hospitals.

CHAPTER 13

Children of 2010

Parents of several children may see a marked difference between children born in 2010 and those born more than two years ago, because the cosmic atmosphere has changed, which should imprint the personalities of this year's children.

Astrologers look to the slow-moving outer planets—Uranus, Neptune, and Pluto—to describe a generation. When an outer planet changes signs, this indicates a significant shift in energy, which is the case in 2010. In the first half of the year, Uranus and Jupiter in Pisces continue the visionary and creative influence of that sign, which will be reflected in the children born then. However, Uranus moves briefly into fiery Aries in June, which will be accompanied by Jupiter, the planet of expansion, indicating a very astrologically active summer of 2010. Children born during the warm months will reflect this with more drive and energy. After Uranus retrogrades back into Pisces in mid-August for the remainder of the year, the atmosphere becomes somewhat calmer. Neptune still passing through Aquarius and Pluto in Capricorn should add vision and practicality to the personality of this year's children. This generation will be focused on saving the planet and on making things work in order to clear the path for the future. Saturn in Libra will enter the mixture, teaching them diplomacy in getting along with others.

Astrology can be an especially helpful tool when used to design an environment that enhances and encourages each child's positive qualities. Some parents start before conception, planning the birth of their child as far as possible to harmonize with the signs of other family members. However, each baby has its own schedule, so if yours arrives a week early or late, or elects a different sign than you'd planned, recognize that the new sign may be more in line with the mission your child is here to accomplish. In other words, if you were hoping for a Libra child and he arrives during Virgo, that Virgo energy may be just what is needed to stimulate or complement your family. Remember that there are many astrological elements besides the sun sign that indicate strong family ties. Usually each child will share a particular planetary placement, an emphasis on a particular sign or house, or a certain chart configuration with his parents and other family members. Often there is a significant planetary angle that will define the parent-child relationship, such as family sun signs that form a T-square or a triangle.

One important thing you can do is to be sure the exact moment of birth is recorded. This will be essential in calculating an accurate astrological chart. The following descriptions can be applied to the sun or moon sign (if known) of a child—the sun sign will describe basic personality and the moon sign indicates the child's emotional needs.

The Aries Child

Baby Aries is quite a handful. This energetic child will walk—and run—as soon as possible, and perform daring feats of exploration. Caregivers should be vigilant. Little Aries seems to know no fear (and is especially vulnerable to head injuries). Many Aries children, in their rush to get on with life, seem hyperactive, and they are easily frustrated when they can't get their own way. Violent temper tantrums and dramatic physical displays are par for the course with this child, requiring a time-out mat or naughty chair.

The very young Aries should be monitored carefully, since he is prone to take risks and may injure himself. Aries love to take things apart and may break toys easily, but with encouragement, the child will develop formidable coordination. Aries's bossy tendencies should be molded into leadership qualities, rather than bullying, which should be easy to do with this year's babies. Encourage these children to take out aggressions and frustrations in active, competitive sports, where they usually excel. When young Aries learns to focus energies long enough to master a subject and learns consideration for others, the indomitable Aries spirit will rise to the head of the class.

Aries born in 2010 will be a more subdued version of this sign, but still loaded with energy. The Capricorn effect should make little Aries easier to discipline and more focused on achievement. A natural leader!

The Taurus Child

This is a cuddly, affectionate child who eagerly explores the world of the senses, especially the senses of taste and touch. The Taurus child can be a big eater and will put on weight easily if not encouraged to exercise. Since this child likes comfort and gravitates to beauty, try coaxing little Taurus to exercise to music, or take him or her out of doors, with hikes or long walks. Though Taurus may be a slow learner, this sign has an excellent retentive memory and generally masters a subject thoroughly. Taurus is interested in results and will see each project patiently through to completion, continuing long after others have given up. This year's earth sign planets will give him a wonderful sense of support and accomplishment.

Choose Taurus toys carefully to help develop innate talents. Construction toys, such as blocks or erector sets, appeal to their love of building. Paints or crayons develop their sense of color. Many Taurus have musical talent and love to sing, which is apparent at a young age.

This year's Taurus will want a pet or two, and a few plants of his own. Give little Taurus a small garden, and watch the natural green thumb develop. This child has a strong sense of acquisition and an early grasp of material value. After filling a piggy bank, Taurus graduates to a savings account, before other children have started to learn the value of money.

Little Taurus gets a bonanza of good luck from Jupiter in compatible Pisces, supported by Pluto in Capricorn and Saturn retrograding back into Virgo, a compatible earth sign. These should give little Taurus an especially easygoing disposition and provide many opportunities to live up to his sign's potential.

The Gemini Child

Little Gemini will talk as soon as possible, filling the air with questions and chatter. This is a friendly child who enjoys social contact, seems to require company, and adapts quickly to different surroundings. Geminis have quick minds that easily grasp the use of words, books, and telephones, and will probably learn to talk and read at an earlier age than most. Though they are fast learners, Gemini may have a short attention span, darting from subject to subject. Projects and games that help focus the mind could be used to help them concentrate. Musical instruments, typewriters, and computers help older Gemini children combine mental with manual dexterity. Geminis should be encouraged to finish what they start before they go on to another project. Otherwise, they can become jack-of-all-trade types who have trouble completing anything they do. Their disposition is usually cheerful and witty, making these children popular with their peers and delightful company at home.

This year's Gemini baby is impulsive and full of energy, with a strong Aries influence in his life. He will be highly independent and original, a go-getter. When he grows up, Gemini may change jobs several times before he finds a position that satisfies his need for stimulation and variety.

The Cancer Child

This emotional, sensitive child is especially influenced by patterns set in early life. Young Cancers cling to their first memories as well as their childhood possessions. They thrive in calm emotional waters, with a loving, protective mother, and usually remain close to her (even if their relationship with her was difficult) throughout their lives. Divorce and death—anything that disturbs the safe family unit—are devastating to Cancers, who may need extra support and reassurance during a family crisis.

They sometimes need a firm hand to push the positive, creative side of their personality and discourage them from getting swept away by emotional moods or resorting to emotional manipulation to get their way. If this child is praised and encouraged to find creative expression, Cancers will be able to express their positive side consistently, on a firm, secure foundation.

This year's Cancer baby may run against type, thanks to a meeting of Jupiter and Uranus in hyperactive Aries, which might make him much more outgoing and energetic than usual. He should have natural leadership tendencies, which should be encouraged, and the parents' challenge will be to find positive outlets for his energy.

The Leo Child

Leo children love the limelight and will plot to get the lion's share of attention. These children assert themselves with flair and drama, and can behave like tiny tyrants to get their way. But in general, they have a sunny, positive disposition and are rarely subject to blue moods.

At school, they're the types voted most popular, head cheerleader, or homecoming queen. Leo is sure to be noticed for personality, if not for stunning looks or academic work; the homely Leo will be a class clown, and the unhappy Leo can be the class bully.

Above all, a Leo child cannot tolerate being ignored for long. Drama or performing-arts classes, sports, and school politics are healthy ways for Leo to be a star. But Leos must learn to take lesser roles occasionally, or they will have some painful putdowns in store. Usually, their popularity is well earned; they are hard workers who try to measure up to their own high standards—and usually succeed.

This year's Leo should be a highly active version of the sign, with Saturn in Libra teaching lessons of balance and diplomacy in relationships, while Jupiter and Uranus in Aries amp up the energy level and Pluto in Capricorn demands focus and results. Good use of this energy could produce pioneers, fearless natural leaders who could change the world for the better.

The Virgo Child

The young Virgo can be a quiet, rather serious child, with a quick, intelligent mind. Early on, little Virgo shows far more attention to detail and concern with small things than other children. Little Virgo has a built-in sense of order and a fascination with how things work. It is important for these children to have a place of their own, which they can order as they wish and where they can read or busy themselves with crafts and hobbies. This child's personality can be very sensitive. Little Virgo may get hyper and overreact to seemingly small irritations, which can take the form of stomach upsets or delicate digestive systems. But this child will flourish where there is mental stimulation and a sense of order. Virgos thrive in school, especially in writing or language skills, and they seem truly happy when buried in books. Chances are, young Virgo will learn to read ahead of classmates. Hobbies that involve detail work or that develop fine craftsmanship are especially suited to young Virgos.

Baby Virgo of 2010 is likely to be an early talker, and will show concern for the welfare of others. This child should be a natural communicator and may show an interest in the arts or the legal profession.

The Libra Child

The Libra child learns early about the power of charm and appearance. This is often a very physically appealing child with an enchanting dimpled smile, who is naturally sociable and enjoys the company of both children and adults. It is a rare Libra child who is a discipline problem, but when their behavior is unacceptable, they respond better to calm discussion than displays of emotion, especially if the discussion revolves around fairness. Because young Libras without a strong direction tend to drift with the mood of the group, these children should be encouraged to develop their unique talents and powers of discrimination, so they can later stand on their own.

In school, this child is usually popular and will often have to choose between social invitations and studies. In the teen years, social pressures mount as the young Libra begins to look for a partner. This is the sign of best friends, so Libra's choice of companions can have a strong effect on his future direction. Beautiful Libra girls may be tempted to go steady or have an unwise early marriage. Chances are, both sexes will fall in and out of love several times in their search for the ideal partner.

Little Libra of 2010 is an especially creative, expressive child, who may have strong artistic talents. This child is endowed with much imagination, as well as social skills.

The Scorpio Child

The Scorpio child may seem quiet and shy, but will surprise others with intense feelings and formidable willpower. Scorpio children are single-minded when they want something and intensely passionate about whatever they do. One of a caregiver's tasks is to teach this child to balance activities and emotions, yet at the same time to make the most of his great concentration and intense commitment.

Since young Scorpios do not show their depth of feelings easily, parents will have to learn to read almost imperceptible signs that troubles are brewing beneath the surface. Both Scorpio boys and girls enjoy games of power and control on or off the playground. Scorpio girls may take an early interest in the opposite sex, masquerading as tomboys, while Scorpio boys may be intensely competitive and loners. When her powerful energies are directed into work, sports, or challenging studies, Scorpio is a superachiever, focused on a goal. With trusted friends, young Scorpio is devoted and caring—the proverbial friend through thick and thin, loyal for life.

Scorpio 2010 has a strong emphasis on achievement and success. Uranus and lucky Jupiter in Pisces in their house of creativity should put them on the cutting edge of whichever field they choose.

The Sagittarius Child

This restless, athletic child will be out of the playpen and off on explorative adventures as soon as possible. Little Sagittarius is remarkably well-coordinated, attempting daredevil feats on any wheeled vehicle from scooters to skateboards. These natural athletes need little encouragement to channel their energies into sports. Their cheerful friendly dispositions earn them popularity in school, and once they have found a subject where their talent and imagination can soar, they will do well academically. They love animals, especially horses, and will be sure to have a pet or two, if not a home zoo. When they are old enough to take care of themselves, they'll clamor to be off on adventures of their own, away from home, if possible.

This is a child who loves to travel, who will not get homesick at summer camp, and who may sign up to be a foreign-exchange student or spend summers abroad. Outdoor adventure appeals to little Sagittarius, especially if it involves an active sport, such as skiing, cycling or mountain climbing. Give them enough space and encouragement, and their fiery spirit will propel them to achieve high goals.

Baby Sagittarius of 2010 has a natural generosity of spirit and an optimistic, social nature. Home and family will be especially important to him, though he may have an unconventional family life. He'll have an ability to look past the surface of things to seek out what has lasting value.

The Capricorn Child

These purposeful, goal-oriented children will work to capacity if they feel this will bring results. They're not ones who enjoy work for its own sake—there must be a goal in sight. Authority figures can do much to motivate these children, but once set on an upward path, young Capricorn will mobilize his energy and talent and work harder, and with more perseverance, than any other sign. Capricorn has built-in self-discipline that can achieve remarkable results, even if lacking the flashy personality, quick brainpower, or penetrating insight of others. Once involved, young Capricorn will stick to a task until it is mastered. This child also knows how to use others to his advantage and may well become the team captain or class president.

A wise parent will set realistic goals for the Capricorn child, paving the way for the early thrill of achievement. Youngsters should be encouraged to express their caring, feeling side to others, as well as their natural aptitude for leadership. Capricorn children may be especially fond of grandparents and older relatives, and will enjoy spending time with them and learning from them. It is not uncommon for young Capricorns to have an older mentor or teacher who guides them. With their great respect for authority, Capricorn children will take this influence very much to heart.

The Capricorn born in 2010 should be a good talker, with sharp mental abilities. He is likely to be social and outgoing, with lots of friends and closeness to brothers and sisters.

The Aquarius Child

The Aquarius child has a well-focused, innovative mind that often streaks so far ahead of peers that this child seems like an oddball. Routine studies never hold the restless youngster for long; he or she will look for another, more experimental place to try out his ideas and develop his inventions. Life is a laboratory to the inquiring Aquarius mind. School politics, sports, science, and the arts offer scope for their talents. But if there is no room for expression within approved social limits, Aquarius is sure to rebel. Questioning institutions and religions comes naturally, so these children may find an outlet elsewhere, becoming rebels with a cause. It is better not to force these children to conform, but rather to channel forward-thinking young minds into constructive group activities.

This year's Aquarius will have special financial talent. Luck and talent are his and fame could be in the stars!

The Pisces Child

Give young Pisces praise, applause, and a gentle, but firm, push in the right direction. Lovable Pisces children may be abundantly talented, but may be hesitant to express themselves, because they are quite sensitive and easily hurt. It is a parent's challenge to help them gain self-esteem and self-confidence. However, this same sensitivity makes them trusted friends who'll have many confidants as they develop socially. It also endows many Pisces with spectacular creative talent.

Pisces adores drama and theatrics of all sorts; therefore, encourage them to channel their creativity into art forms rather than indulging in emotional dramas. Understand that they may need more solitude than other children may as they develop their creative ideas. But though daydreaming can be creative, it is important that these natural dreamers not dwell too long in the world of fantasy. Teach them practical coping skills for the real world.

Since Pisces are sensitive physically, parents should help them build strong bodies with proper diet and regular exercise. Young Pisces may gravitate to more individual sports, such as swimming, sailing, and skiing, rather than to team sports. Or they may prefer more artistic physical activities, like dance or ice-skating.

Born givers, these children are often drawn to the underdog (they quickly fall for sob stories) and attract those who might take advantage of their empathic nature. Teach them to choose friends wisely, to set boundaries in relationships, and to protect their emotional vulnerability—invaluable lessons in later life.

With the planet Uranus now in Pisces along with lucky Jupiter, the 2010 baby belongs to a generation of Pisces movers and shakers. This child may have a rebellious streak that rattles the status quo. But this generation also has a visionary nature, which will be much concerned with the welfare of the world at large.

CHAPTER 14

Give the Perfect Gift to Every Sign

So often we're in a quandary about what to give a loved one, someone who has everything, that hard-to-please friend, or a fascinating new person in your life, or about the right present for a wedding, birthday, or hostess gift. Why not let astrology help you make the perfect choice by appealing to each sun sign's personality. When you're giving a gift, you're also making a memory, so it should be a special occasion. The gift that's most appreciated is one that touches the heart, reminds you both of a shared experience, or shows that the giver has really cared enough to consider the recipient's personality.

In general, the water signs (Cancer, Pisces, Scorpio) enjoy romantic, sentimental, and imaginative gifts given in a very personal way. Write your loved one a poem or a song to express your feelings. Assemble an album of photos or mementos of all the good times you've shared. Appeal to their sense of fantasy. Scorpio Richard Burton had the right idea when he gave Pisces Elizabeth Taylor a diamond bracelet hidden in lavender roses (her favorite color).

Fire signs (Aries, Leo, Sagittarius) appreciate a gift presented with lots of flair. Pull out the drama, like the actor who dazzled his Aries sweetheart by presenting her with trash cans overflowing with daisies.

Air signs (Gemini, Libra, Aquarius) love to be surprised with unusual gifts. The Duke of Windsor gave his elegant Gemini duchess, Wallis Windsor, fabulous jewels engraved with love notes and secret messages in their own special code.

Earth signs (Taurus, Virgo, Capricorn) value solid, tangible gifts or ones that appeal to all the senses. Delicious gourmet treats, scented body lotions, the newest CDs, the gift of a massage, or stocks and bonds are sure winners! Capricorn Elvis Presley once received a gold-plated piano from his wife.

Here are some specific ideas for each sign:

Aries

These are the trendsetters of the zodiac, who appreciate the latest thing! For Aries, it's the excitement that counts, so present your gift in a way that will knock their socks off. Aries is associated with the head, so a jaunty hat, hair ornaments, chandelier earrings, sunglasses, and hair-taming devices are good possibilities. Aries love games of any kind that offer a real challenge, like war video games, military themes, or rousing music with a beat. Anything red is a good bet: red flowers, red gems, and red accessories. How about giving Aries a way to let off steam with a gym membership or aerobic-dancing classes? Monogram a robe with a nickname in red.

Taurus

These are touchy-feely people who love things that appeal to all their senses. Find something that sounds, tastes, smells, feels, or looks good. And don't stint on quality or comfort. Taurus know the value of everything and will be aware of the price tag. Taurus foodies will appreciate chef-worthy kitchen gadgets, the latest cookbook, and gourmet treats. Taurus is a great collector. Find out what their passion is and present them with a rare item or a beautiful storage container such as an antique jewelry box. Green-thumb Taurus would love some special plants or flowers, garden tools, beautiful plant containers. Appeal to their sense of touch with fine fabrics—high-thread-count sheets, cashmere, satin, and mohair. One of the animal-loving signs, Taurus might appreciate a retractable leash or soft bed for the dog or cat. Get them a fine wallet or checkbook cover. They'll use it often.

Gemini

Mercury-ruled Gemini appreciates gifts that appeal to their mind. The latest book or novel, a talked-about film, a CD from a hot new singer, or a high-tech gadget might appeal. A beautiful diary or a tape recorder would record their adventures. Since Geminis often do two things at once, a telephone gadget that leaves their hands free would be appreciated. In fact, a new telephone device or superphone would appeal to these great communicators. Gloves, rings, and bracelets accent their expressive hands. Clothes from an interesting new designer appeal to their sense of style. You might try giving Gemini a variety of little gifts in a beautiful box or a Christmas stocking. A tranquil massage at a local spa would calm Gemini's sensitive nerves. Find an interesting way to wrap your gift. Nothing boring, please!

Cancer

Cancer is associated with home and family, so anything to do with food, entertaining at home, and family life is a good bet. Beautiful dishes or serving platters, silver items, fine crystal and linen, gourmet cookware, cooking classes or the latest DVD from a cooking teacher might be appreciated. Cancer designers Vera Wang and Giorgio Armani have perfected the Cancer style and have many home products available, as well as their elegant designer clothing. Naturally, anything to do with the sea is a possibility: pearls, coral, or shell jewelry. Boat and water-sports equipment might work. Consider cruise wear for traveling Cancers. Sentimental Cancer loves antiques and silver frames for family photos. Cancer people are often good photographers, so consider frames, albums, and projectors to showcase their work. Present your gift in a personal way with a special note.

Leo

Think big with Leo and appeal to this sign's sense of drama. Go for the gold (Leo's color) with gold jewelry, designer clothing, or big attention-getting accessories. Follow their signature style, which could be superelegant, like Jacqueline Onassis, or superstar, like Madonna or Jennifer Lopez. This sign is always ready for the red carpet and stays beautifully groomed, so stay within these guidelines when choosing your gift. Feline motifs and animal prints are usually a hit. The latest grooming aids, high-ticket cosmetics, and mirrors reflect their best image. Beautiful hairbrushes tame their manes. Think champagne, high-thread-count linens, and luxurious loungewear or lingerie. Make Leo feel special with a custom portrait or photo shoot with your local star photographer. Be sure to go for spectacular wrapping, with beautiful paper and ribbons. Present your gift with a flourish!

Virgo

Virgo usually has a special subject of interest and would appreciate relevant books, films, lectures, or classes. Choose health-oriented things: gifts to do with fitness and self-improvement. Virgo enjoys brainteasers, crossword puzzles, computer programs, organizers, and digital planners. Fluffy robes, bath products, and special soaps appeal to Virgo's sense of cleanliness. Virgo loves examples of good, practical design: efficient telephones, beautiful briefcases, computer cases, desk accessories. Choose natural fibers and quiet colors when choosing clothes for Virgo. Virgo has high standards, so go for quality when choosing a gift.

Libra

Whatever you give this romantic sign, go for beauty and romance. Libra loves accessories, decorative objects, whatever makes him or his surroundings more aesthetically pleasing. Beautiful flowers in pastel colors are always welcome. Libras are great hosts and hostesses, who might appreciate a gift related to fine dining: serving pieces, linens, glassware, flower vases. Evening or party clothes please since Libra has a gadabout social life. Interesting books, objets d'art, memberships to museums, and tickets to cultural events are good ideas. Fashion or home-decorating magazine subscriptions usually please Libra women. Steer away from anything loud, garish, or extreme. Think pink, one of their special colors, when giving Libra jewelry, clothing, or accessories. It's a very romantic sign, so be sure to remember birthdays, holidays, and anniversaries with a token of affection.

Scorpio

Scorpios love mystery, so bear that in mind when you buy these folks a present. You could take this literally and buy them a good thriller DVD, novel, or video game. Scorpios are power players, so a book about one of their sign might please. Bill Gates, Jack Welch, Condoleezza Rice, and Hillary Clinton are hot Scorpio subjects. Scorpios love black leather, suede, fur, anything to do with the sea, power tools, tiny spy tape recorders, and items with secret compartments or intricate locks. When buying a handbag for Scorpio, go for simple shapes with lots of interior pockets. Sensuous Scorpios appreciate hot lingerie, sexy linens, body lotions, and perfumed candles. Black is the favored color for Scorpio clothing—go for sexy textures like cashmere and satin in simple shapes by designers like Calvin Klein. This sign is fascinated with the occult, so give them an astrology or tarot-card reading, beautiful crystals, or an astrology program for the computer.

Sagittarius

For these outdoor people, consider adventure trips, designer sportswear, gear for their favorite sports. A funny gift or something for their pets pleases Sagittarius. For clothing and accessories, the fashionista of this sign tends to like bright colors and dramatic innovative styles. Otherwise, casual sportswear is a good idea. These travelers usually have a favorite getaway place; give them a travel guide, DVD, novel, or history book that would make their trip more interesting. Luggage is also a good bet. Sleek carry-ons, travel wallets, ticket holders, business-card cases, and wheeled computer bags might please these wanderers. Anything that makes travel more comfortable and pleasant is good for Sagittarius, including a good book to read en route. This sign is the great gambler of the zodiac, so gifts related to their favorite gambling venue would be appreciated.

Capricorn

For this quality-conscious sign, go for a status label from the best store in town. Get Capricorns something good for their image and career. They could be fond of things Spanish, like flamenco or tango music, or of country-and-western music and motifs. In the bookstore, go for biographies of the rich and famous, or advice books to help Capricorn get to the top. Capricorns take their gifts seriously, so steer away from anything too frivolous. Garnet, onyx, or malachite jewelry, Carolina Herrera fragrance and clothing, and beautiful briefcases and wallets are good ideas. Glamorous status tote bags carry business gear in style. Capricorns like golf, tennis, and sports that involve climbing, cycling, or hiking, so presents could be geared to their outdoor interests. Elegant evening accessories would be fine for this sign, which often entertains for business.

Aquarius

Give Aquarius a surprise gift. This sign is never impressed with things that are too predictable. So use your imagination to present the gift in an unusual way or at an unexpected time. With Aquarius, originality counts. When in doubt, give them something to think about, a new electronic gadget, perhaps a small robot, or an advanced computer game. Or something New Age, like an amethyst-crystal cluster. Aquarius like innovative materials with a space-age look. They are the ones with the wraparound glasses, the titanium computer cases. This air sign loves to fly—an airplane ticket always pleases. Books should be on innovative subjects, politics, or adventures of the mind. Aquarius goes for unusual color combinations—especially electric blue or hot pink—and abstract patterns. They like the newest, coolest looks on the cutting edge of fashion and are not afraid to experiment. Think of Paris Hilton's constantly changing looks. Look for an Aquarius gift in an out-of-the-way boutique or local hipster hangout. They'd be touched if you find out Aquarius's special worthy cause and make a donation. Spirit them off to hear their favorite guru.

Pisces

Pisces respond to gifts that have a touch of fantasy, magic, and romance. Look for mystical gifts with a touch of the occult. Romantic music (a customized CD of favorite love songs) and love stories appeal to Pisces sentimentalists. Pisces is associated with perfume and fragrant oils, so help this sign indulge with their favorite scent in many forms. Anything to do with the ocean, fish, and water sports appeals to Pisces. How about a whirlpool, a water-therapy spa treatment, or a sea salt rub. Appeal to this sign with treats for the feet: foot massages, pedicures, ballet tickets, and dance lessons. Cashmere socks and metallic evening sandals are other Pisces pleasers. A romantic dinner overlooking the water is Pisces paradise. A case of fine wine or another favorite liquid is always appreciated. Write a love poem and enclose it with your gift.

CHAPTER 15

Your Pet-Scope for 2010: How to Choose Your Best Friend for Life

With Jupiter, the planet of luck and expansion, in compassionate Pisces, this is a great time to bring joy into your life by adopting an animal friend. At this writing, 63 percent of all American households have at least one pet, according to a recent survey by the American Pet Product Manufacturers Association. And we spend billions of dollars on the care and feeding of our beloved pets. Our pets are counted as part of the family, often sharing our beds and accompanying us on trips.

Whether you choose to adopt an animal from a local shelter or buy a Thoroughbred from a breeder, try for an optimal time of adoption and sun sign of your new friend. If you're rescuing an animal, however, it's difficult to know the sun sign of the animal, but you can adopt on a day when the moon is compatible with yours, which should bless the emotional relationship. Using the moon signs listed in the daily forecasts in this book, choose a day when the moon is in your sign, a sign of the same element, or a compatible element. This means fire and air signs should go for a day when the moon is in fire signs Aries, Leo, Sagittarius or air signs Gemini, Libra, or Aquarius. Water and earth signs should choose a day when the moon is in water signs Cancer, Scorpio, or Pisces or earth signs Taurus, Virgo, or Capricorn. If possible, aim for a new moon, good for beginning a new relationship.

Here are some sign-specific tips for adopting an animal that will be your best friend for life.

Aries: The Rescuer

Aries gets special pleasure from rescuing animals in distress and rehabbing them, so do check your local shelters if you're thinking of adopting an animal. As an active fire sign, you'd be happiest with a lively animal that can accompany you, and you might do well with a rescue animal such as a German shepherd or Labrador retriever. You'd also enjoy training such an animal. Otherwise look for intelligence, alertness, playfulness and obedience in your friend. Since Aries tend to have an active life, look for a sleek, low maintenance coat on your dog or cat. Cat lovers would enjoy the more active breeds such as the Siamese or Abyssinian.

An Aries sun-sign dog or cat would be ideal. Aries animals have a brave, energetic, rather combative nature. They can be mischievous, so the kittens and puppies should be monitored for safety. They'll dare to jump higher, run faster, and chase more animals than their peers. They may require stronger words and more obedience training than other signs. Give them plenty of toys and play active games with them often.

Taurus: The Toucher

Taurus is a touchy-feely sign, and this extends to your animal relationships. Look for a dog or cat that enjoys being petted and groomed, is affectionate, and adapts well to family life. As one of the great animal-loving signs, Taurus is likely to have several pets, so it is important that they all get along together. Give each one its own special safe space to minimize turf wars.

Taurus animals are calm and even tempered, but do not like being teased and could retaliate, so be sure to instruct children in the proper way to handle and play with their pet. Since this sign has strong appetites and tends to put on weight easily, be careful not to overindulge them in caloric treats and table snacks. Sticking to a regular feeding schedule could help eliminate between-meal snacking.

Taurus female animals are excellent mothers and make good breeders. They tend to be clean and less destructive of home furnishings than other animals.

Gemini: The Companion

A bright, quick-witted sign like yours requires an equally interesting and communicative pet. Choose a social animal that adapts well to different environments, since you may travel or have homes in different locations.

Gemini animals can put up with noise, telephones, music, and different people coming and going. They'll want to be part of the action, so place a pillow or roost in a public place. They do not like being left alone, however, so, if you will be away for long periods, find them an animal companion to play with. You might consider adopting two Gemini pets from the same litter.

Animals born under this sign are easy to teach and some enjoy doing tricks or retrieving. They may be more vocal than other animals, especially if they are confined without companionship.

Cancer: The Nurturer

Cancer enjoys a devoted, obedient animal who demonstrates loyalty to its master. An affectionate, home-loving dog or cat who welcomes you and sits on your lap would be ideal. The emotional connection with your pet is most important; therefore, you may depend on your powerful psychic powers when choosing an animal. Wait until you feel that strong bond of psychic communication between you both. The moon sign of the day you adopt is very important for moon-ruled Cancer, so choose a water sign, if possible.

Cancer animals need a feeling of security; they don't like changes of environment or too much chaos at home. If you intend to breed your animal, the Cancer pet makes a wonderful and fertile mother.

Leo: The Prideful Owner

The Leo owner may choose a pet that reminds you of your own physical characteristics, such as similar coloring or build. You'll be proud of your pet, keep the animal groomed to perfection, and choose the most spectacular example of the breed. Noble animals with a regal attitude, beautiful fur, or striking markings are often preferred, such as the Himalayan or red tabby Persian cat, the standard poodle, the chow chow dog. An attention getter is a must.

Under the sign of the King of Beasts, Leo-born animals have proud noble natures. They usually have a cheerful, magnanimous disposition and rule their domains regardless of their breed, holding their heads with pride and walking with great authority. They enjoy grooming, like to show off and be the center of attention. Leo animals are naturals for the show ring, thriving in the spotlight and applause. They'll thrive with plenty of petting, pampering, and admiration.

Virgo: The Caregiver

Virgo owners will be very particular about their pets, paying special attention to requirements for care and maintenance. You need a pet who is clean, obedient, intelligent, yet rather quiet. A highly active, barking or meowing pet that might get on your nerves is a no-no.

Cats are usually very good pets for Virgo. Choose one of the calm breeds, such as a Persian. Though this is a high-maintenance cat, its beauty and personality will be rewarding.

You are compassionate with animals in need, and you might find it rewarding to volunteer at a local shelter or veterinary clinic or to train service dogs.

Virgo animals can be fussy eaters, very particular about their environment. They are gentle and intelligent, and respond to kind words and quiet commands, never harsh treatment.

Virgo is an excellent sign for dogs that are trained to do service work, since they seem to enjoy being useful and are intelligent enough to be easily trained.

Libra: The Beautifier

The Libra owner responds to beauty and elegance in your pet. You require a well-mannered, but social companion, who can be displayed in all of nature's finery. An exotic variety such as a graceful curly-haired Devon Rex cat would be a show-stopper. Libra often prefers the smaller varieties, such as a miniature schnauzer, a mini-greyhound or a teacup poodle.

Pets born under Libra are usually charming, well-mannered gentlemen who love the comforts of home life. They tend to be more careful than other signs, not rushing willfully into potentially dangerous situations. They'll avoid confrontations and harsh sounds, responding to words of love and gentle corrections.

Scorpio: The Powerful

Scorpios enjoy a powerful animal with a strong character. They enjoy training animals in obedience, would do well with service dogs, guard dogs, or police animals. Some Scorpios enjoy the more exotic, edgy pets, such as hairless Sphynx cats or Chinese chin dogs. Scorpios could find rescuing animals in dire circumstances and finding them new homes especially rewarding, as Matthew McConaughey did during Hurricane Katrina.

Animals born under this sign tend to be one-person pets, very strongly attached to their owners and extremely loyal and possessive. They are natural guard animals who will take extreme risks to protect their owners. They are best ruled by love and with consistent behavior training. They need to respect their owners and will return their love with great devotion.

Sagittarius: The Jovial Freedom Lover

Sagittarius is a traveler and one of the great animal lovers of the zodiac. The horse is especially associated with your sign, and you could well be a "horse whisperer." You generally respond most to large, active animals. If a small animal, like a Chihuahua, steals your heart, be sure it's one that travels well or tolerates your absence. Outdoor dogs like hunting dogs, retrievers, and border collies would be good companions on your outdoor adventures.

Sagittarius animals are freedom-loving, jovial, happy-go-lucky types. They may be wanderers, however, so be sure they have the proper identification tags and consider embedded microchip identification. These animals tend to be openly affectionate, companionable, untemperamental. They enjoy socializing and playing with humans and other animals and are especially good with active children.

Capricorn: The Thoroughbred

Capricorn is a discriminating owner, with a great sense of responsibility toward your animal. You will be concerned with maintenance and care, will rarely neglect or overlook any health issues with your pet. You will also discipline your pet wisely, not tolerating any destructive or outrageous antics. You will be attracted to good breeding, good manners, and deep loyalty from your pet.

The Capricorn pet tends to be more quiet and serious than other pets, perhaps a lone wolf who prefers the company of its owner, rather than a sociable or mischievous type. This is another good sign for a working dog, such as a herder, as Capricorn animals enjoy this outlet for their energy.

Aquarius: The Independent Original

Aquarius owners tend to lead active, busy lives and need an animal who can either accompany them cheerfully or who won't make waves. Demanding or high-maintenance dogs are not for you. You might prefer unusual or oddball types of pets, such as dressed-up Chihuahuas who travel in your tote bag or scene-stealing, rather shocking hairless cats. Or you will acquire a group of animals who can play with one another when you are pursuing outside activities, as Oprah Winfrey does. You can relate to the independence of cats, who require relatively little care and maintenance.

Aquarius animals are not loners—they enjoy the companionship of humans or groups of other animals. They tend to be more independent and may require more training to follow the house rules. However, they can have unique personalities and endearing oddball behavior.

Pisces: The Soul Mate

This is the sign that can "talk to the animals." Pisces owners enjoy a deep communication with their pets, love having their animals accompany them, sleep with them, and show affection. Tenderhearted Pisces will often rescue an animal in distress or adopt an animal from a shelter.

Tropical fish are often recommended as a Pisces pet, and seem to have a natural tranquilizing effect on this sign. However, Pisces may require an animal that shows more affection than their fish friends.

Pisces animals are creative types, can be sensually seductive and mysterious, mischievous and theatrical. They make fine house pets, do not usually like to roam far from their owners, and have a winning personality, especially with the adults in the home. Naturally sensitive and seldom vicious, they should be treated gently and given much praise and encouragement.

CHAPTER 16

Your Cancer Personality and Potential: The Roles You Play in Life

The more you understand your Cancer personality and potential, the more you'll benefit from using your special solar power to help create the life you want. There's a life coach, personal trainer, career adviser, fashion expert, and matchmaker all built into your Cancer sun sign. Whether you want to make a radical change in your life or simply choose a new wardrobe or paint a room, your sun sign can help you discover new possibilities and make good decisions. You could tap into your Cancer power to deal with relationship issues such as getting along with your boss or spicing up your love life. Maybe you'll be inspired by a celebrity sign mate who shares your special traits.

Let the following chapters help you move in harmony with your natural Cancer gifts. As the ancient oracle of Delphi advised, "Know thyself." To know yourself, as astrology helps you to do, is to gain confidence and strength.

You may wonder how astrologers determine what a Cancer personality is like. To begin with, we use a type of recipe, blending several ingredients. First there's your Cancer element: water. Cancer operates like a cardinal sign: an active doer. Then there's your sign's polarity, which adds a reactive, feminine, yin dimension. Let's not forget your planetary ruler: the moon, the planet of emotion. Add your sign's place in the zodiac: fourth, in the house of the home, family, roots. Finally, stir in your symbol, the Crab, with a hard protective shell and soft vulnerable interior.

This cosmic mix influences everything we say about Cancer. For example: Your sun sign occupies the place of home and family, making Cancer a home-loving type. With the moon as a ruler, you operate intuitively. Like the Crab, you're likely to be a bit self-protective and concerned with security.

But all Cancers are not alike! Your individual astrological personality contains a blend of many other planets, colored by the signs they occupy, plus factors such as the sign coming over the horizon at the exact moment of your birth. However, the more Cancer planets in your horoscope, the more likely you'll recognize yourself in the descriptions that follow. On the other hand, if many planets are grouped together in a different sign, they will color your horoscope accordingly, sometimes making a low-key mellow sun sign come on much stronger. So if the Cancer traits mentioned here don't describe you, there might be other factors flavoring your cosmic stew. (Look up your other planets in the tables in this book to find out what they might be!)

The Cancer Man: Sixth Sense

The Cancer man operates very much like his symbol, the Crab. You're a sidewalker who moves indirectly at a situation, never confronting it head-on, but always obliquely, subtly, and cleverly. Some might call you shrewd, others surreptitious. But what you are doing is reacting to your keen intuitive understanding of the hidden motives and agendas of others. You'll tune in to your powerful sixth sense before you listen to objective reason.

You sometimes wear a hard outer shell to protect yourself from the harsh realities of life. But inside you're vulnerable and tender, afraid of being exploited if you show this nurturing side to the world. Usually, it comes forth in a professional way, through your choice of a career where you can express your feelings safely in a creative context. Many Cancer men choose nurturing fields in medicine, child care, psychology, hotel work, family businesses, or restaurants. Or they'll extend their nurturing to a family tribe, like the Cancer writer Ernest Hemingway, who was called "Papa" by all who knew him personally.

You have an uncanny ability to read the feelings of others, which gives you great emotional power and understanding. You know exactly how to nurture people by giving them what they need when they need it. On the other hand, you know where to inflict the most hurt—often by withholding what is needed. But your negative side, which can be cool and cruel, is actually a form of resentment if you yourself have not been nurtured enough. If you can learn how to release the past and any hurts rendered to you, and how to nurture yourself, you have a much better chance to reach your full potential. Many Cancers have found psychotherapy extremely helpful in doing this.

A Cancer man's mother is especially important to him, even more so than to other men. If this relationship is lacking, you may try to replace it by mothering (or smothering) others or by looking for someone else to mother you.

The Cancer man, though virile and sensual, rarely embodies the stereotypical masculine attitude. There is always a special communication of tenderness in your treatment of women, which makes you one of the zodiac's great lovers. You can tap into a woman's emotional needs and treat her with great understanding and sensitivity. This subtle vulnerability is evident in Cancer celebrities such as Robin Williams, Tom Cruise, Harrison Ford, and Geraldo Rivera. The shy blue-eyed gaze of England's Prince William is ever so effective with the opposite sex. The Cancer man's special sensitivity is far more attractive to women than the muscle-flexing of macho types.

In a Relationship

Like the Crab, the Cancer man hangs on. You're extremely possessive of whatever and whoever belongs to you. You'll hang on to old memories, old sweaters, often your first dollar. In a committed relationship or marriage, you're at last free to show your tender, caring, protective side. Your home is supremely important to you. It's the place where you feel most secure. Here you can thrive in the supportive atmosphere of a long-term love. You treasure the mother of your children, who probably resembles your own mother in some way. You are usually not attracted to independent women (unless your mother was independent), preferring the more maternal, nurturing type or a romantic, creative partner. You'd like her to be interested in domestic life and be an excellent cook. (If your partner is on the go all the time, she'll come home to a crabby mate.) Since you are usually materially successful, your home can be a private paradise for enjoying the good life together.

The Cancer Woman: Mother Goddess

Ruled by the moon and associated with the breast, motherhood, and nurturing, the Cancer woman is one of the most feminine of the zodiac. As an active cardinal sign, you know how to capitalize creatively on your deeply sensitive feelings by finding ways to satisfy or feed others. Many Cancer women have become successful in business by providing the right product at the right time, like cosmetics tycoon Estée Lauder. However, you can be quite acquisitive, hoarding money or objects as if to store up for hard times. It has been said that nothing upsets a Cancer woman more than an empty refrigerator or an empty closet.

Because of your deep feelings and uncanny intuition, you easily grasp the inner motivations of others. This knowledge becomes your shell of protection. Cancer women in high places often extend their shell to become mother figures for their country, such as the late Princess Diana, Imelda Marcos, or Nancy Reagan. The wisest and wealthiest members of your sign use their intuition for personal and professional benefit.

You are especially affected by the moon's phases, especially during the full moon, when you could become supersensitive and overreact to imagined slights. Let creative projects come to the rescue, turning your negative energies into positive ones again. You can find emotional fulfillment by providing food and shelter to others; cooking a delicious family dinner is excellent therapy for the Cancer moody blues.

Family influences are more potent with Cancer than with many other signs. It is especially important that you try to conquer or reprogram negative relationships. This way you can express your creative talents fully. You keep strong family ties throughout life and you are often able to combine your career with your home life either by working at home or in a family business.

In a Relationship

You need a partner who is devoted and demonstrative, who will give you tangible proof of his love, and who will provide you with the stable home life you need. Your choice of a mate is especially important. A good relationship can draw you out of your shell and provide the emotional security you crave.

Usually, you are quite possessive of your husband and anxious to fulfill his needs. And if his needs include a beautiful home and strong family ties, you will make him happy indeed. Many of you marry someone wealthy, powerful, and protective, and then provide an indispensable support system for him. That could include transforming your shy self into a public person and perfect hostess if your husband's role demands it, like Nancy Reagan and the late Princess Diana did. You make a perfect wife for a chief executive, as you are able to embody the feminine power role. You can be seen as a maternal figure, a supportive coruler with your mate. There are several stellar examples of Cancer women who became as famous and powerful as their husbands: Leona Helmsley, Imelda Marcos, and the late Princess Diana come to mind.

Cancer in the Family

The Cancer Parent

As the mother figure of the zodiac (even if you're the dad), you're in your element as a parent. You're at your best cuddling a tiny vulnerable child. This nurturing quality may extend to all children, who arouse your deepest caring instincts. You can be fiercely protective of your brood and also possessive, hanging on to the mother role long after your children have left the nest. Often the Cancer parent will have a dynasty, sustaining their parental role by bringing the children into a family business. One of your greatest lessons will be to let go when the time comes, and to find constructive outlets for your nurturing energies as you evolve out of the parental role.

The Cancer Stepparent

Since a broken home is probably one of the most traumatic events that can happen to a Cancer, you will be full of compassion for your stepchildren. You will intuitively understand their unspoken feelings and their need for emotional support. Much depends, however, on how secure you yourself feel in the new family situation, and if you are getting the emotional support you require from your mate. If not, you may have difficulty sharing your mate with a previous family. If you can be open with your feelings, this situation can be remedied. Establishing open communications can sidestep power struggles and emotional manipulation. You'll easily win the children over when your caring, protective nature is channeled in the right direction. Then you can provide a warm, welcoming, extended family.

The Cancer Grandparent

Grandparenthood is a liberating experience for Cancer. Now you're free to enjoy young children without chores or responsibilities. You can fuss over the babies to your heart's content. You'll actually love babysitting the toddlers, pampering them with presents. Family get-togethers, when your brood gathers over a delicious meal, will be important seasonal events. You'll keep close ties with everyone in the family. Your grandchildren will always have a home with you, and there usually will be some young visitor toddling about. Especially concerned that your dynasty's future will be secure, you probably have provided a substantial nest egg. As you grow older, you'll pass on your family traditions, recipes, and stories to each new generation.

CHAPTER 17

Cancer Fashion and Decor Tips: Elevate Your Mood with Cancer Style!

In this year of serious concerns, why not put joy and imagination into your life by creating a harmonious environment and expressing your sun sign's natural flair in everything you do and wear? There are colors, sounds, fashion, and decor tips that fit Cancer like the proverbial glove and that could brighten every day. Even small changes in decor could make you feel "home at last." A simple change of color in your walls or curtains, your special music in the air, and a wardrobe makeover inspired by a Cancer designer or celebrity are natural mood elevators that boost your confidence and energy level. Even your vacations might be more fun if you tailor them to your natural Cancer inclinations. Try these tips to enhance your lifestyle and express the Cancer in you.

Cancer's Fashion Secrets

Cancer has an intuitive fashion sense that cues you on the right dress for every occasion. Like the late Princess Diana, you look best in fluid, romantic lines that play up your intense femininity. Soft, flowing, shimmering evening wear brings out the luminous moon maiden in you. Wear silver and pearls, iridescent fabrics, and wavy hair to play up this quality. Accent your expressive eyes with subtle makeup and take care of your sensitive skin, which can react to emotional upsets or overexposure to the sun.

Cancer women, like Pamela Anderson, often have (or acquire via cosmetic surgery) spectacular breasts, which you can play up with discreetly plunging necklines. (Choose undergarments that play up your best assets and give you the support you need.)

Cancer Colors

As one of the zodiac's most emotional signs, you'll feel and look your best when you wear your Cancer colors, which are soft, subtle shades, nothing garish or shouting. All the moonbeam shades of pearly white, silver, and taupe are yours. Wear colors of the sea, plus moss green, midnight blue, and coral. Cancer designers like Giorgio Armani and Vera Wang are specialists in using subtle colors and filmy fabrics to evoke romantic moods and create a dreamlike atmosphere.

Your Cancer Fashion Role Models

There are many chic fashion leaders and designers under your sun to inspire you. These designers understand the many moods and the perfect styles for your sign: Giorgio Armani, Vera Wang, Oscar de la Renta, and Norma Kamali. Trendy Cancers like Lindsay Lohan, Jessica Simpson, Liv Tyler, and Courtney Love always look best when they are accenting their beautiful eyes and luminous skin, and when they project an ethereal moonbeam quality. Cancer fashion models have always ruled the runway. In recent years, the Brazilian sensation Gisele Bundchen's curvaceous body and undulating walk have captured the sensual mood of the moment.

Cancer Home Makeover Tips

There's a good reason why some of the world's most famous decorators have been born under the sign of Cancer. Yours is the sign associated with the fourth house in the astrological chart, the place that governs family ties and the home, where you feel most secure. As a Cancer, you take to home decorating like a crab to water, and you instinctively know how to create a nurturing shell for yourself and others.

You couldn't do better than follow the advice of the late Sister Parish, who was the First Lady of decorating for the rich and famous. "Sister's" infallible Cancer intuition helped her create the kinds of rooms where everyone felt at home. She created a mood that was comforting, secure, and relaxing by using crystal, candlelight, silver, and mirrors; the room looked especially good at night, when Cancer shines brightest. Not for her the cold minimalist look! Sister enhanced the personality of the owner with carefully selected accessories and sentimental touches. She was not afraid to express emotion in her rooms, and neither should you be. Recently fashion designers Giorgio Armani and Vera Wang have translated their aesthetic into furniture and accessories for the home, using subtle subdued colors to create a restful relaxing atmosphere.

You tend to accumulate sentimental treasures, so be sure there is storage space for favorite items and memorabilia you've saved over the years. Since you love to cook, your kitchen and dining room should be equipped to prepare frequent family feasts. It will probably be the favorite gathering place in your home. A large dining table will be needed to accommodate your extended family and friends.

One room should be done in tranquil, restful colors—a place for solitary meditation. Incorporate the water element in some way in your decor, perhaps with a tiny waterfall or fountain, an aquarium, or a painting of a favorite beach. A swimming pool or a Jacuzzi tub are water-loving Cancer luxuries. Why not turn a bathroom into a home spa as a private place to relax and rejuvenate?

More than any other sign, you understand how to use color

to evoke emotion. Your favorites are sure to be the soft, subtle moonlight shades, though Sister Parish was known to use dramatic dark walls, spectacular at night. Generally, you can't go wrong using all the colors of the sea and ships in your environment: Atlantic blue, surf white, pearly pastels, and plenty of silver touches.

Cancer Sounds

Your kind of music stirs deep feelings or reminds you of happy times. Though you gravitate to blues and love songs, you should collect upbeat music that lifts your spirits as well as cool jazz that soothes your nerves. Make special tapes of your favorite songs, themed to evoke moods for romance, relaxation, or high energy, as the perfect background music to intimate occasions, festive meals, and family parties.

Cancer Getaways

Water-loving Cancers are in their element on cruises, at seaside resorts, or in tropical island paradises. Rather than an impersonal resort, you might prefer a home-away-from-home with a family feeling. Or invite a relative or intimate friend for company. Investigate renting your own villa or condominium at a resort rather than staying in a big hotel. This would give you both privacy and a place to entertain new friends. Cancer will actually enjoy shopping at the local food markets and serving regional specialties.

One of the zodiac's great shoppers, you'll probably bring home souvenirs for everyone in the family. Stash an extra collapsible suitcase or ballistic nylon tote bag in your baggage to hold all your finds. Most Cancers love to take photos, so bring a small camera with you at all times. The new disposable cameras are perfect for casual snapshots, and eliminate worry about theft.

Since stomach upsets are your travel foe, take along proper medication. Another sensitive Cancer area is your skin, so include a high-SPF sunscreen in all your travel kits.

Cancer likes to be upon or under the waves; ocean liners are the perfect floating vacation homes, ideal for family vacations. Or you may rent a sailboat to cruise the Caribbean or the Greek Islands. Scuba vacations also appeal. Go where the reefs are unspoiled: Australia, Belize, Samoa. Exotic places like Nairobi, Singapore, Istanbul, Venice, and the highlands of Scotland suit your many travel moods.

CHAPTER 18

The Cancer Way to Stay Healthy and Age Well

This year we'll be focused on staying healthy to avoid the high costs of health care and to cope with stressful events. Some signs have an easier time than others committing to a health and diet regimen. Cancer is an active, moon-ruled sign that responds to emotional needs and loves to be near your favorite water element. Dieting may require extra discipline for your food-loving sign. Astrology can clue you in to the specific Cancer tendencies that contribute to good or ill health. So follow these sun-sign tips to help yourself become the healthiest Cancer possible.

Nuture Yourself Emotionally and Physically

Dieting can be difficult for Cancers, who love good food, find emotional solace with goodies, and fill up with comfort foods in tough times. There are sure to be conflicts within the Cancer who wants to be fashionably thin but also to please the family with Grandma's favorite dishes. Cancer food conflicts sometimes lead to eating disorders, as with Princess Diana. Remember that you must be nurtured emotionally as well as physically. A diet therapy group might help you deal with issues surrounding food and give you the support you need to stick to a diet. Find nonfood ways to baby yourself, such as a visit to a spa, walks along the beach, beauty treatments to help you feel good about yourself while you lose weight.

Get the family behind you when you diet. You'll never lose weight if they insist on eating caloric favorites in front of you. Challenge yourself to create diet-conscious variations of family recipes so the whole family can eat healthy.

Head for the Water

Your natural water-sign element is also your best therapy. Sometimes just a walk by a pond or a brief stop by a fountain can do wonders to relieve emotional stress and tension. You will more likely stick to an exercise routine if it's in or near water. Pool aerobics, swimming, fishing, sailing, and all other water sports provide ideal ways for you to stay fit.

Protect Your Vulnerable Areas

Health-wise, Cancer is associated with the breast area. Cancer women should have regular checkups, according to your age and family health history of breast-related illness, and be sure to wear a well-fitting supportive bra.

Cancer is also prone to digestive difficulties, especially gastric ulcers and eating disorders. When emotionally caused digestive problems from those stomach-knotting insecurities crop up, baby yourself with extra pampering. The comforts of home have special health benefits for Cancer, so try to live in a cozy, harmonious atmosphere. If you feel blue, a visit with loved ones, old friends, and family could provide the support you need. Planning special family activities that bring everyone closer together will further benefit your health and well-being.

Stay Forever Young

Cancer is family-oriented in the elder years and thrives on close contact with loving relatives. It is even better if your home is near water, where you can exercise with long walks on the beach and swimming. If not, join a local water aerobics class at your local pool. Cancer can be a moody sign, so combat any tendency to get depressed by doing creative projects and spending time with loved ones. A positive attitude is one of your best antiaging techniques.

CHAPTER 19

Add Cancer Star Power to Your Career: What It Takes to Succeed in 2010

In today's tight job market, you'll need to pull out all the stops to land a great job. Cancers have a combination of talents and abilities that can make you a natural winner. Tops on the list is your uncanny intuition, which helps you size up the market and connect with the public's wants and needs. Trust those gut feelings! You know what others want before they do. Your natural nurturing instincts and creative ability also give you the edge in many industries. If you develop your Cancer talents, you'll be more likely to find a career you truly enjoy, as well as one that rewards you financially. Here's to your success!

Where to Look for Your Perfect Job

Cancer has proven to be one of the most financially successful signs. From behind your thick protective shell, you can figure out just what a job requires, or intuit what the public wants and needs, then put your creativity to work finding ways to fulfill those needs. It's no wonder that many billionaires were born under your sign! Your natural acquisitiveness makes you a shrewd judge of quality. And, as self-protective as your symbol, the Crab, you will build your personal nest egg at the same time as you're increasing company profits.

Your emotional sensitivity can be your greatest strength, if you use it properly. It gives you a powerful way to connect with the public wants and needs. Then apply your natural creativity to market your wares.

Follow your natural Cancer tendencies. Cancer often thrives in the security of a family business, or brings the family into a successful business. Creative fields give the needed self-expression: photography, theater, music, fashion. The food, shelter, home-maintenance, and child-related businesses are other natural Cancer meccas, as well as interior design and architecture. Many successful Cancers have made their fortunes in hotels, restaurants, and real estate. Marine businesses such as shipping, yacht sales, and marine biology are water-sign havens that would put you in the seaside environment you love.

Live Up to Your Leadership Potential

There is no such thing as an uninvolved Cancer, especially one at the helm of a profitable business. You are extremely possessive of your means of security, and you hang on to your position despite all odds. As a boss, you operate intuitively rather than openly, which could lead others to suspect a hidden agenda. Your secretiveness can project paranoia, but you usually make up for this with a very protective attitude toward your underlings. Your emotional sensitivity is a plus when negotiating a deal, helping you intuit when to sign on the dotted line and when the competition is about to act. Though your moods may be baffling to associates, they have learned never to underestimate you and to wait out your downtime for a few days until your mood changes.

Cancer's emotional sensitivity is your greatest strength and enables you to connect with what the public wants and needs. Richard Branson's Virgin Records began when he saw an opportunity to sell pop records at a discount. Later he started Virgin Airlines when he sensed that the public wanted more personal services at more reasonable prices than other airlines were providing. Estée Lauder was a self-made cosmetics tycoon who had a finger on the pulse of women's needs and buying habits. She knew that offering a free sample of her creams and perfumes would entice the customer to buy more product. As the business began to thrive, she brought her family into the company, which is run by her relatives today.

How to Work with Others

You work best in a traditional, nurturing atmosphere. Here you can express your creativity and surprise everyone with your organizational talent and perseverance. Once you feel secure, you really produce. It is very important for Cancer to work with supportive and congenial people, because you are easily upset by criticism and office politics. While you may appear quiet and shy, you are really taking everyone's measure. This is your way of protecting yourself before you reveal your tender, caring side.

You'd like your office to be a home away from home, where you are taking care of people and fulfilling their needs. Though you may have up-and-down days, you should guard against bringing your personal problems into the workplace. Emphasize your excellent sense of marketing and your shrewd eye for quality, plus your innate good taste.

The Cancer Way to Get Ahead

As a Cancer, you bring some important assets to the table. It's up to you to decide how to best utilize your talents and abilities to bring you the very highest return on the investment of your time and energy. When you job hunt, choose a company with a supportive atmosphere and creative opportunities. Play up your finest attributes:

- Creativity
- Intuitive insight into the market
- Perseverance
- Shrewd judgment
- Caring, nurturing qualities
- Organizational talent

CHAPTER 20

Learn from Cancer Celebrities

You know how much fun it is when you find a famous person who shares your sun sign—and even your birthday! Why not turn your brush with fame into an education in astrology? Celebrities who capture the media's attention reflect the current planetary influences, as well as the unique star quality of their sun sign. Who's in this year may be out next year. You can learn from the hottest stellar spotlight stealers what the public is responding to and what this says about our current values.

If one of your famous sign mates intrigues you, explore his personality further by looking up his other planets using the tables in this book. You may even find his horoscope posted on astrology-related Internet sites like www.astrodatabank. com or www.stariq.com, which have charts of world events and headline makers. Then apply the effects of Venus, Mars, Saturn, and Jupiter to his sun-sign traits. It's a way to get up close and personal with your famous friend, maybe learn some secrets not revealed to the public.

You're sure to have lots in common with your famous sign mates. Consider how Lindsay Lohan and Camilla, Duches of Cornwall, have handled scandal. Do you admire the Cancer style of Giorgio Armani? Perhaps you were a fan of the watery TV series *Lost*, which brought together four stars born under Cancer (Michelle Rodriguez, Josh Holloway, Matthew Fox, and Terry O'Quinn). There are caring Cancers whose lives can inspire you to crusade for worthy causes like Nelson Mandela, Princess Diana, and the Dalai Lama.

Get to know these famous Cancers better and learn what makes their stars shine brightly.

Cancer Celebrities

Jane Russell (6/21/21)
Mariette Hartley (6/21/40)
Meredith Baxter (6/21/47)
Juliette Lewis (6/21/73)
Prince William (6/21/82)
Bill Blass (6/22/22)
Kris Kristofferson (6/22/36)
Klaus-Maria Brandauer (6/22/44)
Meryl Streep (6/22/49)
Lindsay Wagner (6/22/49)
Tracy Pollan (6/22/60)
Carson Daly (6/22/73)
Alfred Kinsey (6/23/1894)
Selma Blair (6/23/72)
Michelle Lee (6/24/42)
Peter Weller (6/24/47)
Nancy Allen (6/24/50)
Carly Simon (6/25/45)
George Michael (6/25/63)
Pearl S. Buck (6/26/1892)
Peter Lorre (6/26/1904)
Chris Isaak (6/26/56)
Chris O'Donnell (6/26/70)
Derek Jeter (6/26/74)
Ross Perot (6/27/30)
Vera Wang (6/27/49)
Isabelle Adjani (6/27/55)
Tobey Maguire (6/27/75)
Mel Brooks (6/28/26)
Pat Morita (6/28/32)
Kathy Bates (6/28/48)
Mary Stuart Masterson (6/28/66)

John Cusack (6/28/66)
Ruth Warrick (6/29/15)
Gilda Radner (6/29/46)
Lena Horne (6/20/17)
Mike Tyson (6/30/66)
Michael Phelps (6/30/85)
Charles Laughton (7/1/1899)
Estée Lauder (7/1/1908)
Olivia de Havilland (7/1/16)
Farley Granger (7/1/25)
Leslie Caron (7/1/31)
Karen Black (7/1/42)
Geneviève Bujold (7/1/42)
Deborah Harry (7/1/45)
Dan Aykroyd (7/1/52)
Princess Diana (7/1/61)
Pamela Anderson (7/1/67)
Liv Tyler (7/1/77)
Imelda Marcos (7/2/31)
Richard Perry (7/2/37)
Ron Silver (7/2/46)
Jerry Hall (7/2/56)
Lindsay Lohan (7/2/86)
Betty Buckley (7/3/47)
Montel Williams (7/3/56)
Aaron Tippin (7/3/58)
Tom Cruise (7/3/62)
Jaime Pressley (7/3/77)
Louis Armstrong (7/4/1900)
Geraldo Rivera (7/4/43)
P. T. Barnum (7/5/1810)
Edie Falco (7/5/63)
Nancy Reagan (7/6/21)
Merv Griffin (7/6/25)
Dalai Lama (7/6/35)
Ned Beatty (7/6/36)
George W. Bush (7/6/46)
Sylvester Stallone (7/6/46)
Geoffrey Rush (7/6/51)

Pierre Cardin (7/7/22)
Ringo Starr (7/7/40)
John D. Rockefeller (7/8/1839)
Anjelica Huston (7/8/51)
Marianne Williamson (7/8/52)
Kevin Bacon (7/8/58)
Barbara Cartland (7/9/1901)
Brian Dennehy (7/9/39)
O. J. Simpson (7/9/49)
John Tesh (7/9/52)
Jimmy Smits (7/9/55)
Tom Hanks (7/9/56)
Kelly McGillis (7/9/57)
Courtney Love (7/9/64)
David Brinkley (7/10/20)
Jessica Simpson ((7/10/80)
Tab Hunter (7/11/31)
Giorgio Armani (7/11/34)
Sela Ward (7/11/56)
Richie Sambora (7/11/59)
Lisa Rinna (7/11/65)
L'il Kim (7/11/75)
Henry David Thoreau (7/12/1817)
Milton Berle (7/12/1908)
Bill Cosby (7/12/37)
Richard Simmons (7/12/48)
Cheryl Ladd (7/12/51)
Rolanda Watts (7/12/59)
Kristi Yamaguchi (7/12/71)
Michelle Rodriguez (7/12/78)
Patrick Stewart (7/13/40)
Harrison Ford (7/13/42)
Ingmar Bergman (7/14/18)
Harry Dean Stanton (7/14/26)
Polly Bergen (7/14/30)
Matthew Fox (7/14/66)
Linda Ronstadt (7/15/46)
Jesse Ventura (7/15/51)
Terry O'Quinn (7/15/52)

Brigitte Nielsen (7/15/63)
Orville Redenbacher (7/16/1907)
Ginger Rogers (7/16/11)
Ruben Blades (7/16/48)
Michael Flatley (7/16/58)
Phoebe Cates (7/16/63)
Corey Feldman (7/16/71)
Art Linkletter (7/17/12)
Diahann Carroll (7/17/35)
Donald Sutherland (7/17/35)
Camilla, Duches of Cornwall (7/17/47)
Lucie Arnaz (7/17/51)
David Hasselhoff (7/17/52)
Hume Cronyn (7/18/11)
Red Skelton (7/18/13)
Nelson Mandela (7/18/18)
Ann Landers and Abigail van Buren (7/18/18)
John Glenn (7/18/21)
James Brolin (7/18/40)
Richard Branson (7/18/50)
Pat Hingle (7/19/24)
Diana Rigg (7/20/38)
Josh Holloway (7/20/69)
Sandra Oh (7/20/71)
Ernest Hemingway (7/21/1899)
Robin Williams (7/21/52)
Josh Hartnett (7/21/78)
Alex Trebek (7/22/40)
Danny Glover (7/22/47)
Don Henley (7/22/47)
Rob Estes (7/22/63)
David Spade (7/22/64)
Carson Daly (7/22/73)

CHAPTER 21

Your Cancer Relationships with Every Other Sign: The Green Lights and Red Flags

Are you looking for insight into a relationship? Perhaps it's someone you've met online, a new business partner, a roommate, or the proverbial stranger across a crowded room. After an initial attraction, you may be wondering if you'll still get along down the line. Or why supposedly incompatible signs sometimes have a magical attraction to each other. If things aren't working out, astrology could give you some clues as to why he or she is "not that into you."

Astrology has no magic formula for success in love, but it does offer a better understanding of the qualities each person brings to the relationship and how your partner is likely to react to your sun-sign characteristics. Knowing your potential partner's sign and how it relates to yours could give you some clues about what to expect down the line.

There is also the issue of the timing of a new relationship. From an astrological perspective, the people you meet at any given time provide the dynamic that you require at that moment. If you're a home-loving Cancer, you might benefit from a more social Libra or a globe-trotting Sagittarius companion at a certain time in your life.

The celebrity couples in this chapter can help you visualize each sun-sign combination. You'll note that some legendary lovers have stood the test of time, while others blazed, then broke up, and still others existed only in the fantasy world of film or television (but still captured our imagination). Traditional astrological wisdom holds that signs of the same element are naturally compatible. For Cancer, that would be fellow water signs Scorpio and Pisces. Also favored are signs of complementary elements, such as water signs with earth signs (Taurus, Virgo, Capricorn). In these relationships communication supposedly flows easily, and you'll feel comfortable together.

As you read the following matches, remember that there are no hard-and-fast rules; each combination has perks as well as peeves. So, when sparks fly and an irresistible magnetic pull draws you together, when disagreements and challenges fuel intrigue, mystery, passion, and sexy sparring matches, don't rule the relationship out. That person may provide the diversity, excitement, and challenge you need for an unforgettable romance, a stimulating friendship, or a successful business partnership!

Cancer/Aries

THE GREEN LIGHTS:

Cancer will give Aries hero worship and nurturing, plus shrewd business sense and a solid home base to operate from. Aries gives Cancer romance, positive energy, and courage.

THE RED FLAGS:

Aries detests complaining or whining, so you'll have to suffer in silence. Sulking and possessive behavior are other Aries turnoffs. You may balk when Aries pushes, finding the behavior too insensitive and self-centered.

SIGN MATES:

Cancer President Gerald Ford and Aries Betty Ford

Cancer/Taurus

THE GREEN LIGHTS:

In theory, this should be one of the best combinations. Taurus can't get too much affection, which Cancer provides. And Taurus protects Cancer from the cold world, with solid secure assets. Both are home loving, emotional, and sensual.

THE RED FLAGS:

Cancer's dark mood plus Taurus's stubbornness could create some muddy moments. Both partners should look for constructive ways to let off steam rather than brooding and sulking over grievances.

SIGN MATES:

Cancer James Brolin and Taurus Barbra Streisand

Cancer/Gemini

THE GREEN LIGHTS:

This is a very public pair with charisma to spare. Gemini charm sets off Cancer poise with the perfect light touch. Cancer adds warmth and emotional appeal to Gemini. You can go places together.

THE RED FLAGS:

It's not easy for Gemini to deliver the emotional intimacy Cancer demands. There are too many other exciting options. Cancer possessiveness versus Gemini restlessness could sink this one if you don't have strong mutual interests or projects.

SIGN MATES:

Cancer Tracy Pollan and Gemini Michael J. Fox

Cancer/Cancer

THE GREEN LIGHTS:

Ideally, here is someone who understands your moods, gives you the mothering care you crave, and protects you from the cold cruel world. Your home can be a loving sanctuary for your extended family and a secure nest for each other.

THE RED FLAGS:

You both take slights so personally that disagreements can easily get blown out of proportion. And if you are both in a down mood at the same time, your relationship can explode. You'll need outside activities for balance and time away from each other to regain perspective. Creative expression can save the day by providing an outlet for your emotions.

SIGN MATES:

Cancers Donna Dixon and Dan Aykroyd

Cancer/Leo

THE GREEN LIGHTS:

These neighboring signs come through for each other like good buddies. Cancer gives Leo total attention, backup support, and the VIP treatment the Lion craves. Here is someone who won't fight for the spotlight. Leo gives you confidence, and this sign's positive mental outlook is good medicine for your moods.

THE RED FLAGS:

Cancer's blue moods and tendency to cling tenaciously can weigh Leo down. High-handed Leo behavior can steamroll your sensitive Cancer feelings.

Cancer Kevin Bacon and Leo Kyra Sedgwick

Cancer/Virgo

THE GREEN LIGHTS:

You two vulnerable signs protect and nurture each other. Moody Cancer needs Virgo to refine and focus emotions creatively. Virgo gives Cancer protective care and valuable insight. The charming romantic tenderness of Cancer nurtures the shy side of Virgo. You'll have good communication on a practical level, respecting each other's shrewd financial acumen.

THE RED FLAGS:

Cancer's extreme self-protection could arouse Virgo suspicions. Why must Cancer be so secretive? Virgo's protectiveness could become smothering, making Cancer overdependent. Virgo must learn to offer suggestions instead of criticism.

SIGN MATES:

Sopranos costars Cancer Edie Falco and Virgo James Gandolfini

Cancer/Libra

THE GREEN LIGHTS:

You'll bring out each other's creativity, as Cancer's sensitivity merges with the balanced Libra aesthetic sense. Libra's innate sense of harmony could create a serenely elegant atmosphere where Cancer flourishes. You'll create an especially beautiful and welcoming home together.

THE RED FLAGS:

Libra's detachment could be mistaken for rejection by Cancer, while your Cancer hypersensitivity could throw the Libra scales off-balance. Emotions and emotional confrontations are territories Libra avoids, so Cancer may look elsewhere for sympathy and nurturing.

SIGN MATES:

Cancer Pamela Anderson and Libra Tommy Lee

Cancer/Scorpio

THE GREEN LIGHTS:

Cancer actually enjoys Scorpio intensity and possessiveness—it shows how much they care! And like Prince Charles and Camilla Parker Bowles (or Diana), this pair cares deeply about those they love. Strong emotions are a great bond that can survive heavy storms.

THE RED FLAGS:

Mysterious and melancholy Scorpio moods can leave Cancer feeling isolated and insecure. And the more Cancer clings, the more Scorpio withdraws.

SIGN MATES:

Cancer President George W. Bush and Scorpio Laura Bush
Cancer Harrison Ford and Scorpio Callista Flockhart

Cancer/Sagittarius

THE GREEN LIGHTS:

Sagittarius gets a sensual partner who will keep the home fires burning and the coffers full, while Cancer gets a strong dose of optimism that could banish the blues. The carefree, outgoing, outdoor Sagittarius lifestyle expands the sometimes narrow Cancer point of view and gets you physically active.

THE RED FLAGS:

This joy ride could reach a dead end when Sagittarius shows little sympathy for the Cancer need for mothering or runs roughshod over sensitive Cancer feelings.

SIGN MATES:

Cancer Tom Cruise and Sagittarius Katie Holmes

Cancer/Capricorn

THE GREEN LIGHTS:

A serious sense of duty, family pride, and a basically traditional outlook bring you together. The zodiac mother (Cancer) and father (Capricorn) establish a strong home base. Cancer's tender devotion brings out Capricorn's earthy and sensual side. This couple gets closer over the years.

THE RED FLAGS:

Melancholy moods could muddy this picture. Develop a strategy for coping if depression hits. Capricorn is a lone wolf who may withdraw emotionally. Cancer could look elsewhere for comfort and consolation.

SIGN MATES:

Cancer Prince William and Capricorn Kate Middleton
Cancer Beth Ostrosky and Capricorn Howard Stern

Cancer/Aquarius

THE GREEN LIGHTS:

The key to success for this one-of-a-kind couple is basic ideals. If you two share goals and values, there is no limit to how far you can go. Cancer is turned on by the security of a high position and offers Aquarius strong support and caring qualities that touch everyone's heart, the perfect counterpoint to Aquarius charisma. Former President Ronald Reagan and his wife, Nancy, are a case in point.

THE RED FLAGS:

Cancer is best one on one, while Aquarius loves a crowd. Cancer has to learn to share love with many. Aquarius has to learn to show warmth and emotion rather than turn off Cancer moods.

SIGN MATES:

Cancer Nancy Reagan and Aquarius President Ronald Reagan

Cancer/Pisces

THE GREEN LIGHTS:

You both love to swim in emotional waters, where your communication flows easily. Cancer protective attention and support help Pisces gain confidence and direction. Pisces gives Cancer dreamy romance and creative inspiration. A very meaningful relationship develops over time.

THE RED FLAGS:

You two emotionally vulnerable signs know where the soft spots are and can really hurt each other. Pisces has a way of slipping through clingy Cancer clutches, possibly to dry out after too much emotion. Learn to give each other space. Find creative projects to defuse negative moods and to give a sense of direction.

SIGN MATES:

Cancer David Gest and Pisces Liza Minnelli

CHAPTER 22

The Big Picture for Cancer in 2010

Welcome to 2010! This will be a year about relationships, teamwork, cooperation, and an exploration of your spiritual beliefs and worldview. You may go back to college or on to graduate school. You could be taking seminars and workshops—or teaching them.

Mercury, the ruler of communication and travel, begins the year in retrograde motion. On January 15, it turns direct again, in your seventh house, so things in the communication department improve dramatically. Venus—the planet that rules romance and love, the arts, and money—also begins the year in Capricorn, your opposite sign, your seventh house. So right away, the focus is on partnerships (personal or professional). You and your partner will be discussing your respective needs and desires for the partnership, and the relationship should be pleasantly romantic during this transit, which ends on January 18.

Mars, the planet that symbolizes our sexuality and aggression, begins the year retrograde in Leo, your fourth house, and turns direct again on March 10. Until then, there may be disagreements and heated discussions with family members. Not all the time, but more frequently than you like. After March 10, your sex life should improve dramatically, and you'll feel physically invigorated.

Saturn begins the year in Libra, your fourth house, turns retrograde on January 13, moves back into Virgo, then finally on July 21 enters Libra again. While in Virgo, Saturn urges you to be precise in your communications, in your relationships with relatives, and to meet your obligations with these individuals. During its two-and-a-half year transit of Libra, your home and family are impacted. There could be delays in moving and restrictions concerning parents or your family generally. But you also find strong structures in terms of family and the foundations of relationships. Your creative work will become more structured and disciplined.

Pluto, the planet of profound transformation, continues its long journey through Capricorn, your seventh house, and brings about change in your romantic and business partnerships. But because Pluto will be in this sign until 2024, none of the change happens overnight. If you have Scorpio rising, then you will want to see where Pluto is in your natal chart to get an accurate picture of where in your life this profound change will occur.

Pluto turns retrograde on April 6 and doesn't turn direct again until September 13. During this retrograde period, pay close attention to everything that happens concerning partnerships. Follow synchronicities; listen to your intuition.

Neptune—the planet that symbolizes our illusions, idealism, all forms of escapism, and our higher selves—continues its journey through Aquarius and your eighth house. Neptune has been in this position since 1998, so by now you're well aware of how it impacts resources you share with others. Your partner's money, insurance, taxes, mortgages and loans falls into this house. But the eighth house also governs the weird, the strange, the inexplicable, and the mysterious. Reincarnation. Hauntings. Things that go bump in the night. Life after death. Mediumship. All things psychic. So you may have many experiences in these areas.

When Neptune turns retrograde between May 31 and November 6, it essentially goes to sleep. Any mundane stuff you're dealing with—like taxes and insurance, for instance—may not function smoothly.

Uranus—the planet that symbolizes our individualism and sudden and unexpected change—enters Aries on May 27, for a period of about seven years. Check your birth chart to find out exactly what area of your life will be affected by this transit. That area will experience sudden, unexpected change, new and exciting experiences and insights. Uranus's job is to shake up the status quo and get us out of the comfortable ruts into which we often fall. The best way to navigate this seven-year transit is to embrace change. Try new things, go back to school, find a new career path, change jobs, or do whatever you feel will expand your universe and help you to evolve and achieve your potential. This transit should benefit you, because it will be forming a harmonious angle with your sun.

Uranus turns retrograde on July 5 and doesn't turn direct again until December 5. During this period, it retrogrades back into Pisces, your ninth house, and brings unexpected changes to education, foreign travel, your worldview, and higher education.

Jupiter, the planet of expansion and luck, enters Pisces and your ninth house on January 17, speeds through it without any retrogrades, and enters Aries on June 6. On July 23, it turns retrograde, slips back into Pisces in early September, and remains there throughout the rest of the year. It enters Aries again in late January 2011, where it remains until early June 2011. So look for expansion and good luck generally in ninth-house areas: education, foreign travel, sales, worldview, and spirituality. If you have a copy of your natal chart, by all means check to see where both Pisces and Aries fall in your chart. This will tell you a great deal about the specific area of your life where expansion is what you're doing.

Romance and Creativity

There are two notable time periods this year that favor romance and creative endeavors. Between May 19 and June 14, Venus will be in your sign. This transit increases your sex appeal, charisma, and general self-confidence. If you're uninvolved when the transit begins, you probably won't be when the transit ends. Venus in your sign accentuates all your normal traits and characteristics. If you get involved under this transit, your passions will be running the show! But your intuition and emotions will be your guidance system.

The second great time period for romance falls between September 8 and the end of the year, when Venus is in fellow water sign Scorpio, transiting your fifth house of romance and creativity. This period should be very romantic if you're already involved and incredibly exciting if you're just getting involved. It's also a creative time, when your muse is so up close and personal that you feel you simply have to do something creative. So dust off those manuscripts and portfolios!

However, Venus will be retrograde between October 8 and November 18. A few bumps and bruises in relationship and creative endeavors could result.

Career

The best career dates this year occur when Venus transits your tenth house and Aries—from March 7 to March 31—and between June 6 and July 23, when Jupiter is transiting Aries. Then, between May 27 and July 5, Uranus is moving direct in Aries. Wow. How's this translate? Venus brings ease and artistic sensibilities to your career. Jupiter brings luck, serendipitous experiences, and expansion. And Uranus brings excitement and unpredictability. With these three planets in pioneering Aries, be prepared for fresh, exciting opportunities that change or alter the direction of your career.

Another great time falls around the new moon and solar eclipse in Cancer on July 11. This moon happens just once a year and sets the tone for the next year. Solar eclipses are like double new moons, so expect both opportunities and the completion of other obligations. This new moon should usher in many opportunities in your personal life as well.

Best Times For

Buying or selling a home: August 6 to September 8, when Venus transits Leo and your fourth house.

Family reunions: July 10 to September 8.

Financial matters: June 14 to July 10.

Signing contracts: When Mercury is moving direct!

Overseas travel, publishing, and higher-education endeavors: February 11 to March 7.

Mercury Retrogrades

Every year, Mercury—the planet of communication and travel—turns retrograde three times. During this period, it's wise not to sign contracts (unless you don't mind renegotiating when Mercury is moving direct), to check and recheck travel plans, and to communicate as succinctly as possible. Refrain from buying any big-ticket items or electronics during this time too. Often, computers and appliances go on the fritz, cars act up, data is lost—you get the idea. Be sure to back up all files before the dates below:

April 17—May 11: Mercury retrograde in Taurus. Communicate clearly and succinctly with friends and the members of any group to which you belong.

August 20—September 12: Mercury retrograde in Virgo, your third house of communication. The third house also rules travel, relatives, neighbors, and your community.

December 10—30: Mercury retrograde in Capricorn, your seventh house of partnerships.

Eclipses

Solar eclipses tend to trigger external events that bring about change according to the sign and the house in which they fall. Lunar eclipses trigger inner, emotional events according to the sign and house in which they fall. Any eclipse marks both beginnings and endings. The solar and lunar eclipse in a pair fall in opposite signs.

If you were born under or around the time of an eclipse, it's to your advantage to take a look at your birth chart to find out exactly where the eclipses will impact you.

Most years feature four eclipses—two solar, two lunar, with the set separated by about two weeks. In 2009, there was a lunar eclipse in Cancer on December 31, so the first eclipse in 2010 is a solar eclipse in the opposite sign, Capricorn. This year, three of the eclipses occur either in your sign or your opposite sign, Capricorn. Below are the dates for this year's eclipses:

January 15: solar, Capricorn, your seventh house. Events concerning the affairs of this house—friends, business and romantic partnerships—are highlighted. Venus is also close to the eclipse degree, adding a protective quality and a nice touch of romance!.

June 26: lunar, Capricorn. Your seventh house is hit again. Emotions stirred concerning the areas mentioned above.

July 11: solar, Cancer, your sun sign, your personal life.

December 21: lunar, Gemini, your second house. This one impacts your finances.

Luckiest Day of the Year

There's at least one day a year when the Sun and Jupiter link up in some way. This year, March 2 looks to be that day, with a nice backup on July 26.

Now let's find out what's in store for you, day by day!

CHAPTER 23

Eighteen Months of Day-by-Day Predictions: July 2009 to December 2010

Moon sign times are calculated for Eastern Standard Time and Eastern Daylight Time. Please adjust for your local time zone.

JULY 2009

Wednesday, July 1 (Moon in Libra to Scorpio 1:20 a.m.) Uranus turns retrograde in Pisces, your ninth house. Between now and December 1, you'll be scrutinizing your spiritual beliefs and worldview. If you're still in school, you'll be taking a closer look at your educational goals. Sudden insights into all areas of your life are going to enable you to make better decisions.

Thursday, July 2 (Moon in Scorpio) Whether you're leaving town for the weekend or people are congregating at your place, it's a good idea to have all your ducks lined up, Cancer. Be organized. Keep your most intense and private feelings private.

Friday, July 3 (Moon in Scorpio to Sagittarius 11:12 a.m.) Just in time for the July 4 weekend, Mercury moves into Cancer—the sign that most aptly embodies the concept of home, family, and country. This transit brings about lively

216

discussions over the weekend that span the gamut of topics, but stay away from politics and religion!

Saturday, July 4 (Moon in Sagittarius)   Happy Independence Day. Regardless of where you are or what you're doing, read the Bill of Rights and find out what makes the U.S. great. Are our rights still intact? Are we still a free nation? Or have current government actions curtailed our freedoms?

Sunday, July 5 (Moon in Sagittarius to Capricorn 11:08 p.m.)   Venus enters Gemini, your twelfth house, today and doesn't move on until July 31. This transit could indicate a secretive romance or affair. Perhaps you and your new partner simply want to keep the relationship under wraps for now. Or there may be other reasons for keeping things secret. Once Venus moves into your sign on July 31, however, it becomes less likely that the relationship will be kept a secret.

Monday, July 6 (Moon in Capricorn)   Here are the moon and Pluto together again. Whether it's your first day back to work after the weekend or part of your weekend, take notice of what happens between you and a partner. With a lunar eclipse in Capricorn coming up tomorrow, you could be feeling the effects already. Prepare yourself by discussing your relationship with your partner. Talk about each other's expectations.

Tuesday, July 7 (Moon in Capricorn)   Today's lunar eclipse in Capricorn occurs opposite your sign. Saturn forms a beneficial angle to the eclipse degree, suggesting that you find an ideal vehicle to express your feelings. It could be through a letter or e-mail that you write to your partner (or someone else you're close to). In fact, writing your feelings down will help you organize them.

Wednesday, July 8 (Moon in Capricorn to Aquarius 12:04 p.m.)   The moon enters your eighth house. As usual, this transit brings up all kinds of strange and sometimes disturbing feelings. When the feelings are disturbing, it's usually because things happen over which you feel you have no control. If you're disturbed about an event, relationship, or situation, try to step back a little and figure out what you're supposed to learn.

Thursday, July 9 (Moon in Aquarius)   Let's take stock. Venus is in air sign Gemini, your twelfth house. The moon, Neptune, and Jupiter are also in an air sign—Aquarius. And the other six planets are in compatible earth and water signs. This arrangement sets up a struggle between your inner needs and your responsibilities in the outer world. Your intuition and your reasoning mind could be sending you different messages. Balance and precision are called for. Are you up to the task?

Friday, July 10 (Moon in Aquarius)   The moon enters Pisces, joining Uranus in your ninth house. No doubt about it. With this duo, there's always excitement. And today it seems to come out of nowhere, shaking up the status quo. But all of this will probably be quite positive once the dust settles.

Saturday, July 11 (Moon in Aquarius to Pisces 12:44 a.m.)   Mars joins Venus in Gemini, your twelfth house. Anytime these two travel closely together, there's a potential for a love affair that is highly charged sexually. Since the pair is in Gemini, it's likely the attraction is, at first, intellectual. With the pair in your twelfth house, the relationship will be secret and private at least until July 31, when Venus enters your sign.

Sunday, July 12 (Moon in Pisces)   It's possible that your spiritual beliefs take precedence today. Whether you're dealing with in-laws, foreign-exchange students, foreign-business interests, attorneys, or courts, stick to what you know and believe. Don't allow others to sway your opinions.

Monday, July 13 (Moon in Pisces to Aries 11:40 a.m.)   The moon enters your tenth house. Once again, your focus is on your career, the public, or perhaps your father. Your interaction with people in the public sector of your chart should be tempered somewhat. Be assertive, but not aggressive. Be firm, but not stubborn.

Tuesday, July 14 (Moon in Aries)   You're passionate about something today, and it shows in your work, your presentations, and your general behavior. You're able to gather the support you need to pitch an idea or agenda. Make sure this idea or agenda is approved before Mercury turns retrograde on September 6.

Wednesday, July 15 (Moon in Aries to Taurus 6:30 p.m.)   Your focus is on groups and friends today and how these people bolster your dreams and ambitions. If you have a friend who is a constant naysayer, you should really take a closer look at this friendship and decide whether you want this person in your life.

Thursday, July 16 (Moon in Taurus)   Stubbornness is your friend today. It enables you to hold your own ground against the competition or against those who don't support what you do. Even though you generally aren't known as someone who surrenders to peer pressure, there are times when you do it just to keep the peace.

Friday, July 17 (Moon in Taurus to Gemini 11:42 p.m.)   Mercury enters Leo, your second house. Between now and August 2, your daily activities and conscious thought are focused on money and how you can express yourself in a way that allows your genuine self to shine. You may be doing a lot of writing, e-mailing, and phoning to touch base with clients, coworkers, peers, or people who share your values.

Saturday, July 18 (Moon in Gemini)   The moon joins Venus and Mars in Gemini, your twelfth house. This trio of planets certainly heightens the romantic and sexual aspects of a relationship. One thing is sure: You're clearing mental, emotional, and spiritual space in your life for tomorrow's moon in your sign.

Sunday, July 19 (Moon in Gemini)   The moon enters your sign, and another power day begins. Apply the day's energy to the area of your life that you feel needs a boost.

Monday, July 20 (Moon in Gemini to Cancer 12:52 a.m.)   Your intuitive flow is excellent and leads you, serendipitously, to the place you need to be, with the people you need to talk to and know. Gone is the battle between head and heart; today, you're all about empathetic knowing.

Tuesday, July 21 (Moon in Cancer)   Today's solar eclipse in Cancer is important for you. It indicates that sudden, unexpected events occur that impact your personal life. This event is ultimately positive for you.

Wednesday, July 22 (Moon in Cancer to Leo 12:28 a.m.)   You're in a spending state of mind today. Whether it's a big-ticket item or something small, you may be buying to mollify an inner condition. Resist the urge to buy; instead, examine the feelings beneath the urge.

Thursday, July 23 (Moon in Leo)   Finally, a friendly moon in a compatible fire sign! Today, you and an older relative or neighbor take it upon yourselves to do something for your neighborhood or community. This work you perform is on a volunteer basis and could be for a local charity or some other nonprofit organization.

Friday, July 24 (Moon in Leo to Virgo 12:24 a.m.)   Attend to details you've overlooked and shoved aside to attend to more pressing issues or deadlines. These details could include making dental and doctor appointments, taking your car in for an oil change, or even catching up on all that e-mail that has accumulated in your in-box.

Saturday, July 25 (Moon in Virgo)   If you're throwing a party or having some sort of gathering, be sure you've got all the details worked out. This party or gathering brings you out of the shell you've been in for the last several weeks and puts you back in touch with your social self! A Taurus figures in the day's events.

Sunday, July 26 (Moon in Virgo to Libra 2:26 a.m.) The moon enters your fourth house. Transitions and activities involve home and family. Stay away from heated discussions and debates.

Monday, July 27 (Moon in Libra) Your artistic side is showing today. Whether it expresses itself through music, art, dance, photography, or writing, you feel very good about it. If this artistic expression is something you can do in private, so much the better. The position of Venus favors it.

Tuesday, July 28 (Moon in Libra to Scorpio 7:57 a.m.) Between now and July 31, you and your partner may be discussing making your relationship more public. It's possible that you decide to move in together, get engaged, or even get married. If you're not involved at this time, then you may be getting ready to submit a creative project.

Wednesday, July 29 (Moon in Scorpio) Someone around you may be acting out. If this person is close to you, ask yourself if this person's antics actually fit your own mood. Sometimes, the people around us reflect how we ourselves feel.

Thursday, July 30 (Moon in Scorpio to Sagittarius 5:10 p.m.) A work situation surfaces today. Rather than getting bent out of shape about it, step back. Take an honest look at the situation. If the problem is personal, don't make any decisions until after Venus enters your sign tomorrow.

Friday, July 31 (Moon in Sagittarius) Venus enters Cancer, your first house. This transit marks one of the most romantic and creative times for you this year. It lasts until August 26, so use this window of opportunity to take on anything your heart desires. For one day, on August 25, Mars and Venus both will be in your sign, so plan for something special on that day.

Saturday, August 1 (Moon in Sagittarius) Today is problematic in that it creates a struggle between your professional and personal responsibilities. To minimize stress, have your priorities laid out and approach everything with practicality in mind.

Sunday, August 2 (Moon in Sagittarius to Capricorn 5:09 a.m.) Mercury enters compatible earth sign Virgo, your third house. Between now and August 25, you've got the ideal window of opportunity to finish a manuscript, pitch a project, or publicize your product. This transit stirs up a lot of activity, such as short-distance travel or more contact than usual with relatives. You may be looking at neighborhoods, too, during this time, in anticipation of a move.

Monday, August 3 (Moon in Capricorn) You are infused with a sense of your personal power. You're able to evaluate other people's criticisms, and if you find them petty, shrug them off. You and a partner are able to talk honestly and openly about your relationship.

Tuesday, August 4 (Moon in Capricorn to Aquarius 6:08 p.m.) The moon joins Neptune and Jupiter in your eighth house. You may get together with a group of people whose interests support and complement your own. There's an emotional earthquake bubbling up just beneath the surface. Don't worry about it. You're feeling the effects already of tomorrow's lunar eclipse in Aquarius.

Wednesday, August 5 (Moon in Aquarius) Today's lunar eclipse in Aquarius could stir up your emotions surrounding resources you share with others or vice versa. Mars forms a beneficial angle to this moon, indicating that you take decisive action. The overall tone of this eclipse is positive, but may require an attitude adjustment on your part.

Thursday, August 6 (Moon in Aquarius) Air signs—Gemini, Libra, Aquarius—play a vital role in the day's events and activities. It's a people day, when you network, discuss, brainstorm, make and receive calls, and answer e-mails. These activities involve both your professional and your personal lives and may include tax and insurance matters.

Friday, August 7 (Moon in Aquarius to Pisces 6:35 a.m.) The moon joins Uranus in Pisces. This combination also occurs once a month and usually brings about unusual emotional re-actions on your part. You might, for instance, get stressed out or explode over some inconsequential event, but not react at all to something that would drive someone else right over the edge.

Saturday, August 8 (Moon in Pisces)   You perform a ser-vice for someone today out of the goodness of your heart.

Sunday, August 9 (Moon in Pisces to Aries 5:24 p.m.)   The moon enters your tenth house. This transit usually highlights career issues and relationships with bosses and peers. But since today is Sunday, you probably have the day off. Even so, your focus could be on work, your standing at your job, or on how you can make the next career leap without undermining your present position. Line up your priorities for this week; then tackle them one by one.

Monday, August 10 (Moon in Aries)   Mercury is still in Virgo, providing you with the communication skills to con-vince your boss about the validity of a project or the sound-ness of an idea. You may feel that the people around you can't do the job as well as you can, so that makes you reluctant to delegate. But you may need to do exactly that so you can place your energy where it needs to be focused.

Tuesday, August 11 (Moon in Aries)   Take a deep breath and step back from whatever or whoever is making you feel impatient. Once you have some emotional distance from the situation, you'll do fine. Just remember you don't have to do everything yourself!

Wednesday, August 12 (Moon in Aries to Taurus 1:51 a.m.)   Finally, an earth-friendly moon that brings some sanity and grounding back to your life. It's a good time to hang out with friends and people who think like you do or share your interests and passions.

Thursday, August 13 (Moon in Taurus)   You're in it for the long haul—in a relationship, on a project, or with a creative endeavor. Whatever it is that you're pursuing, you won't give up until it's completed or resolved to your satisfaction. This particular moon also stimulates your artistic side, so you may want to surround yourself with beauty—paintings, fresh flowers, bold colors.

Friday, August 14 (Moon in Taurus to Gemini 7:27 a.m.)   It may be one of those wild spending days when you see something you absolutely must buy. Maybe you feel that you deserve this special purchase—and you undoubtedly do—or that it's time to treat yourself to something special. If so, buy it and love it! But if you're buying to appease inner turmoil, think again.

Saturday, August 15 (Moon in Gemini)   You're clearing out old stuff in your life—from clothes you no longer wear to beliefs that no longer serve you. In a sense, you're making space for new experiences, situations, relationships, and emotions. After all, tomorrow the moon enters your sign, and that's always a power day.

Sunday, August 16 (Moon in Gemini to Cancer 10:14 a.m.)   Sleep in, kick back, and get lost in doing what you love. The lunar transits that bring the moon into your sun sign are usually gifts. We may not always notice or appreciate them the way we should, though, so take a few moments at some point today and express gratitude for the life you're living.

Monday, August 17 (Moon in Cancer)   Mercury, Saturn, and Pluto are in compatible earth signs, and Uranus is in a fellow water sign. That's six out of ten planets stacked in your favor. Use this energy to take on difficult challenges today, and watch the obstacles melt away. There's nothing too large or insurmountable for you once you make up your mind to dive in.

Tuesday, August 18 (Moon in Cancer to Leo 10:57 a.m.)   The moon enters your second house. If you feel disorganized today, or if your life seems chaotic, it's time to untangle yourself and dive into a creative project. Shut your door, and don't feel guilty about it.

Wednesday, August 19 (Moon in Leo)   You're building foundations in some area of your life, and your efforts attract the attention of someone who can make a difference financially or professionally. You're on time for everything today, perhaps because you feel pressed for time. But try not to let stress eat you up. Just do the best that you can with what you have.

Thursday, August 20 (Moon in Leo to Virgo 11:01 a.m.)   The new moon in Virgo ushers in new financial opportunities. You could land a second job to supplement your income, get a raise at your present job, or receive money someone owes you. In some way, shape, or form, your income improves. Mars in Gemini forms a harmonious angle to this moon, indicating action.

Friday, August 21 (Moon in Virgo)   Your attention to details pays off. Whether you're dealing with a communication project or a relationship, be aware of how the small parts fit together to form a cohesive whole. Once you have all the pieces of the puzzle, you're in good shape. And by the way, Cancer, there's someone nearby who is interested in you.

Saturday, August 22 (Moon in Virgo to Libra 12:12 p.m.)   The moon enters your fourth house. You need to balance professional and personal responsibilities today. Since it's the weekend, one way to do that is to work at home, catching up on stuff you'll tackle early next week. If you have chil-

225

dren who are home for the summer, you may want to divide your time between them and your work.

Sunday, August 23 (Moon in Libra)   Most of the month's transits happen in the next few days. Mercury, Venus, and Mars will all change signs, and Saturn is moving toward its big change at the end of October, from Virgo to Libra. Prepare for the changes today by lining up your priorities for the week ahead. And then remember to do something for yourself!

Monday, August 24 (Moon in Libra to Scorpio 4:17 p.m.)   It's a bottom-line kind of day. Whether you're conducting research on a new product or a new way of ferrying people around town, your psychic sense is reading the atmosphere and the moods of people around you. This gives you an edge on the competition.

Tuesday, August 25 (Moon in Scorpio)   Mercury enters Libra; Mars enters your sign and will be there until October 16. This transit in particular provides a very nice window of opportunity to get things done. In your personal life, you can expect a whirlwind of activity that includes travel, heightened sexuality, and an abundance of physical energy. Check out what the Mercury transit means in tomorrow's entry.

Wednesday, August 26 (Moon in Scorpio)   Venus enters Leo, your second house, and Mercury is now in Libra, your fourth house. These two planets should bring more income and greater balance into your family life. Mercury reaches out more to other people, and one of those people could be a special romantic interest who shares your values.

Thursday, August 27 (Moon in Scorpio to Sagittarius 12:16 a.m.)   This moon is also compatible with the positions of both Mercury and Venus, and brings a work situation or health issue into greater clarity. You may be in a party mood over the weekend, Cancer, and could be seeing some of your coworkers and employees at the gatherings.

226

Friday, August 28 (Moon in Sagittarius)   Mercury will turn retrograde on September 6 and again on December 26. Be sure you start backing up computer files several days early. It's also a good idea to have basic maintenance done to your car. And be sure that between now and October 16, you don't speed. Mars in your sign increases the likelihood of tickets and accidents.

Saturday, August 29 (Moon in Sagittarius to Capricorn 11:45 a.m.)   The moon joins Pluto in your seventh house. You're in the driver's seat today—or, at any rate, you think that you are. Either way, you aren't easily swayed by what other people think you should do, and you refuse to give in just to appease a partner.

Sunday, August 30 (Moon in Capricorn)   Your business plan has a few chinks in it. Not to worry. There are experts in your circle of friends and acquaintances who have the knowledge or information that you need. The big question is whether you're willing to make the changes that are necessary. Remain flexible.

Monday, August 31 (Moon in Capricorn)   Beginnings and endings—that's what today is made of. Events aren't necessarily dramatic, although they can be. Most likely, the beginnings and endings are merely a reflection of the change that is rippling through the undercurrents of your life.

SEPTEMBER 2009

Tuesday, September 1 (Moon in Capricorn to Aquarius 12:43 a.m.)   Jupiter is working tirelessly to expand your opportunities in many areas of your life. One of those areas involves resources that you share with others. It's now easier for you to obtain mortgages and loans, your spouse or a partner may have gotten a raise, which impacts your life as well, and your spiritual beliefs may be undergoing a positive change.

Wednesday, September 2 (Moon in Aquarius)　Turn inward today for answers. The insights you're looking for are inside you; once you start looking, your innate wisdom will surface. It may sound much too simple, but when you're in the flow, that's how it works. And no sign is more consistently in the flow than you are, Cancer.

Thursday, September 3 (Moon in Aquarius to Pisces 12:59 p.m.)　The moon links up with Uranus in your ninth house. Once again, erratic or surprising emotions are highlighted. Either you feel these emotions or someone close to you experiences them, almost as if they have picked up on your mood. With this combination, there can be telepathic communication.

Friday, September 4 (Moon in Pisces)　Today's full moon in Pisces should be quite romantic for you. In fact, whatever you can imagine today, you can manifest. On a more mundane level, you'll be mulling over things like your educational goals, political beliefs, or even where you're going on your vacation.

Saturday, September 5 (Moon in Pisces to Aries 11:15 p.m.)　Tomorrow, Mercury turns retrograde in Libra, your fourth house. So back up all computer files today, double-check travel plans, and if possible, delay major purchases until after September 29. If you have to buy something that can break down—an appliance, for instance—then be sure you read the fine print in the contract.

Sunday, September 6 (Moon in Aries)　With the moon in Aries and Mercury turning retrograde in Libra, you may be spending at least some of your Sunday working. Whether you brought work home or you go into the office, you need to get things straightened out in your own mind before you can tackle them tomorrow.

Monday, September 7 (Moon in Aries)　The week gets off to a running start, with five million things landing on your desk simultaneously, the phone ringing off the hook, and your in-box filling up. You'll need to delegate today, even if you don't want to, and the sooner you surround yourself with dependable people, the better off you'll be.

Tuesday, September 8 (Moon in Aries to Taurus 7:19 a.m.)   Mars is still moving through your sign, and today's moon forms a beneficial angle to it. The combination should facilitate the flow of intuitive information that you rely upon so readily. You may get together at some point with a few close friends.

Wednesday, September 9 (Moon in Taurus)   If you feel at all out of sorts today, then reach out and do something for someone else. The world probably doesn't have enough of that, and perhaps if more of us did it more frequently, we could raise global consciousness and eventually manage to live at peace.

Thursday, September 10 (Moon in Taurus to Gemini 1:18 p.m.)   You're entering a dormant phase for the next few days. You may get together with people and attend a party or two, but essentially, you'll be reserved. Your focus will be on yourself: your motives, ambitions, and personal unconscious.

Friday, September 11 (Moon in Gemini)   Pluto turns direct today. The effects of this movement will be subtle, unfolding over the rest of the year. But it should help your intimate relationships and your own sense of confidence and power. Right now, you're gearing up for the moon moving into your sign late tomorrow afternoon.

Saturday, September 12 (Moon in Gemini to Cancer 5:20 p.m.)   This afternoon, the moon enters your sign, and you're ready! Whatever you do today, you're buoyant. Remember how you feel under this moon, and try to bring about that mood when the moon is in a more challenging sign.

Sunday, September 13 (Moon in Cancer)   Nurturing women feature in the day's events. Your mother, a sister, or a friend who is like family has insights and wisdom from which you can benefit. You may be hosting a gathering at your place—a dinner, a party, or even an impromptu celebration of some kind.

Monday, September 14 (Moon in Cancer to Leo 7:40 p.m.) What brings you out before the public today? A speaking engagement? A promotional tour of some kind? Or is it just that you're the center of attention at work or among the members of a group to which you belong? Whatever it is, Cancer, put on your public persona.

Tuesday, September 15 (Moon in Leo) If Mercury's retrograde movement is creating havoc for you in some area of your life, the only way to mitigate the damage is to communicate clearly and succinctly to everyone with whom you come into contact. If you have to travel during the retrograde period, prepare yourself for unexpected changes in your plans.

Wednesday, September 16 (Moon in Leo to Virgo 8:56 p.m.) The moon joins Saturn in your third house. You have to play by the rules of whatever game you're playing. If you do, then Saturn provides a solid foundation and enables you to ground yourself effectively.

Thursday, September 17 (Moon in Virgo) Details are part and parcel for the moon in Virgo. But there's something else, too, that bears mentioning. You're able to analyze and critique emotionally, as though your emotions are a filter through which the rest of your life flows.

Friday, September 18 (Moon in Virgo to Libra 10:26 p.m.) Today's new moon in Virgo ushers in opportunities related to your daily life. It's possible that you'll be looking at new neighborhoods in anticipation of a move. You may be traveling more frequently and have more contact with relatives. Opportunities surface concerning writing and communication in general.

Saturday, September 19 (Moon in Libra)   You may decide to take a computer course or some other kind of course that enables you to be more self-sufficient. If you're having computer problems during this Mercury retrograde period, then the computer course may be the best route to take.

Sunday, September 20 (Moon in Libra)   Venus enters Virgo and remains there until October 14. This transit puts a whole new spin on the new moon of two days ago. It now looks as if romance is headed your way, and it's much closer than you think. A neighbor or someone in your immediate community is a distinct romantic possibility.

Monday, September 21 (Moon in Libra to Scorpio 1:52 a.m.)   With Venus now in a compatible earth sign and Mars in your own sign, the chance for a sexually charged romantic relationship is heightened considerably. The Scorpio moon is intensely passionate, too, so tread carefully today. Be sure that whatever actions you take are the result of genuine feelings and not just hormones!

Tuesday, September 22 (Moon in Scorpio)   As Saturn prepares to transit its way into Libra, which happens at the end of October, you'll feel the change. Its transit through Libra won't be as beneficial for you as its transit during the past two and a half years. The Saturn square to the sun is one of the more challenging aspects. However, if you're in a solid place within yourself, Saturn will help strengthen that.

Wednesday, September 23 (Moon in Scorpio to Sagittarius 8:44 a.m.)   Just another six days until Mercury turns direct again. Until then, continue to revise whatever you're working on. In relationships, maintain your clarity of communication. You could feel impatient with coworkers or employees today. Just remember that qualities you find annoying in other people may be qualities that you yourself possess.

Thursday, September 24 (Moon in Sagittarius)   The stars provide you with ample opportunities to grasp the big picture. What will you do with this knowledge?

Friday, September 25 (Moon in Sagittarius to Capricorn 7:19 p.m.)   You and a partner are building a solid foundation for your relationship. Business or personal, this relationship is important to you. The main thing is to talk to each other honestly.

Saturday, September 26 (Moon in Capricorn)   Kick back, relax, and do whatever you enjoy. Leo figures prominently in the day's events. In fact, a Leo may suggest getting out of town for the weekend.

Sunday, September 27 (Moon in Capricorn)   October has a number of transits that are sure to leave you gasping for air, time, and relaxation. So enjoy whatever free time you have today; don't worry about deadlines, people who aren't living up to their end of the bargain, or naysayers who continually try to thwart your best efforts.

Monday, September 28 (Moon in Capricorn to Aquarius 8:07 a.m.)   It may be time for a group meeting—with co-workers, family, or even friends. You may be planning a special celebration for someone, or perhaps you're already looking forward to the holidays and want to find out who is going to be where.

Tuesday, September 29 (Moon in Aquarius)   Mercury turns direct so get in touch with your e-mail group again. Life moves forward. Anything that has been delayed now untangles itself.

Wednesday, September 30 (Moon in Aquarius to Pisces 8:27 p.m.)   On the last day of September, you're feeling pretty good about things. If seasons change where you are, there's a distinct new flavor in the air, which fills you with hope for the last three months of the year. Change is inevitable. Flow with it.

Thursday, October 1 (Moon in Pisces)   With the moon and Uranus in a fellow water sign and Mars in your sign, your intuition and imagination are heightened. Tackle any challenges today by using Mars's energy to overcome them; move the way water moves. Flow around the challenges and the people who create them.

Friday, October 2 (Moon in Pisces)   It's wiser to allow yourself to feel than to suppress. Good or bad, our emotions are messengers that inform us about the state of our inner world. If you understand the source of the emotion, you can deal with any external situation or relationship.

Saturday, October 3 (Moon in Pisces to Aries 6:21 a.m.)   You may be feeling the effects of tomorrow's full moon in Aries. There's a certain tension in the air that's hard to pin down, but which you feel. It's time to step back and take an honest look at where you are in your life, as opposed to where you would like to be.

Sunday, October 4 (Moon in Aries)   The full moon in Aries may bring hidden issues to light. These issues could be of a long-standing nature, from childhood or perhaps even past lives. The best way to deal with these issues is to meditate or to seek professional help if you feel you would benefit from it.

Monday, October 5 (Moon in Aries to Taurus 1:34 p.m.)   If you're feeling stubborn today, it's probably with good reason. Someone may want you to do something that you either don't want to do or feel you aren't qualified to do. Dig in your heels. Maybe when the moon moves into your sign, you'll have a different perspective on this.

Tuesday, October 6 (Moon in Taurus)   You're building foundations and laying down goals that could be related to your spiritual or political beliefs. Education is key. Consider taking a couple college or adult-education courses. Or, if you've been thinking about going to graduate school, start collecting your information now.

Wednesday, October 7 (Moon in Taurus to Gemini 6:47 p.m.) Your need to be free of a situation, relationship, or emotion highlights a fundamental tenet of your psyche: You like calling your own shots. If you presently work for someone else, you may want to consider starting your own business. You have the resources and talent to do this.

Thursday, October 8 (Moon in Gemini) If possible, keep to yourself today. You're getting ready for the moon's transit into your sign tomorrow, and you'll need all your physical, emotional, and spiritual reserves for that. Once again, some internal housecleaning may be in order.

Friday, October 9 (Moon in Gemini to Cancer 10:48 p.m.) Late this evening, the energy shifts, and you're aware of it. The moon has joined Mars in your sign. You may be obsessed with an idea, a project, or even a relationship. You can accomplish virtually anything today if you put your energy into it. Just follow your intuition.

Saturday, October 10 (Moon in Cancer) With the weekend spread out before you like a banquet of possibilities, you aren't sure what to sample first. Since the stars are stacked so nicely in your favor, why not sample a little of everything? You've got the whole weekend to do that, so make good use of your time!

Sunday, October 11 (Moon in Cancer) A surprise visit from your mother or another nurturing female in your life could throw off your routine if the stars were arranged just a little differently. But you take the visit in stride and bring the woman, whoever she is, along on the weekend's wild, enjoyable ride.

Monday, October 12 (Moon in Cancer to Leo 2:03 a.m.) Jupiter turns direct in Aquarius, your eighth house. This movement frees up Jupiter's expansive energy. It will now be much easier for you to obtain loans and mortgages. If your partner has been hoping for a raise, it could happen between now and the end of the year.

Tuesday, October 13 (Moon in Leo)   You're in a position today to work cooperatively with someone else. It could be any kind of project—a creative endeavor, part of your long-range business plan, or something specifically for work. Whatever it is, two get the job done faster than one. Follow your instincts.

Wednesday, October 14 (Moon in Leo to Virgo 4:46 a.m.)   Venus enters Libra and your fourth house. This transit lasts until November 7 and should bring smoothness and balance to your home life. It should also bolster your love life, expanding your options if you're not involved or solidifying a current relationship.

Thursday, October 15 (Moon in Virgo)   The moon joins Saturn in your third house for the last time this year. Actually, it's the last time in thirty years, because that's how long it takes Saturn to traverse the zodiac. Tidy up your daily life so that when Saturn leaves Virgo on October 29, you can spring into action.

Friday, October 16 (Moon in Virgo to Libra 7:30 a.m.)   Mars enters Leo, your second house, and remains there through the end of the year. It turns retrograde on December 20, but until then, you have ample opportunities to increase your income. A second job is one possibility. Or you may get a significant raise.

Saturday, October 17 (Moon in Libra)   The moon joins Venus in your fourth house. This combination certainly enhances your love life and your artistic sensibilities, particularly in your own home and within your family life. In the artistic department, you and your family, for instance, may launch a home beautification project—new paint, new furniture, or perhaps a garden of some kind. Or someone in the family buys a special painting or other object that embodies beauty.

Sunday, October 18 (Moon in Libra to Scorpio 11:23 a.m.)   The new moon in Scorpio opens new doorways related to your home and family. If you've been wanting to start a family, then this new moon helps it happen. If you've wanted to move, this new moon promises that you can. Libra is about social networks, relationships, harmony, and balance, so this new moon brings in those elements as well.

Monday, October 19 (Moon in Scorpio)   In ten days, Saturn leaves Virgo and won't return for another thirty years. So as long as Saturn is in your third house of communication, take advantage of it. Write and send your memos. Submit your manuscripts. Pay close attention to details in all your communications. And if you're going to move, hurry up and get it done before October 29.

Tuesday, October 20 (Moon in Scorpio to Sagittarius 5:50 p.m.)   If a work issue surfaces this afternoon, your best bet is to adjust your own attitude and ask what you're supposed to learn from this situation or event. What is the other person teaching you? Once you approach challenges in this manner, the entire dynamics change.

Wednesday, October 21 (Moon in Sagittarius)   If you're looking for the larger perspective today, you find it. It could be related to your work routine or your health maintenance, but other possible areas are education and spiritual beliefs.

Thursday, October 22 (Moon in Sagittarius)   With both Mercury and Venus in Libra and the moon in Sagittarius, your work and home life are the areas of concentration for you today. It may be that you have an opportunity to travel with coworkers, employees, or your family, and that the journey isn't quite what you anticipate. In fact, the journey could turn into a spiritual quest that leaves you reeling. In a good sense!

Friday, October 23 (Moon in Sagittarius to Capricorn 3:40 a.m.) The moon enters your seventh house, Saturn in Virgo is in your third house, both Mercury and Venus are in Libra, your fourth house, and Mars is in Leo, your second house. So all of these areas could come into play today: your finances, home and family, and partnerships. Maybe it's time, Cancer, to evaluate what you really are seeking in business and personal partnerships. If you don't have what you want, then figure out a way to change the status quo.

Saturday, October 24 (Moon in Capricorn) You and a partner lay out a strategy or long-range plan for your business. If this is a business that already exists, then you may be trying to expand your markets. If this is a business you hope to start, then the success of your long-range plans and goals may depend on what Saturn will be doing in your natal chart once it enters Libra.

Sunday, October 25 (Moon in Capricorn to Aquarius 3:08 p.m.) The moon joins Neptune and Jupiter in your eighth house. Five out of ten planets are in air signs today, so you may be thinking more than feeling or intuiting. Try to strike a balance between the two approaches, if possible. You're at your best when you can intuit your way through a challenge, so before making any decisions, it's wise to wait until the moon is in your sign.

Monday, October 26 (Moon in Aquarius) You get together with your support group today—writers, bridge enthusiasts, actors, or whatever it is. You enjoy the interaction with this group. It buoys your spirits and makes you feel that you are a vital part of a community. If you don't belong to a group like this, then perhaps it's time to try one.

Tuesday, October 27 (Moon in Aquarius) How far can you push the envelope today? It may surprise you. You've got plenty of supporters who are eager for your ideas and projects. Believe in yourself, Cancer, and move forward. One step at a time. That's how everything is done.

Wednesday, October 28 (Moon in Aquarius to Pisces 3:46 a.m.)   Mercury enters Scorpio, your fifth house. This transit lasts until November 15 and creates an atmosphere in which honest discussion with a romantic partner is much easier. In fact it's a two-way conversation, and you and a partner are able to make significant strides in your relationship. This transit also favors all creative projects and endeavors.

Thursday, October 29 (Moon in Pisces)   Saturn enters Libra, your fourth house. This transit, which will last for about two and a half years, is a major shift in energy. This planet demands that we fulfill our obligations and responsibilities, and if we do this, then it provides support, structure, and grounding.

Friday, October 30 (Moon in Pisces to Aries 1:57 p.m.) Career and professional issues are highlighted today and tomorrow. Even though you're entering the weekend, you may be taking work home with you. Be sure to make your e-mail address and phone number available to coworkers and employees.

Saturday, October 31 (Moon in Aries)   Happy Halloween! If you celebrate, it may be with people from work or people who work in the same profession that you do. If you have kids and are celebrating with them, be sure to make it as different and memorable as possible. The Aries moon loves marching to its own drummer.

NOVEMBER 2009

Sunday, November 1—Daylight Saving Time Ends (Moon in Aries to Taurus, 7:45 p.m.)   The moon enters earth-friendly Taurus, your eleventh house. This transit favors all kinds of activities with friends and groups. You may decide to toss a party at your house today or attend a gathering at someone else's place. Either way, your appreciation for good friends deepens.

Monday, November 2 (Moon in Taurus)   The Taurus full moon should be incredibly enjoyable for you. The only possible challenge is that you'll feel an inner tension about so much socializing because a part of you will want to be working on your creative projects or spending time with a partner or your kids.

Tuesday, November 3 (Moon in Taurus to Gemini 11:53 p.m.)   The moon enters your twelfth house. This transit is usually best utilized as an internal housecleaning day. You can still go about your business, of course, but do so with awareness.

Wednesday, November 4 (Moon in Gemini)   Neptune turns direct in Aquarius, your eighth house. The effects will be subtle because Neptune moves with such slowness. However, over the course of the next several months, you'll be better able to integrate your ideals into your spirituality. You may also become more aware of your esoteric interests.

Thursday, November 5 (Moon in Gemini)   Tomorrow, the moon enters your sign. Prepare for it by lining up your priorities for tomorrow and Saturday so that you can maximize your time. Or decide if you would rather kick back and chill for a couple days. It all depends on your moods and your needs.

Friday, November 6 (Moon in Gemini to Cancer 2:43 a.m.)   Once again, it's a power day. The moon is in your sign and you are raring to go somewhere or do something. This is why prioritizing yesterday was a good idea! Do whatever you need to today; your inner dialogue will be much quieter.

Saturday, November 7 (Moon in Cancer)   Venus enters Scorpio, your fifth house. Between now and December 1, you'll be in one of the most romantic, sexually intense, and creative periods this year. Venus forms a harmonious angle to your sun, so there will be a nice flow of information and emotions between you and your partner. If a relationship begins under this transit, then you are in for a wild, intriguing time.

Sunday, November 8 (Moon in Cancer to Leo 5:23 a.m.) The moon enters your second house and brings your focus to money. Today, that focus may be on spending for a big-ticket item that you need. You've got the money in the bank—despite your fretting about lack of money—and you need the item, so make the purchase!

Monday, November 9 (Moon in Leo) On November 15, Mercury enters Sagittarius and your sixth house. Sagittarius isn't as compatible with your sign as Scorpio is, where Mercury is now, so complete all research projects and prepare yourself for a lot more contact with employees and coworkers. Part of that contact, by the way, will be due to the holidays.

Tuesday, November 10 (Moon in Leo to Virgo 8:31 a.m.) With the moon entering earth-compatible Virgo, your attention is on details and perhaps on health matters as well. You may be scheduling a dentist or a doctor appointment, joining a gym, or signing up for a yoga class. One way or another, maintenance of your health plays into the day's events.

Wednesday, November 11 (Moon in Virgo) If you have siblings, you may have more contact than usual with them today—a slew of e-mails, calls, or perhaps even a surprise visit. Or relatives are on your mind today for some reason. Aries individuals play into the day's events.

Thursday, November 12 (Moon in Virgo to Libra 12:23 p.m.) The moon joins Saturn in Libra, your fourth house. This combination has a whole new flavor compared to when Saturn was alone in Libra. For one thing, your focus is more on your personal relationships and balancing the many facets of your life. Today, Taurus individuals have tips for you.

Friday, November 13 (Moon in Libra) It's party time at your house. But be sure that you follow the rules on this one—Saturn demands that you must. In other words, if you're a teenager having a party while your parents are out of town, you probably are breaking the rules right there.

Saturday, November 14 (Moon in Libra to Scorpio 5:25 p.m.) The moon joins Mercury and Venus in your fifth house. You and your partner may be talking late into the night, planning for the future. If you're not involved, then this energy manifests itself through your creative drive. It's a wonderful combination if you're a writer or in the communications or travel business.

Sunday, November 15 (Moon in Scorpio) Mercury enters Sagittarius, your sixth house. Even though it's Sunday, you may be exchanging e-mails and calls with coworkers or employees today. It's also possible that you'll be filling out college or graduate-school applications for next fall. If you're a writer, this is a great day to either start a book or finish one!

Monday, November 16 (Moon in Scorpio) The new moon in Scorpio brings opportunities for romantic relationships, creative endeavors, and children, if you've been hoping to start a family. It's to your advantage to use whatever visualization techniques you know to help manifest your desires.

Tuesday, November 17 (Moon in Scorpio to Sagittarius 12:23 a.m.) The moon joins Mercury in your sixth house. This combination should energize you. If you're working today, it could be a challenge to focus on work and your usual routine. You may feel restless, with a need to travel and connect with people.

Wednesday, November 18 (Moon in Sagittarius) If yesterday's restlessness repeats itself today, then the message probably is that you should take the day off and burn off some of that excessive energy. Putter around your home. Go shopping. Browse through the new titles at a bookstore. Go to the gym.

Thursday, November 19 (Moon in Sagittarius to Capricorn 10:01 a.m.) The moon enters your seventh house. A partner—business or romantic—needs more of your attention today. Or the relationship itself needs attention. You'll have to decide which it is. You and your partner discuss your long-range plans—for yourself as individuals and for the relationship.

Friday, November 20 (Moon in Capricorn)   How far can you and a business partner take your idea? As it turns out, pretty far. You have similar goals. If you're working for someone else, you may be tired of doing so. In fact, self-employment looks increasingly appealing.

Saturday, November 21 (Moon in Capricorn to Aquarius 10:11 p.m.)   Brainstorm with your support group today. Test your new business ideas on others and get feedback.

Sunday, November 22 (Moon in Aquarius)   Your spiritual beliefs come into play today. It may be that you are veering away from the spiritual paradigm with which you were brought up, and the people around you—family, friends—may be offended. But in the end, does that matter? You're here to define who you are.

Monday, November 23 (Moon in Aquarius)   You're building foundations today in some area of your life. Whether it's a relationship you're working on, an educational or spiritual goal, or something else altogether, you've got plenty on your plate. Be patient.

Tuesday, November 24 (Moon in Aquarius to Pisces 11:08 a.m.)   Once in a great while, you have an epiphany that completely rearranges your life. It may start with something small, but by the time you're done, the issue is huge. That's where you are today.

Wednesday, November 25 (Moon in Pisces)   Getting ready for the Thanksgiving holidays? Going out of town or staying close to home? Whichever it is, today your mind is really not on that issue.

Thursday, November 26 (Moon in Pisces to Aries 10:11 p.m.)   For the next two and a half days, your career should

242

be your focus. You won't be into it at all, not with Thanksgiving right in your face and so many demands on your time. But perhaps you can send Thanksgiving greetings to the people in your life who matter.

Friday, November 27 (Moon in Aries)   Take time to touch base with clients, bosses, peers, coworkers, or whoever populates your daily work world, and send out your best greeting for the holidays. It may feel like a shallow gesture to you, but to the people you contact, the gesture will be appreciated.

Saturday, November 28 (Moon in Aries)   Feeling a tad restless? Feeling like something is lacking in your life? Feeling that you aren't quite getting it? The moon's square to your sun always creates tension of some kind. Sometimes, we can use it constructively. Today, the end result falls in your court, Cancer.

Sunday, November 29 (Moon in Aries to Taurus 5:35 a.m.)   It's always nice to end the month on a friendly lunar transit, and the Taurus moon is certainly that. Friends, groups, your own wishes and dreams—all these elements come into play. You're going to be starting the New Year on a whole new foundation, Cancer. You're setting the groundwork.

Monday, November 30 (Moon in Taurus)   Friends gather around. All of them may not be physically present, but they are there, nonetheless, offering support, feedback, whatever it is that you need right now. Your wishes and dreams for yourself are changing, but that's a good thing.

DECEMBER 2009

Tuesday, December 1 (Moon in Taurus to Gemini 9:24 a.m.)   Venus enters Sagittarius and your sixth house, and Uranus turn direct, in your ninth house. The Venus transit promises that an office flirtation could become something much more between now and December 25. The Uranus movement portends a shift in your relationship with things like educational goals, overseas travels, or spirituality.

Wednesday, December 2 (Moon in Gemini)   Today's full moon in Gemini highlights what is hidden in your life. Issues you thought were resolved could surface—hidden fears or addictions, for instance, or even a past-life challenge that has carried over into this life. Confront the issue and move on.

Thursday, December 3 (Moon in Gemini to Cancer 11:01 a.m.)   The moon enters your sign today. With every planet now moving in direct motion, you have enormous energy at your disposal. Whether you use it to enjoy yourself, tackle some challenging project, or make strides in your personal or professional life, you succeed regardless.

Friday, December 4 (Moon in Cancer)   Get the jump on holiday shopping and head out to the mall with a friend, partner, or family member. Your spirits are soaring today; it's a good idea to remember what this kind of mood feels like so that later in the month, if you feel down, you can try to conjure up these same emotions.

Saturday, December 5 (Moon in Cancer to Leo 12:08 p.m.)   Mercury enters Capricorn and your seventh house. This transit, which lasts into next year, facilitates communication with a partner. You and your partner may travel together during this period. Keep in mind, though, that Mercury turns retrograde on December 26, which may mess up your New Year's Eve plans.

Sunday, December 6 (Moon in Leo)   You're spending money today on gifts and holiday stuff, and preparing for your getaway out of town for the holidays or for the arrival of relatives. Either way, you may be stressed out, so slow down and be secure in the knowledge that everything will get done.

Monday, December 7 (Moon in Leo to Virgo 2:07 p.m.)   With the moon, Mercury, and Pluto all in earth

244

signs, you've got plenty of grounding today. Keep a close eye on details and avoid conflict and confrontation with a business or romantic partner. If a neighbor has been troubling you, that problem disappears on its own.

Tuesday, December 8 (Moon in Virgo) You get together with people in your neighborhood or community for some sort of group volunteer project. It could concern a charitable event or a neighborhood beautification project for the holidays. If you have children, you could be involved in some school event today.

Wednesday, December 9 (Moon in Virgo to Libra 5:48 p.m.) The moon joins Saturn in your fourth house. If you recently moved, then Saturn helps you get settled so that by the holidays your new home is really a home, rather than stacks of boxes! If you've been thinking about moving, it's best to wait until Saturn leaves Libra, two and a half years from now.

Thursday, December 10 (Moon in Libra) The Libra moon seeks emotional harmony and balance. It dislikes confrontations and disagreements, and tries to please everyone. Be careful today that you don't bend like a straw to accommodate the needs of people around you.

Friday, December 11 (Moon in Libra to Scorpio 11:32 p.m.) You're researching or investigating an issue or situation, and won't settle for anything less than the absolute truth. The Scorpio moon is one of the most emotionally intense, so whatever you're researching really has your passions boiling.

Saturday, December 12 (Moon in Scorpio) Your emotions are so powerful today that they barrel through any obstacles you face. When you combine such strong emotions with focused intent, you can begin to change what you experience.

Sunday, December 13 (Moon in Scorpio) One facet of the Scorpio moon that can turn against you is a need to get even. If someone has injured you in some way, ask yourself what you're supposed to learn from this. Make the necessary adjustments in your attitude. Then forgive the person.

Monday, December 14 (Moon in Scorpio to Sagittarius 7:25 a.m.)   Holiday shopping is on your to-do list, but this time it's for employees or coworkers or you're shopping for an office party. Rather than delegating the task, do it yourself. You'll enjoy it.

Tuesday, December 15 (Moon in Sagittarius)   Get ready for tomorrow's new moon in Capricorn by making up a list of what you hope to manifest in terms of your work routine and health maintenance. There's a celebratory aspect to the Sagittarius moon that's hard to resist. So don't resist it!

Wednesday, December 16 (Moon in Sagittarius to Capricorn 5:32 p.m.)   Today's new moon in Capricorn opens a chapter for your work routine and health maintenance. You may try a diet or nutritional program, or join a gym or sign up for yoga or Pilates classes. If you've been sending out résumés, then you begin to get positive responses and may end up changing jobs.

Thursday, December 17 (Moon in Capricorn)   The moon enters your seventh house. There's plenty to talk about today with a partner, but where do you start? Let him or her begin. Then get into the flow of it and have your say.

Friday, December 18 (Moon in Capricorn)   On December 20, this beautiful period of every planet moving direct ends, when Mars turns retrograde in Leo, your second house. Prepare for it by making sure your finances are in order—know your budget for holiday buying, pay in cash if possible, and be sure your payments are up-to-date.

Saturday, December 19 (Moon in Capricorn to Aquarius 5:39 a.m.)   The moon joins Neptune and Jupiter in your eighth house. Both of these planets are moving direct now. Your vision about what is possible for you and a partner is expanded in some way today. Your ideals are heightened and validated.

Sunday, December 20 (Moon in Aquarius)   Mars turns retrograde in Leo, your second house. This retrograde lasts until mid-March 2010 and could play havoc with your finances. If you have a natal moon or rising in Leo, you may be more accident-prone, run the risk of getting ticketed if you speed, and experience emotional tumult.

Monday, December 21 (Moon in Aquarius to Pisces 6:42 p.m.)   The moon enters fellow water sign Pisces, your ninth house. Some of today will feel surreal, but once the moon enters Pisces this evening, you feel more at home in your own body and head. Your thoughts this evening turn to spiritual matters.

Tuesday, December 22 (Moon in Pisces)   Be imaginative today if you do last-minute shopping, particularly if you're buying for the special people in your life. Buy a gift that fits the person.

Wednesday, December 23 (Moon in Pisces)   In three days, Mercury turns retrograde in Capricorn, your seventh house. So start backing up computer files, tying up contract negotiations, and generally consolidating your resources. Be sure to let your partner know about the retrograde, too, just so you're both aware that communication and travel snafus are likely.

Thursday, December 24 (Moon in Pisces to Aries 6:40 a.m.) Whether you're celebrating at home or elsewhere—or not at all—the energy favors lively discussions and a celebratory mood. Just be sure to take some time out today to back up any recent work on the computer. Mercury turns retrograde on December 26.

Friday, December 25 (Moon in Aries)   What a nice transit for Christmas Day: Venus enters Capricorn and your seventh house. Despite the fact that Mercury is turning retrograde in the same house and sign tomorrow, the Venus transit should add smoothness and spice to your love life.

Saturday, December 26 (Moon in Aries to Taurus, 3:27 a.m.) Mercury's retrograde in Capricorn won't end until January 15. More immediately, though, it may mess up your New Year's plans, particularly if you're traveling. Remain flexible. Approach everything as an adventure.

Sunday, December 27 (Moon in Taurus) This friendly earth moon heightens your artistic sense and your mystical interests. Whether you're traveling or at home, this moon may put you in a kitchen, whipping up gourmet foods, or in a restaurant, enjoying the gourmet delights that someone else has cooked.

Monday, December 28 (Moon in Taurus to Gemini, 8:15 p.m.) Take time for yourself today. You're preparing for the moon moving into your sign on December 30 and for a lunar eclipse in your sign on New Year's. Double-check your New Year's Eve plans. If you're going to be traveling, you might want to reconsider and travel on New Year's Day instead.

Tuesday, December 29 (Moon in Gemini) Information and networking are highlights for the day. Your networking, though, may occur through e-mail and blogs rather than in person. Time to make up your New Year's resolutions, too, Cancer.

Wednesday, December 30 (Moon in Gemini to Cancer 9:46 p.m.) Late this evening, the moon enters your sign, and you welcome it. The shift in energy invigorates you and turns your thoughts toward the New Year. What surprises are in store for you in 2010?

Thursday, December 31 (Moon in Cancer) Today's lunar eclipse in your sign triggers emotions related to your personal life. Whatever you feel could include nostalgia for the good old days. Sometimes it's easier to look back than forward. But tonight, embrace the future.

HAPPY NEW YEAR!

JANUARY 2010

Friday, January 1 (Moon in Cancer to Leo 10:42 p.m.)   The year begins on a number 9 day with the moon in Cancer. So the focus is on the home, endings, and beginnings. How can you make improvements to your home or home life now?

Saturday, January 2 (Moon in Leo)   The moon is in your second house today. Expect emotional experiences related to money. You could be feeling quite magnanimous and impulsive, especially related to finances. Your generosity is appreciated. However, watch your spending. You feel best in the home setting, surrounded by family, friends, and familiar objects.

Sunday, January 3 (Moon in Leo to Virgo 10:53 p.m.)   Cooperation is highlighted today. You're intuitive, especially when you focus on relationships. Romance and love play a role in your day. Let things develop. Put off any major purchases for a few days.

Monday, January 4 (Moon in Virgo)   Take what you know, and share it with others. However, keep conscious control of your emotions when communicating, especially with family members. Your thinking is unduly influenced by things of the past.

Tuesday, January 5 (Moon in Virgo)   Take care of details, especially related to your health. Follow your resolutions. Start exercising; watch your diet. Exercise your mind as well. Stop worrying. You could be getting involved in a challenging mental activity, such as online gaming, a debate, or a game of chess.

Wednesday, January 6 (Moon in Virgo to Libra 12:59 a.m.) Change and variety are highlighted now. Think freedom; think outside the box. It's a number 5 day. No restrictions. Your creativity, personal grace, and magnetism are highlighted.

Thursday, January 7 (Moon in Libra) With the moon in your fourth house, you feel a close tie to your roots. A parent plays a role. Work on a home-improvement project. You're dealing with the foundations of who you are and who you will be.

Friday, January 8 (Moon in Libra to Scorpio 6:01 a.m.) Secrets, intrigue, and confidential information play a role. Something mysterious is going on. You explore the unknown. Investigate, research, and dig deep. Be aware of things happening behind closed doors and possible deception.

Saturday, January 9 (Moon in Scorpio) Yesterday's energy flows into your Saturday. Expect intense, emotional experiences today. You investigate, analyze, or simply observe what's going on now. You quickly come to a conclusion and wonder why others don't see what you see. You detect deception and recognize insincerity with ease.

Sunday, January 10 (Moon in Scorpio to Sagittarius 2:10 p.m.) Complete a project. Clear up odds and ends. Take an inventory of where things are going in your life. It's a good day to make a donation to a worthy cause. Make room for something new. Clear your desk for tomorrow's new cycle. But don't start anything new today.

Monday, January 11 (Moon in Sagittarius) It's a service day. You improve, edit, and refine the work of others. Help others, but don't deny your own needs. Once again, remember to keep your resolutions about exercise and diet.

Tuesday, January 12 (Moon in Sagittarius) Make use of your sense of humor. You see the big picture, not just the details. Publishing or the law and the justice system play a role in your day. You're restless, impulsive, and inquisitive. Spiritual values arise. Worldviews are emphasized.

Wednesday, January 13 (Moon in Sagittarius to Capricorn 12:54 a.m.)   Saturn goes retrograde in your fourth house today until May 30. Expect more restrictions and delays related to your home or family life. You take a deeper look at your family matters. It's *not* a good time to try to start a family.

Thursday, January 14 (Moon in Capricorn)   The moon is in your seventh house today. The focus turns to relationships, business and personal ones. You get along well with others now. You can fit in just about anywhere. Loved ones and partners are more important than usual.

Friday, January 15 (Moon in Capricorn to Aquarius 1:17 p.m.)   There's a solar eclipse and a new moon in your seventh house today. That indicates a time of completion and a new beginning, especially related to a partnership. With Mercury going direct in this same house, there's much discussion now about personal relationships. A legal matter might come to a head.

Saturday, January 16 (Moon in Aquarius)   The moon is in your eighth house now. You have a strong sense of duty and feel obligated to fulfill your promises. Security is an important issue with you right now. You could be dealing with your feelings about belongings and things you possess, as well as things that you share with others.

Sunday, January 17 (Moon in Aquarius)   Jupiter moves into your ninth house today. It's a good time to set off on a long trip or to plan one. You're feeling intuitive and lucky. It's a great day to pursue any interest in psychology, philosophy, or religion. A foreign culture could play a role in your day. You expand your intellectual horizons now.

Monday, January 18 (Moon in Aquarius to Pisces 2:18 a.m.)   Venus moves into your eighth house today. You prosper or move ahead with your plans as a result of a close personal relationship, especially one in which you share possessions or resources. You could be dealing with people who are interested in the mysteries of the unknown.

Tuesday, January 19 (Moon in Pisces)   The moon is in your ninth house today. You're a dreamer and a thinker. You may feel a need to get away. You're feeling restless; you yearn for a new experience. You can create positive change through your ideas.

Wednesday, January 20 (Moon in Pisces to Aries 2:37 p.m.)   You're at the top of your cycle today. Be independent and creative; refuse to be discouraged by naysayers. Take the lead; get a fresh start. Stress originality, and don't be afraid to turn in a new direction. Trust your hunches. Intuition is highlighted.

Thursday, January 21 (Moon in Aries)   Business or professional matters are highlighted. You gain an elevation of prestige. You're more responsive to the needs and moods of a group and of the public in general. Your life is more public today, but avoid emotional displays.

Friday, January 22 (Moon in Aries)   It's a great time for initiating projects, launching new ideas, and brainstorming. You're passionate but impatient. Emotions could be volatile. You're extremely persuasive, especially if you're passionate about what you're doing or selling or trying to convey.

Saturday, January 23 (Moon in Aries to Taurus 12:41 a.m.)   Your organizational skills are highlighted. Control your impulses. Take care of obligations. You're building foundations for an outlet for your creativity. Persevere to get things done, but emphasize quality.

Sunday, January 24 (Moon in Taurus)   Friends play an important role in your day, especially a Scorpio and a Pisces. You find strength in numbers. You find meaning through friends and groups, especially if you're involved in a project to raise social awareness. Take time to focus on your wishes and dreams.

Monday, January 25 (Moon in Taurus to Gemini 7:12 a.m.)   Service to others is the theme of the day. You offer advice and support. Do a good deed for someone. Be sympathetic and kind, generous and tolerant. Focus on making people happy, but avoid scattering your energies.

Tuesday, January 26 (Moon in Gemini)   You might feel a need to withdraw and work on your own. Think carefully before you act. There's a tendency to undo all the positive actions you've taken. Avoid any self-destructive tendencies. Be aware of hidden enemies.

Wednesday, January 27 (Moon in Gemini to Cancer 10:02 a.m.)   It's your power day. Unexpected money comes your way. You attract financial success. Open your mind to a new approach that could bring in big bucks, but avoid acting in a way that would hurt others.

Thursday, January 28 (Moon in Cancer)   The moon is in your first house today. Take care of yourself, especially any health issues. You're sensitive to other people's feelings. You may feel moody, withdrawn one moment, happy the next, then sad. It's all about your health and emotional self. Your feelings and thoughts are aligned.

Friday, January 29 (Moon in Cancer to Leo 10:10 a.m.)   You're at the top of your cycle again, a number 1 day. You make connections that others overlook. You're determined and courageous today. Explore, discover, and create. In romance, something new is developing. Refuse to deal with people who have closed minds.

Saturday, January 30 (Moon in Leo)   There's a full moon today in your second house. It's a time of completion. You reap what you have sown, and you move aggressively forward. Money comes your way. You equate your financial assets with emotional security now. However, put off any major purchases for a few days. Look at your priorities in handling your new income.

Sunday, January 31 (Moon in Leo to Virgo 9:23 a.m.) You're innovative and creative; you communicate well. Enjoy the harmony, beauty, and pleasures of life. Your imagination is keen. You're curious and inventive. It's a good day to beautify your home.

FEBRUARY 2010

Monday, February 1 (Moon in Virgo) The moon is in your third house. You write from a deep place. It's a good day for journaling. Your thinking may be unduly influenced by things from the past. Visits from relatives are likely. You accept an invitation to a social event.

Tuesday, February 2 (Moon in Virgo to Libra 9:42 a.m.) The spotlight is on cooperation. Marriage or a partnership plays a key role now. Use your intuition to get a sense of the day. Show your appreciation to others. Help comes through friends and loved ones.

Wednesday, February 3 (Moon in Libra) The moon is in your fourth house today. Spend time with your family and loved ones. Stick close to home, if possible. A parent plays a role in your day. Work on a home-repair project. Beautify your home.

Thursday, February 4 (Moon in Libra to Scorpio 12:56 p.m.) Persevere to get things done today. Don't get sloppy. Be methodical and thorough. You're at the right place at the right time. You can overcome bureaucratic red tape.

Friday, February 5 (Moon in Scorpio) Be yourself. In love, there's great emotional depth to a relationship. Your emotions tend to overpower your intellect. You feel strongly attached to loved ones, particularly children. But eventually you need to let go.

Saturday, February 6 (Moon in Scorpio to Sagittarius 8:04 p.m.)   Diplomacy wins the way. Best to avoid confrontations now. Be sympathetic and kind, generous and tolerant. Do so, even if you face an emotional outburst or someone who makes unfair demands on your time.

Sunday, February 7 (Moon in Sagittarius)   Yesterday's energy flows into your Sunday. It's another service-oriented day. Help others, but don't deny your own needs. Visit someone who is sick, but be careful not to be a martyr.

Monday, February 8 (Moon in Sagittarius)   Make use of your sense of humor. See the big picture, not just the details. Think abundance and prosperity. Spiritual values arise. World-views are emphasized. It's a good time to take a workshop or seminar.

Tuesday, February 9 (Moon in Sagittarius to Capricorn 6:45 a.m.)   Finish what you started. Visualize the future, set your goals, and get to work. Clear up odds and ends. Make room for something new. Take an inventory of where things are going in your life.

Wednesday, February 10 (Moon in Capricorn)   Mercury moves into your eighth house today. You take a renewed interest in matters of life and death, and what comes afterward. You investigate and dig deep. While you may read an interesting book on the subject, much of what you conclude comes through your intuition.

Thursday, February 11 (Moon in Capricorn to Aquarius 7:25 p.m.)   Venus moves into your ninth house. It's a good time for a long trip. You're feeling a love of learning and travel now. A relationship could develop with a person from another country.

255

Friday, February 12 (Moon in Aquarius) There's a new moon in your eighth house today. You can expect opportunities to arise, especially related to shared resources, taxes, insurance, or investments. Alternately, a doorway opens related to a pursuit of a metaphysical subject.

Saturday, February 13 (Moon in Aquarius) Yesterday's energy flows into your Saturday. Sex, death, rebirth, rituals, and relationships play a role. Managing shared resources takes on new importance. Security is an important issue with you right now.

Sunday, February 14 (Moon in Aquarius to Pisces 8:24 a.m.) Release old structures; get a new point of view. Think outside the box. Promote new ideas; follow your curiosity. A change of scenery would work to your advantage. You could be moving to a new location.

Monday, February 15 (Moon in Pisces) You're feeling restless. You're a dreamer and a thinker now. Your mind is active, and you yearn for a break from the routine. You can create positive change through your ideas.

Tuesday, February 16 (Moon in Pisces to Aries 8:31 p.m.) You work best on your own today. Knowledge is essential to success. Gather information, but don't make any absolute decisions until tomorrow. Just go with the flow. Express your desires, but avoid self-deception.

Wednesday, February 17 (Moon in Aries) Professional concerns are your focus. It's a good day for sales and dealing with the public. You get a boost in status; you're admired. But don't blur the boundary between your personal and professional lives.

Thursday, February 18 (Moon in Aries) It's a good day for an adventure, such as starting a new project or taking up a physical challenge. Go rock climbing, take a ride on a fast roller coaster, ride down a mountain bike trail, or parachute out of a plane. Imprint your style, but avoid recklessness. Athletics could be highlighted. Sports events are possible.

Friday, February 19 (Moon in Aries to Taurus 6:56 a.m.)   You're at the top of your cycle again. Be independent and creative. Following the energy of the last two days; take the lead in something new. You get a fresh start; don't be afraid to turn in a new direction.

Saturday, February 20 (Moon in Taurus)   Friends play an important role today, especially a Pisces and a Scorpio. You find strength in numbers. You could join a group of like-minded individuals to work for the common good. At the same time, keep an eye on your own wishes and dreams.

Sunday, February 21 (Moon in Taurus to Gemini 2:47 p.m.)   Your attitude determines everything today. Ease up on routines. Spread your good news. You communicate well. You're warm and receptive to what others say. Your popularity is on the rise.

Monday, February 22 (Moon in Gemini)   The moon is in your twelfth house today. Best to work behind the scenes and avoid any conflicts and confrontations, especially with women. Keep your feelings secret. Unconscious attitudes can be difficult.

Tuesday, February 23 (Moon in Gemini to Cancer 7:29 p.m.)   It's a number 5 day. Change and variety are highlighted now. Think freedom, no restrictions. Think outside the box. Approach the day with an unconventional mind-set. You're versatile and changeable. Be careful not to spread out and diversify too much.

Wednesday, February 24 (Moon in Cancer)   The moon is in your first house and on your ascendant. The way you see yourself is the way others see you. You're recharged for the month ahead, and this makes you more appealing to the public. You're physically vital, and relations with the opposite sex go well.

Thursday, February 25 (Moon in Cancer to Leo 9:09 p.m.) Knowledge is essential to success. Gather information, but don't make any absolute decisions until tomorrow. Maintain your emotional balance. Avoid confusion and conflicts. Keep any secrets entrusted to you.

Friday, February 26 (Moon in Leo) Expect emotional experiences related to money. You feel best when surrounded by familiar objects. It's not the objects themselves that are important, but the feelings and memories you associate with them.

Saturday, February 27 (Moon in Leo to Virgo 8:53 p.m.) It's a number 9 day. Clear your desk for tomorrow's new cycle. Accept what comes your way now, but don't start anything new. Use the day for reflection, expansion, and concluding projects.

Sunday, February 28 (Moon in Virgo) You reap what you've sown. It's a time of completion, especially related to the way you communicate with others and deal with friends, neighbors, and family in your everyday life. With Pluto trining the moon, you're in the power seat now. You call the shots.

MARCH 2010

Monday, March 1 (Moon in Virgo to Libra 8:32 p.m.) Mercury moves into your ninth house, the house of higher learning. Over the next couple of weeks, you could be feeling a renewed interest in a publishing project, philosophy, religion, the law, or education. It's a good time to work on a writing project. You might also have a strong interest in foreign cultures.

Tuesday, March 2 (Moon in Libra) The moon is in your fourth house, the house of the home. It's a good day to spend time with your family and loved ones. A parent could be involved in your day. You feel close to your roots. See if you can remember a dream from last night.

Wednesday, March 3 (Moon in Libra to Scorpio 10:12 p.m.) Have some fun today in preparation for tomorrow's discipline and focus. Remain flexible. Make time to listen to others. Play your hunches. Take time to relax and recharge your batteries.

Thursday, March 4 (Moon in Scorpio) The moon is in your fifth house today. Be yourself. Be emotionally honest. In love, there's great emotional depth to a relationship. Your emotions tend to overpower your intellect today. You're emotionally in touch with your creative side. You're protective and nurturing toward children.

Friday, March 5 (Moon in Scorpio) Intense, emotional experiences are key. You're passionate; your sexuality is heightened. Control issue might arise. Forgive and forget; try to avoid going to extremes. Be aware of things happening in secret and of possible deception.

Saturday, March 6 (Moon in Scorpio to Sagittarius 3:37 a.m.) Focus on making people happy today. Be sympathetic, kind, and compassionate. Avoid scattering your energies. Do a good deed for someone. Visit someone who is ill or in need of help.

Sunday, March 7 (Moon in Sagittarius) Venus moves into your tenth house. It's a good day for appearing in public. A partner could help you in a career matter. You could be dealing with the arts, diplomacy, fashion, or entertainment.

Monday, March 8 (Moon in Sagittarius to Capricorn 1:15 p.m.) It's your power day. Open your mind to a new approach that could bring in big bucks. You have a chance to gain recognition, fame, and power. Be aware that you're playing with power, so try not to hurt anyone.

Tuesday, March 9 (Moon in Capricorn) The focus turns to relationships, business and personal ones. You get along well with others. You can fit in just about anywhere. A legal matter comes to your attention. Women play a prominent role. Be careful that others don't manipulate your feelings.

Wednesday, March 10 (Moon in Capricorn)   Mars goes direct in your second house. It's a good day to put your energy into making money. Finances are highlighted. A risk or whatever you're working on pays off handsomely. However, budget your spending.

Thursday, March 11 (Moon in Capricorn to Aquarius 1:44 a.m.)   The spotlight is on cooperation. Show your appreciation to others. Be aware that there could be some soul-searching related to relationships. Emotions and sensitivity are highlighted. Don't make waves. Don't rush or show resentment. Let things develop.

Friday, March 12 (Moon in Aquarius)   The moon is in your eighth house. It's a good day for dealing with mortgages, insurance, and investments, especially if shared possessions or resources are involved. Security is an important issue with you right now. If you are planning on making a major purchase, make sure that you and your partner are in agreement. Otherwise, you could encounter intense emotional resistance.

Saturday, March 13 (Moon in Aquarius to Pisces 2:44 p.m.)   Tear down the old in order to rebuild. Revise; rewrite. Be methodical and thorough. Persevere to get things done. Remember that you're building a creative base for your future.

Sunday, March 14—Daylight Saving Time Begins (Moon in Pisces)   The moon is in your ninth house. It's a good time to plan a journey to a foreign country. Alternately, you take new interest in worldviews, ideas, philosophy, and mythology. Sign up for a workshop or seminar. Follow whatever opportunity opens for you.

Monday, March 15 (Moon in Pisces)   There's a new moon in your ninth house today. Yesterday's energy related to travel continues as a door opens for you to pursue your interests, whether it's a trip to a foreign country or enrolling in a seminar or workshop.

Tuesday, March 16 (Moon in Pisces to Aries 3:32 a.m.)   You work best on your own today. You investigate, analyze, or simply observe what's going on now. Knowledge is essential to success. Gather information, but don't make any absolute decisions until tomorrow.

Wednesday, March 17 (Moon in Aries)   Mercury moves into your tenth house. You can use your speaking and writing abilities to move ahead in your profession. You get along well with others at work, but you don't feel any strong emotional attachments. You can work out a strategy to advance your career.

Thursday, March 18 (Moon in Aries to Taurus, 1:30 p.m.)   Finish what you started. Take an inventory of where things are going in your life. Visualize the future, set your goals, and get to work. Make room for something new. It's a good day to make a donation to a worthy cause.

Friday, March 19 (Moon in Taurus)   The moon is in your eleventh house today. Friends play an important role, especially a Scorpio and a Pisces. You find strength in numbers. You find meaning through friends and groups, especially a group of like-minded people working for the common good.

Saturday, March 20 (Moon in Taurus to Gemini 9:29 p.m.)   It's a number 2 day. That means that cooperation and partnership are highlighted again. There's a beginning or an opportunity arises. Your intuition focuses on relationships. Don't make waves. Don't rush or show resentment. Let things develop.

Sunday, March 21 (Moon in Gemini)   A change of scenery feels good. Take a car trip to visit relatives. Contact neighbors. It's a good day to get out and have fun. But you also may feel an urge to pursue a creative task, especially writing, such as in a journal.

Monday, March 22 (Moon in Gemini)   The moon is in your twelfth house today. Think carefully before you act or speak. If you're not careful, there's a tendency to undo all the positive actions you've taken. You might feel a need to withdraw. Take time to reflect and meditate.

Tuesday, March 23 (Moon in Gemini to Cancer 3:16 a.m.)   Get ready for some adjustments that could include a possible move or relocation. You're versatile and changeable now. Variety is the spice of life. Let go of old structures now; get a new point of view. It's a great day to experiment.

Wednesday, March 24 (Moon in Cancer)   Everything you do is filtered through your sense of self. Your self-awareness and appearance are highlighted. Your feelings and thoughts are aligned. You get recharged for the month ahead.

Thursday, March 25 (Moon in Cancer to Leo 6:40 a.m.)   It's a number 7 day. Knowledge is essential to success. You investigate, analyze, or simply observe what's going on now. Gather information, but don't make any absolute decisions until tomorrow. Go with the flow.

Friday, March 26 (Moon in Leo)   It's a great day for dealing with your finances and planning how to spend your income. You feel emotionally tied to certain possessions that make you feel secure. Alternately, you discuss your values openly, and you're clearly understood.

Saturday, March 27 (Moon in Leo to Virgo 7:58 a.m.)   Look beyond the immediate. Strive for universal appeal. Spiritual values surface. Use the day for reflection, expansion, and concluding projects. Take an inventory of where things are going in your life.

Sunday, March 28 (Moon in Virgo)   You're dealing with your home life, and you're thinking about health issues. Stop fretting. Remember to exercise and watch your diet. You get your ideas across, but you could be over-influenced by past events. Stay in control of your emotions when talking with others, especially family members.

Monday, March 29 (Moon in Virgo to Libra 8:22 a.m.)   There's a full moon in your fourth house. It's a good time to complete a project related to your home. Spend time with your family and loved ones. Stick close to home. You can now be the person you've always wanted to be.

Tuesday, March 30 (Moon in Libra)   Romance is highlighted. Relationship issues figure prominently. You work to create harmony and peace with those around you. Your personal grace and magnetism are appreciated. Visit an art gallery, attend a concert, or go to a movie or the theater. If you can't go today, make plans to do so in the near future.

Wednesday, March 31 (Moon in Libra to Scorpio 9:42 a.m.)   Venus moves into your eleventh house today. You put others at ease in social situations. You benefit from friends and social contacts; you work smoothly with a group, especially if you're dealing with something artistic and creative.

APRIL 2010

Thursday, April 1 (Moon in Scorpio)   The moon is in your fifth house today. You're emotionally in touch with your creative side. You also might be more involved with kids. Animals play a role in your day. Take a chance or experiment. Be emotionally honest.

Friday, April 2 (Moon in Scorpio to Sagittarius 1:54 p.m.)   Mercury moves into your eleventh house. You get along well with others; you're admired for your thoughts and ideas, even though your ideas are somewhat unusual. You're willing to talk with anyone and exchange ideas. However, your attitude tends to be somewhat impersonal.

Saturday, April 3 (Moon in Sagittarius)   It's a service-oriented day. Help others, but don't deny your own needs. Keep your resolutions about exercise, and watch your diet. Attend to details related to your health. Make a doctor or dentist appointment. You could be feeling somewhat emotionally repressed.

Sunday, April 4 (Moon in Sagittarius to Capricorn 10:08 p.m.)   It's a number 5 day. Promote new ideas; follow your curiosity. Freedom of thought and action is key. A change of scenery would do you good. You're versatile and changeable. However, be careful not to spread out and diversify too much.

Monday, April 5 (Moon in Capricorn)   The moon is in your seventh house today. Secrets, intrigue, and confidential information play a role in your day. You investigate, analyze, or simply observe what's going on now. You detect deception and recognize insincerity with ease. Best to work on your own today.

Tuesday, April 6 (Moon in Capricorn)   Pluto goes retrograde in your seventh house. You tend to spend time scrutinizing your partnerships, both personal and business. By the time Pluto goes direct on September 13, you should be able to integrate your personal power into your relationships.

Wednesday, April 7 (Moon in Capricorn to Aquarius 9:51 a.m.)   It's a number 8 day, your power day! You have a chance to gain recognition, fame, and power. You attract financial success. You pull off a financial coup. It's a good day to buy a lottery ticket.

Thursday, April 8 (Moon in Aquarius)   The moon is in your eighth house today. A mystery of the unknown comes to your attention. Sex, death, rebirth, rituals, and relationships could play a role. Alternately, you could be involved in managing or controlling someone else's resources. You have a strong sense of duty and feel obligated to fulfill your promises.

Friday, April 9 (Moon in Aquarius to Pisces 10:48 p.m.)
You get a chance to prove yourself. Don't be afraid to take a risk by following a new path. Trust your hunches. You make connections that others overlook. Refuse to deal with people with closed minds.

Saturday, April 10 (Moon in Pisces)   The moon is in your ninth house. You're a dreamer and a thinker. You have lots of ideas and the ability to express them well to others. It's a good time for teaching, writing, or learning a foreign language. You may feel a need to get away. Long-distance travel could play a role.

Sunday, April 11 (Moon in Pisces)   Imagination is high-lighted. Watch for psychic events and synchronicities. Keep track of your dreams, including your daydreams. Ideas are ripe. It's a time for deep healing. You pursue universal knowledge, eternal truths, and deep spirituality.

Monday, April 12 (Moon in Pisces to Aries 10:31 a.m.)   It's a number 4 day. Your organizational skills are highlighted. Control your impulses to wander off task. Stay focused; fulfill your obligations. You're building a creative base.

Tuesday, April 13 (Moon in Aries)   The moon is in your tenth house. Business or career matters are highlighted. You gain elevation in prestige. You're warm toward coworkers. You're also in the public eye, so avoid any emotional displays.

Wednesday, April 14 (Moon in Aries to Taurus 7:55 p.m.)   There's a new moon in your tenth house today. Yesterday's energy flows into your Wednesday. A door opens related to your career or profession. You're in the public eye. Make sure you keep your business and personal lives separate.

Thursday, April 15 (Moon in Taurus)   The moon is in your eleventh house today. Group activities are highlighted.

You get along well with others, especially if you're working as a group for a common cause or goal. Take a look at your own goals, and make sure that they're still an expression of who you are.

Friday, April 16 (Moon in Taurus)   You're highly sensual and highly opinionated. There's a tendency to be somewhat fixed in your opinions. Avoid any stubborn behavior. It's a good time for gardening, cultivating ideas, and doing practical things.

Saturday, April 17 (Moon in Taurus to Gemini 3:09 a.m.)   Mercury goes retrograde in your eleventh house. Over the next three weeks, you can expect some communication problems with friends and associates, especially people who belong to a group or share an interest with you. You could be facing delays and confusion related to travel and also computer glitches. Keep in mind that it's temporary.

Sunday, April 18 (Moon in Gemini)   With Mercury going retrograde and the moon in your twelfth house, it's a good day to work behind the scenes and avoid any conflict. You could be dealing with a matter from the past that has returned to haunt you. Keep your feelings secret. Follow your intuition.

Monday, April 19 (Moon in Gemini to Cancer 8:40 a.m.)   The spotlight is on cooperation. Show your appreciation to others. Your emotions and your sensitivity are highlighted. There could be some soul-searching in regard to relationships. A new relationship could form.

Tuesday, April 20 (Moon in Cancer)   Yesterday's energy related to your emotions and sensitivity flow into your Tuesday. You may feel moody one moment, happy the next, then withdrawn and sad. It's all about your health and your emotional self—how you feel and how you feel about yourself. It's difficult to remain detached and objective.

Wednesday, April 21 (Moon in Cancer to Leo 12:43 p.m.)   It's time to get things organized. Revise; rewrite.

Clean out your desk, your closets, your garage, or your attic. Be methodical and thorough. Persevere to get things done, but emphasize quality.

Thursday, April 22 (Moon in Leo)   The moon is in your second house. You identify emotionally with your values or whatever you value. You tend to equate your assets to emotional security. You feel best when surrounded by familiar objects, especially in your home. It's not the objects themselves that are important, but the feelings and memories you associate with them.

Friday, April 23 (Moon in Leo to Virgo 3:25 p.m.)   It's a number 6 day, a service day. Be understanding and avoid confrontations. Diplomacy and compassion win the way. Focus on making people happy, but avoid scattering your energies. Be sympathetic, kind, and understanding.

Saturday, April 24 (Moon in Virgo)   The moon is in your third house. You're busy interacting with neighbors and relatives in a social gathering. You get your ideas across, but try not to get too emotional. A female relative plays an important role.

Sunday, April 25 (Moon in Virgo to Libra 5:18 p.m.)   Venus moves into your twelfth house. You love solitude. You find sustenance in quiet meditation. Your focus turns inward. Your emotions are strong, but you feel it's important to hold them inside.

Monday, April 26 (Moon in Libra)   The moon is in your fourth house. Yesterday's energy flows into your Monday. You're dealing with the foundations of who you are. Take the day off, if possible, or work at home. Spend some time in meditation. Handle repairs or beautify your home. Family and loved ones are important.

Tuesday, April 27 (Moon in Libra to Scorpio 7:30 p.m.) It's a number 1 day. That means you're at the top of your cycle again. You get a fresh start. Be independent, and avoid negative people. Surround yourself with creative and adventurous ones. Trust your hunches; don't be afraid to turn in a new direction.

Wednesday, April 28 (Moon in Scorpio)   There's a full moon in your fifth house today. You gain a sense of fulfillment from a creative endeavor or from your children. It's a time of completion. You reap what you've sown.

Thursday, April 29 (Moon in Scorpio to Sagittarius 11:36 p.m.)   You communicate well, and get your ideas across. Enjoy the harmony, beauty, and pleasures of life. Remain flexible. Your imagination is keen. You're curious and inventive. You're warm and receptive to what others say.

Friday, April 30 (Moon in Sagittarius)   With the moon in your sixth house, the emphasis turns to your daily work and service to others. Attend to details, and be careful not to overlook any seemingly minor matters that could take on importance. Keep up with your exercise plan, and watch your diet.

MAY 2010

Saturday, May 1 (Moon in Sagittarius)   You start the month with the moon in your sixth house of health and daily work. Keep your resolutions about exercise, and watch your diet. Attend to details related to your health. Make a doctor or dentist appointment, if needed. Your personal health occupies your attention.

Sunday, May 2 (Moon in Sagittarius to Capricorn 7:00 a.m.)   Take care of your obligations. You're building a foundation for your future. Emphasize quality. You're at the right place at the right time. Be aware that you could feel inhibited in showing affection.

Monday, May 3 (Moon in Capricorn)   The moon is in your seventh house today. The focus turns to relationships, business and personal ones. You get along well with others. You can fit in just about anywhere. Loved ones and partners are more important than usual.

Tuesday, May 4 (Moon in Capricorn to Aquarius 5:52 p.m.)   Focus on making people happy. It's a service day. Do a good deed for someone. Visit someone who is ill or in need of help. You offer advice and support. A domestic adjustment works out for the best.

Wednesday, May 5 (Moon in Aquarius)   An interest in metaphysics plays a role in your day. You could turn your attention to matters of sex, death, rebirth, rituals, and relationships. Anything involving possessions or resources that you share with someone else could become an issue.

Thursday, May 6 (Moon in Aquarius)   Groups and social events are highlighted. Your individuality is stressed. Your visionary abilities are heightened. You have a greater sense of freedom. You're dealing with new ideas, new options, and originality. You get a new perspective.

Friday, May 7 (Moon in Aquarius to Pisces 6:34 a.m.)   It's a number 9 day. Make room for something new. Clear your desk for tomorrow's new cycle. Visualize the future, set your goals, and get to work. Look beyond the immediate. Strive for universal appeal.

Saturday, May 8 (Moon in Pisces)   The moon is in your ninth house today. You may feel a need to get away. Plan a long trip. Sign up for a workshop or seminar. An interest in ideas, mythology, or philosophy arises.

Sunday, May 9 (Moon in Pisces to Aries 6:30 p.m.)   It's a number 2 day. Use your intuition to get a sense of your day. Be kind and understanding. Don't make waves. Don't rush or show resentment. Let things develop.

Monday, May 10 (Moon in Aries)   The moon is in your tenth house. It's a good day for gaining recognition. You're in the public eye. You get along well with fellow workers; you're much admired. You have a strong desire for high achievement through hard work. Be careful not to blur the distinction between your professional and private lives.

Tuesday, May 11 (Moon in Aries)   Mercury goes direct in your eleventh house. Confusion, delays, and miscommunication related to friends and associates are over. You handle mental work very well, especially dealing with computers and electronic devices. The glitches you've experienced are in the past. A matter related to your association with a group becomes clear.

Wednesday, May 12 (Moon in Aries to Taurus 3:49 a.m.)   It's a number 5 day. Change and variety are highlighted. Think freedom, no restrictions. Change your perspective. Approach the day with an unconventional mind-set. Release old structures; get a new point of view. A change of scenery would work to your advantage.

Thursday, May 13 (Moon in Taurus)   There's a new moon in your eleventh house. That means a doorway related to your wishes and dreams opens. Friends and associates play a role. You could also get help from members of a group.

Friday, May 14 (Moon in Taurus to Gemini 10:19 a.m.)   You could be investigating the unknown. Knowledge is essential to success. Secrets, intrigue, and confidential information play a role. Gather information, but don't make any absolute decisions until tomorrow. Go with the flow.

Saturday, May 15 (Moon in Gemini)   It's a good day to withdraw from the action and work behind the scenes. Matters from the past surface. Take time to turn inward and evaluate where you've been and where you're going. Keep your feelings to yourself, unless you're confiding in a close friend. Remain versatile and adaptable.

Sunday, May 16 (Moon in Gemini to Cancer 2:47 p.m.)   It's a good day to finish up a project, especially one at home. Close a door, and get ready to open a new one. Clear up odds and ends, but don't start anything today. Take time to reflect. Look beyond the immediate. Visualize the future, set your goals, and get to work.

Monday, May 17 (Moon in Cancer)   The moon is in your first house. With the moon in your first house, you're sensitive to other people's feelings. You're malleable and easily change your mind. You may feel moody, withdrawn one moment, happy the next, then sad.

Tuesday, May 18 (Moon in Cancer to Leo 6:07 p.m.)   Use your intuition to get a sense of your day. Be kind and understanding. Your intuition focuses on relationships. Don't make waves. Don't rush or show resentment. Let things develop.

Wednesday, May 19 (Moon in Leo)   Venus moves into your first house. You're feeling more outgoing than usual. You're putting a happy face on life. You also appreciate the good things in life. Your personal grace is noticed and admired.

Thursday, May 20 (Moon in Leo to Virgo 8:59 p.m.)   It's a good day to dig in and get organized. Tidy up your desk. Clean out a closet or the attic. Reorganize the garage. Finish whatever you've been working on, and get ready for something new.

Friday, May 21 (Moon in Virgo)   The moon is in your third house. You write from a deep place. It's a good day for journaling. Your mental abilities are strong; you have an emotional need to reinvigorate your studies, especially regarding matters of the past. You're attracted to historical or archaeological studies. A female relative plays a role.

Saturday, May 22 (Moon in Virgo to Libra 11:50 p.m.)   It's a service day. Do a good deed. Make someone happy today. Keep your resolutions about exercise, and watch your diet. Don't limit yourself or let your fears hold you back. Confront them and move ahead. You could be feeling somewhat emotionally repressed.

Sunday, May 23 (Moon in Libra)   The moon is in your fourth house. It's a good day to stay home, if possible. Work on a home-repair project. Do something to beautify your home environment. You could be dealing with your parents. You feel a close tie to your roots.

Monday, May 24 (Moon in Libra)   Romance is highlighted. Relationships issues figure prominently in your day. Your creativity, personal grace, and magnetism play a role. You try to keep everyone around you in balance. Serve as an arbitrator between two parties in disagreement. You can see both sides of the story.

Tuesday, May 25 (Moon in Libra to Scorpio 3:18 a.m.) Make room for something new; accept whatever comes your way. Clear up odds and ends. Take an inventory of where things are going in your life. Get ready for your new cycle.

Wednesday, May 26 (Moon in Scorpio)   The moon is in your fifth house. Your emotions tend to overpower your intellect. Take a chance or experiment, especially with a creative project. You feel strongly attached to loved ones, particularly children. But eventually you need to let go.

Thursday, May 27 (Moon in Scorpio to Sagittarius 8:16 a.m.)   There's a full moon in your sixth house today. That means it's a time of completion related to a health matter, or you gain a sense of fulfillment regarding your service to others. Uranus moves into your tenth house for the next seven years. As a result, you could see some erratic changes in your career, or you could take an offbeat approach to your career course. You could become your own boss.

Friday, May 28 (Moon in Sagittarius)   Yesterday's service-oriented energy continues into your Friday. Be sympathetic and kind, generous and tolerant. Do a good deed for someone; offer advice and support. Avoid scattering your energies. Take care of any health needs.

Saturday, May 29 (Moon in Sagittarius to Capricorn 3:44 p.m.) Control your impulses. Fulfill your obligations. Persevere to get things done. Emphasize quality. You're building foundations for an outlet for your creativity.

Sunday, May 30 (Moon in Capricorn) Saturn goes direct in your fourth house. You can integrate your family life with your professional responsibilities. There could be some delays, especially if you are attempting to sell your house.

Monday, May 31 (Moon in Capricorn) Neptune goes retrograde in your eighth house. There could be some secret or deceptive practice going on related to joint finances. Expect delays. Be careful with matters related to taxes, insurance payments, or legal dealings. Pay attention to your dreams.

JUNE 2010

Tuesday, June 1 (Moon in Capricorn to Aquarius 2:08 a.m.) You begin the month on a number 4 day. Your organizational skills are called upon. Be methodical and thorough. Stay focused and avoid wandering from task. It's a day of hard work that will make the rest of the week go easier.

Wednesday, June 2 (Moon in Aquarius) The moon is in your eighth house. Some of yesterday's energy flows into your Wednesday. You have a strong sense of duty; you feel obligated to fulfill your promises. You could be involved in managing shared resources. Taxes, mortgages, and insurance take on new importance. Alternately, you could be pursuing an interest in a metaphysical subject, such as life after death.

Thursday, June 3 (Moon in Aquarius to Pisces 2:34 p.m.) It's a service day. Diplomacy is called for, especially when dealing with people who are upset or making unfair demands on

273

your time. You offer advice and support. Be sympathetic, kind, and compassionate, but avoid scattering your energies.

Friday, June 4 (Moon in Pisces)   The moon is in your ninth house. You're feeling restless. You yearn for a new experience. You're a dreamer and a thinker. Plan a long trip or sign up for a seminar or workshop on a subject that interests you, especially if it involves a foreign culture or country.

Saturday, June 5 (Moon in Pisces)   Your imagination is highlighted today. Keep track of your dreams, including your daydreams. Ideas are ripe. Watch for psychic events and synchronicities, but beware of possible self-deception. It's a day for deep healing.

Sunday, June 6 (Moon in Pisces to Aries 2:51 a.m.)   Jupiter moves into your tenth house today. You can expect a big expansion in your career. You should be getting hints of it soon, if not already. Then there will be some delays or possible misgivings related to a partner; then, by early next year, everything works out, and you soar ahead.

Monday, June 7 (Moon in Aries)   Mars moves into your third house today and stays there for six weeks. You're mentally on your toes and resourceful. You're also competitive, abrupt, and direct with people. Try not to get too impatient, especially while driving in traffic. Watch your speed.

Tuesday, June 8 (Moon in Aries to Taurus 12:42 p.m.)   It could be a challenge, but try not to rush too much today. Don't show resentment toward those who are moving up to speed. Let things develop. Don't make waves.

Wednesday, June 9 (Moon in Taurus)   The moon is in your eleventh house. Friends play an important role. You gain success as a result of social contacts. You're warm and receptive to what others say, especially those involved in a group. Your charm and wit are appreciated. You tend to surround yourself with creative people.

Thursday, June 10 (Moon in Taurus to Gemini 7:12 p.m.) Mercury moves into your twelfth house and re-mains there for two weeks. During that time your thoughts are often colored by the past. Your feelings play a stronger role than normal in your decision making, outweighing logic at times. You're secretive about your thoughts, and you keep to yourself more than usual.

Friday, June 11 (Moon in Gemini) The moon joins Mer-cury in your twelfth house. Think carefully before you act. There's a tendency to undo all the positive actions you've taken. You're more sensitive than usual today. Avoid any self-destructive tendencies. Best to back off rather than confront a suspected enemy. Hide your emotions. Keep your feelings secret.

Saturday, June 12 (Moon in Gemini to Cancer 10:51 p.m.) There's a new moon in your twelfth house. The en-ergy of the past two days moves into your Saturday. But you find opportunities by working behind the scenes. You get a chance to delve deeper into your self through meditation, psy-choanalysis, or other means.

Sunday, June 13 (Moon in Cancer) The moon is in your first house. Some of yesterday's energy flows into your Sun-day. You could be feeling moody and out of sorts. You're sen-sitive to other people's feelings. It's all about your health and emotional self.

Monday, June 14 (Moon in Cancer) With Venus in your second house, you love personal adornments and enjoy show-ing them off. It's a good time for making money. You feel good about the status that financial success brings you, especially if you achieve your success through your art or creative en-deavors.

Tuesday, June 15 (Moon in Cancer to Leo 12:55 a.m.) Yes-terday's energy flows into your Tuesday as the moon joins Venus in your second house. Expect emotional experiences related to money and your values. It's a good day for invest-ments, but be practical. Don't make any major purchases. You seek financial and domestic security, and you feel best sur-rounded by familiar objects.

Wednesday, June 16 (Moon in Leo)   You strut your stuff at center stage! Romance and love are highlighted. Financial speculation and gambling play a role. Focus on advertising and publicity. Dress boldly. Showmanship is highlighted.

Thursday, June 17 (Moon in Leo to Virgo 2:41 a.m.)   It's a number 2 day. Expect emotional experiences related to money and your values. It's a good day for investments, but be practical. Don't make any major purchases. You seek financial and domestic security, and you feel best surrounded by famil-iar objects.

Friday, June 18 (Moon in Virgo)   The moon is in your third house. You have an emotional need to pursue ideas and subjects that interest you. Your intellectual curiosity requires continued nurturing. Meanwhile, you're dealing with the ev-eryday world. Expect a lot of running around. Keep your cell phone turned on.

Saturday, June 19 (Moon in Virgo to Libra 5:13 a.m.)   Put off any romantic notions. Stay focused; don't wander off task. Get everything organized. Be methodical and thorough. Keep in mind you're building a creative base for your future.

Sunday, June 20 (Moon in Libra)   The moon is in your fourth house, your native home. It's a good day to stay close to home and take care of domestic matters. Work on a home-repair project. Spend time with your family and loved ones. Get out and enjoy the summer; take time to smell the prover-bial roses.

Monday, June 21 (Moon in Libra to Scorpio 9:14 a.m.)   The week begins on a service day. Diplomacy wins the way. Be sympathetic, kind, and tolerant. Avoid confrontations. Try to make other people happy. An adjustment in your domestic life may be necessary.

Tuesday, June 22 (Moon in Scorpio)   The moon is in your fifth house. You're emotionally in touch with your creative side. Be yourself. In love, there's great emotional depth to a relationship now. Children and pets play a role in your day.

Wednesday, June 23 (Moon in Scorpio to Sagittarius 3:11 p.m.)   It's a number 8 day, your power day. Business dealings go well. You could pull off a financial coup. You're being watched by people in power. Be courageous and honest. Also, be aware that fear of failure can attract tangible experiences that reinforce the feeling.

Thursday, June 24 (Moon in Sagittarius)   The moon is in your sixth house. Help others, but don't ignore your own needs. You're compassionate and sensitive. You tend to feel very strongly about whatever you're involved in. Go with the flow. Diplomacy wins the way.

Friday, June 25 (Moon in Sagittarius to Capricorn 11:22 p.m.)   A part of you is taking a thoughtful look at your life. You're mentally restless; you enjoy connecting with people. You pick up valuable information from your encounters. You adapt quickly to changing circumstances.

Saturday, June 26 (Moon in Capricorn)   There's a lunar eclipse in your seventh house. You tend to react emotionally to unexpected events related to a relationship. Be aware that your partner might be moody and sensitive. It's difficult to remain detached and objective.

Sunday, June 27 (Moon in Capricorn)   Yesterday's energy flows into your Sunday. The focus remains on relationships, business or personal ones. Loved ones and partners are more important than usual. A legal matter comes to your attention.

Monday, June 28 (Moon in Capricorn to Aquarius 9:53 a.m.)   Hard work is called for. Stay focused; get organized. Be methodical and thorough. There's little time to mull over relationships. You may feel inhibited in showing affection. Tear down the old in order to rebuild.

Tuesday, June 29 (Moon in Aquarius)   The moon is in your eighth house. Deal with any emotional discomfort related to possessions you share with another. If you are planning to make a major purchase, be sure that you and your partner are in agreement. Otherwise, you could encounter intense emotional resistance. An interest in metaphysics plays a role in your day. You could be dealing with a mystery.

Wednesday, June 30 (Moon in Aquarius to Pisces 10:11 p.m.)   It's a number 6 day. It's another service day. You offer advice and support. Be diplomatic, kind, and understanding. But don't act like a martyr. Dance to your own tune. A domestic adjustment works out for the best.

JULY 2010

Thursday, July 1 (Moon in Pisces)   Use your intuition as you look into matters dealing with education, philosophy, religion, or travel. A foreign person, country, or culture plays a role in your day. You can create positive change through your ideas.

Friday, July 2 (Moon in Pisces)   Yesterday's energy flows into your Friday. You're dealing with universal knowledge, eternal truths, and deep spirituality. Keep track of your dreams, including your daydreams. Ideas are ripe. Imagination is highlighted. Watch for synchronicities.

Saturday, July 3 (Moon in Pisces to Aries 10:45 a.m.)   You could be looking into a mystery and digging for information. Secrets, intrigue, and confidential information play a role. You investigate, analyze, or simply observe what's going on now.

You quickly come to a conclusion and wonder why others don't see what you see.

Sunday, July 4 (Moon in Aries)   The moon is in your tenth house. Your tenacity is recognized. You gain an elevation in prestige related to your profession and career. Material success and financial security play a role in your day. You make a strong emotional commitment to your profession or to a role in public life.

Monday, July 5 (Moon in Aries to Taurus 9:30 p.m.)   Uranus goes retrograde in your tenth house, which suggests you'll be thinking a lot about your career, your path, and your relationships with peers. Some of your actions related to your career and fellow workers were probably erratic, and you might have some regrets, in spite of your success. Cooperation is highlighted.

Tuesday, July 6 (Moon in Taurus)   The moon is in your eleventh house. Friends play an important role, especially a Scorpio and a Pisces. Take a look at your goals, and make sure that they're still an expression of who you are. You do well in a group setting. You could be dealing with an issue involving social consciousness.

Wednesday, July 7 (Moon in Taurus)   Your health and physical activity are highlighted. It's a good time for gardening, cultivating ideas, and doing practical things. Take care of money matters. You're highly sensual. Your senses are attuned. You're also opinionated and somewhat stubborn.

Thursday, July 8 (Moon in Taurus to Gemini 4:51 a.m.) It's a number 3 day. Your attitude determines everything. Spread your good news. You're innovative and creative; you communicate well. Enjoy the harmony, beauty, and pleasures of life. Beautify your home.

Friday, July 9 (Moon in Gemini)   Mercury moves into your second house. You think quickly, especially related to finances. You can come up with moneymaking ideas. You're very focused, and it's all about finances. Your values are oriented to material gain rather than to the intellect.

Saturday, July 10 (Moon in Gemini to Cancer 8:38 a.m.)   Venus moves into your third house. You're pursuing a creative project with a sense of love and exercising your artistic talents. Your writing skills are strong. You get along well with family members; you do your best to avoid arguments. You exhibit your mastery of compromise.

Sunday, July 11 (Moon in Cancer)   There's a solar eclipse in your first house. It's a very active time for you with personal opportunities arising. Something starts, and something else ends. You get recharged for the month ahead. Your feelings and thoughts are aligned.

Monday, July 12 (Moon in Cancer to Leo 9:54 a.m.)   It's a number 7 day. You work best on your own. Knowledge is essential to success. Gather information, but don't make any absolute decisions until tomorrow. Go with the flow. Express your desires, but avoid self-deception.

Tuesday, July 13 (Moon in Leo)   With the moon in your second house, you're feeling a sense of abundance. You expand your horizons with a new purchase, or new money arrives. You're in a fortunate position, but don't overextend yourself.

Wednesday, July 14 (Moon in Leo to Virgo 10:15 a.m.)   Finish what you started. Make room for something new. Visualize the future, set your goals, and get to work. Take care of details, especially related to your health.

Thursday, July 15 (Moon in Virgo)   Your mental abilities are strong, and you have an emotional need to reinvigorate your studies, especially regarding matters of the past. You're attracted to historical studies or prehistorical explorations. You could be getting involved in a challenging mental activity, such as online gaming, a debate, or a game of chess.

Friday, July 16 (Moon in Virgo to Libra 11:25 a.m.)   Try to keep everything in balance around you. Cooperation is key. You see both sides of the story. Your intuition focuses on relationships. Don't make waves. Don't rush or show resentment. Let things develop.

Saturday, July 17 (Moon in Libra)   The moon is in your fourth house, your native house. Spend time with your family and loved ones. Stick close to home.

Sunday, July 18 (Moon in Libra to Scorpio 2:43 p.m.) Your emotions could get intense this afternoon. Control your impulses. Fulfill your obligations. You're at the right place at the right time. Forgive and forget; try to avoid going to extremes.

Monday, July 19 (Moon in Scorpio)   Your love life takes off now. There's an idealistic turn to whatever you do for pleasure. It's a great time for a creative project, especially fiction writing. A burst of creative energy motors you ahead. It's a good day to get a pet!

Tuesday, July 20 (Moon in Scorpio to Sagittarius 8:49 p.m.)   Service to others is the theme of the day. You offer advice and support. Do a good deed for someone. Focus on making people happy. Domestic purchases are highlighted.

Wednesday, July 21 (Moon in Sagittarius)   Saturn goes direct in your fourth house, your native home. You feel emotionally attached to your home. You take special pride in your home. Upgrade and beautify your living quarters. Make use of your artistic eye in any home-decoration projects. You also feel closer to your roots, especially your parents.

Thursday, July 22 (Moon in Sagittarius)   The moon is in your sixth house. It's a service-oriented day. You improve, edit, and refine the work of others. Help others, but be careful not to act like a martyr. Don't let your fears hold you back. Keep your resolutions about exercise, watch your diet. Attend to details related to your health.

Friday, July 23 (Moon in Sagittarius to Capricorn 5:40 a.m.) It's a number 9 day. Complete a project; get ready to move forward. Look beyond the immediate. Strive for universal appeal. Clear up odds and ends. Take an inventory of where things are going in your life.

Saturday, July 24 (Moon in Capricorn) The moon is in your seventh house. Loved ones and partners are more important than usual. You comprehend the nuance of a situation, but it's difficult to go with the flow. Be careful that others don't manipulate your feelings. You feel a need to be accepted. You're looking for security, but you have a hard time going with the flow.

Sunday, July 25 (Moon in Capricorn to Aquarius 4:39 p.m.) There's a full moon in your eighth house. You reap what you've sown related to shared possessions or resources. Your experiences are more intense than usual. It's all about your feelings concerning belongings and things you possess as well as things you share. Security is an important issue.

Monday, July 26 (Moon in Aquarius) Groups and social events are highlighted. You have a greater sense of freedom. You're dealing with new ideas, new options, and originality. You get a new perspective. Help others, but dance to your own tune. Your wishes and dreams come true.

Tuesday, July 27 (Moon in Aquarius) Mercury moves into your third house. Your mind is particularly active, moving from one thing to another. You're adaptable and versatile, but you're not pondering any deep thoughts. You're too busy for that.

Wednesday, July 28 (Moon in Aquarius to Pisces 5:00 a.m.) It's a number 5 day. Change and variety are highlighted. Focus on freedom, no restrictions. Variety is the spice of life. Think outside the box. Release old structures; get a new point of view.

Thursday, July 29 (Moon in Pisces)   Mars moves into your fourth house today. Now you can put more energy into your home. It's a good time to redecorate or beautify your home with something new. Whatever needs fixing at home, you can do yourself.

Friday, July 30 (Moon in Pisces to Aries 5:42 p.m.)   The focus turns to relationships, business and personal ones. You get along well with others. You can fit in just about anywhere. Loved ones and partners are more important than usual. Be careful that others don't manipulate your feelings. A legal matter comes to your attention.

Saturday, July 31 (Moon in Aries)   The moon is in your tenth house. Even though it's the weekend, you're dealing with professional concerns. You could be involved in a power struggle. Remain responsive to the need and moods of others around you. But avoid making any emotional displays in public.

AUGUST 2010

Sunday, August 1 (Moon in Aries)   It's a great time for initiating projects, launching new ideas, and brainstorming. Emotions could be volatile. You're passionate but impatient. Athletics could be highlighted. It's a good day to attend a sporting event.

Monday, August 2 (Moon in Aries to Taurus 5:13 a.m.) You work best on your own today. Knowledge is essential to success. Express your desires but avoid self-deception. Gather information, but don't make any absolute decisions until tomorrow. Go with the flow.

Tuesday, August 3 (Moon in Taurus)   The moon is in your eleventh house. Friends play an important role in your day, especially a Scorpio and a Pisces. While it was better for you to work on your own yesterday, today you find strength in numbers. You find meaning through friends and groups, especially a group of like-minded people working for the common good.

Wednesday, August 4 (Moon in Taurus to Gemini 1:54 p.m.) It's a number 8 day, your power day. Open your mind to a new approach. Unexpected resources arrive. You can go far with your plans and achieve financial success.

Thursday, August 5 (Moon in Gemini) The moon is in your twelfth house. Unconscious attitudes can be difficult. So can relations with women. You feel best working behind the scenes and keeping your feelings to yourself. Follow your intuition, and work on your self-confidence.

Friday, August 6 (Moon in Gemini to Cancer 6:50 p.m.) With Venus entering your fourth house your native home, it should be a pleasant, comfortable day. You're very domestic-oriented and loving. You can work at home. You take great pride in your home and feel attached to it. Spend time with loved ones.

Saturday, August 7 (Moon in Cancer) The moon is in your first house. You're sensitive to other people's feelings. Your feelings tend to fluctuate by the moment. You focus on how the public relates to you. Your self-awareness and appearance are important. You're dealing with the person you are becoming.

Sunday, August 8 (Moon in Cancer to Leo 8:23 p.m.) It's a number 4 day. Your organizational skills are called upon. You're building foundations for the future and developing outlets for your creativity. Emphasize quality in whatever you're doing.

Monday, August 9 (Moon in Leo) With the new moon in your second house, it's likely that some opportunity will come your way, especially one related to making money. It's a great

284

day for dealing with your finances and planning how to spend your income.

Tuesday, August 10 (Moon in Leo to Virgo 8:02 p.m.)   It's a number 6 day. It's another service day. Be sympathetic and kind, generous and tolerant. Focus on making people happy. Be understanding and avoid confrontations. Dance to your own tune. Attend to any health issues.

Wednesday, August 11 (Moon in Virgo)   The moon is in your third house. It's a good time for expressing yourself through writing. Take what you know, and share it with others. As you go about your everyday life, look to the big picture. Expect an invitation to a social event.

Thursday, August 12 (Moon in Virgo to Libra 9:44 p.m.)   It's another power day. Unexpected money comes your way. Expect a windfall. Business dealings go well, especially if you open your mind to a new approach.

Friday, August 13 (Moon in Libra)   The moon is in your fourth house, a comfortable place. Stick close to home. Finish a home-repair project, or spend time with loved ones. But also take time for some quiet meditation. You're dealing with the foundations of who you are. It's a good day for dream recall.

Saturday, August 14 (Moon in Libra to Scorpio 9:27 p.m.)   You're at the top of your cycle. You get a fresh start. Stress originality. Trust your hunches, follow your intuition, and refuse to deal with people who have closed minds. If you're ready, make room for a new love.

Sunday, August 15 (Moon in Scorpio)   The moon is in your fifth house today. You can move ahead on any creative project. Meanwhile, you have an opportunity to achieve greater depth in a relationship, but it could take hard work to achieve.

Monday, August 16 (Moon in Scorpio)   Expect intense emotional experiences. You're passionate. Your sexuality is heightened. Be aware of things happening in secret and of possible deception. Try to avoid going to extremes. Forgive and forget.

Tuesday, August 17 (Moon in Scorpio to Sagittarius 2:35 a.m.) It's a good day to clean out your closets, your attic, or your garage. Your organizational skills are highlighted. Control your impulses. Make an effort to avoid wandering off task. Tear down the old in order to rebuild.

Wednesday, August 18 (Moon in Sagittarius) The moon is in your sixth house. Delegate some of your responsibilities. Avoid taking on too much work. You help others, but allow them to shoulder some of the burden. Don't become a martyr for someone else's cause. Take care of any health issues.

Thursday, August 19 (Moon in Sagittarius to Capricorn 11:18 a.m.) Yesterday's service-related energy flows into your Thursday. You offer advice and support. Be sympathetic and kind, generous and tolerant, especially toward someone who is hurting. Focus on making people happy.

Friday, August 20 (Moon in Capricorn) Mercury goes retrograde in your third house and stays that way until September 12. That means you can expect some delays and glitches in communication over the next three weeks, especially in dealings with your siblings and neighbors. There also could be delays and confusion related to short-distance travel. Others might misunderstand your motivations.

Saturday, August 21 (Moon in Capricorn to Aquarius 10:38 p.m.) It's your power day. It's a good day to buy a lottery ticket. Expect a windfall. You have a chance to gain recognition, fame, and power. Be aware that you're playing with power, so try not to hurt anyone.

Sunday, August 22 (Moon in Aquarius) The moon is in your eighth house. Things could get emotionally intense today in your dealings with someone of the opposite sex. That's particularly true if you're facing issues related to shared belongings. You're sensitive and intuitive; you could take an interest in a metaphysical topic, such as past lives.

Monday, August 23 (Moon in Aquarius)   Friends play an important role in your day, especially other water signs, Cancer, Scorpio, or Pisces. Groups and social events are highlighted. Your individuality is stressed. Your visionary abilities are heightened. Play your hunches. Look beyond the immediate.

Tuesday, August 24 (Moon in Aquarius to Pisces 11:11 a.m.)   There's a full moon in your ninth house. It's harvesttime related to higher education. You reap what you've sown. A publishing project goes well. The same with publicity and advertising. You also could be heading off on a long-distance journey.

Wednesday, August 25 (Moon in Pisces)   Keep track of your dreams, including your daydreams. Ideas are ripe. Themes of the day: compassion, sensitivity, and inspiration. It's a time of deep healing.

Thursday, August 26 (Moon in Pisces to Aries 11:49 p.m.)   Persevere to get things done. Don't get sloppy. Stay focused. Be methodical and thorough. Put off any romantic notions. However, keep in mind you're building a creative base for your future.

Friday, August 27 (Moon in Aries)   You're more responsive to the needs and moods of a group, especially coworkers, and of the public in general. You're well liked; you gain an elevation in prestige related to your career. Avoid emotional displays in public.

Saturday, August 28 (Moon in Aries)   You're extremely persuasive, especially if you're passionate about what you're doing, selling, or trying to convey. Imprint your style. Wear bright colors. Have an adventure. Do something thrilling.

Sunday, August 29 (Moon in Aries to Taurus 11:36 a.m.)   Secrets, intrigue, and confidential information play a role. Investigate activities taking place behind closed doors. You work best on your own today. Keep your own counsel. Knowledge is essential to success. Gather information, but don't make any absolute decisions until tomorrow.

Monday, August 30 (Moon in Taurus)   With the moon in your eleventh house, friends and associates come to your aid. You get together with a group of like-minded individuals and work toward a common goal. Focus on your wishes and dreams, and make sure that they are still a reflection of who you are.

Tuesday, August 31 (Moon in Taurus to Gemini 9:20 p.m.)   Follow up on yesterday's energy; consider what lies ahead for you. Use the day for reflection, expansion, and concluding projects. Look beyond the immediate. Set your goals and get to work. Consider ways to expand; get ready for a fresh start.

SEPTEMBER 2010

Wednesday, September 1 (Moon in Gemini)   With the moon in your twelfth house, you can communicate your deepest feelings to a trustworthy friend. Otherwise, it's best to keep your thoughts and feelings to yourself. You feel comfortable working behind the scenes. Take time to reflect and meditate.

Thursday, September 2 (Moon in Gemini)   Your mind is particularly active. You're feeling restless, moving from one idea to the next. It's a good time to socialize. Get out and have fun. A change of scenery does wonders.

Friday, September 3 (Moon in Gemini to Cancer 3:51 a.m.)   It's a good day to complete a project. Clear up odds and ends. Don't start anything new today. Take an inventory of where things are going in your life. Strive for universal appeal.

Saturday, September 4 (Moon in Cancer)   The moon is on your ascendant today. You're feeling physically vital and recharged for the rest of the year. You're assertive and out-going. Your appearance and personality shine. You get along well with the opposite sex.

Sunday, September 5 (Moon in Cancer to Leo 6:46 a.m.)   Use your intuition to focus on a relationship issue. Process everything that happened yesterday. Cooperation is highlighted. Be supportive and patient. Don't make waves.

Monday, September 6 (Moon in Leo)   The energy of the past two days continues with an emphasis on finances. The overall financial picture takes a turn for the better. You can apply your values.

Tuesday, September 7 (Moon in Leo to Virgo 6:54 a.m.)   Emphasize quality with whatever you're doing. Be methodical and thorough. Tear down in order to rebuild. Be practical with your money. You may feel inhibited in showing affection.

Wednesday, September 8 (Moon in Virgo)   There's a new moon in your third house, and Venus moves into your fifth house. That means you're very attractive to the opposite sex, and something new regarding a relationship is coming about.

Thursday, September 9 (Moon in Virgo to Libra 6:02 a.m.)   It's a number 6 day. Service to others is the theme of the day. You offer advice and support. Diplomacy wins the way. Do a good deed for someone. Visit someone who is ill or in need of help.

Friday, September 10 (Moon in Libra)   The moon is in your fourth house, your native home. Spend time with your family and loved ones. Stick close to home, if possible. Retreat to a private place for meditation. It's a good day for dream recall. You're dealing with the foundations of who you are and who you will be.

Saturday, September 11 (Moon in Libra to Scorpio 6:22 a.m.) It's your power day. Unexpected money arrives. You can go far with your plans and achieve financial success. Be aware that strong emotional experiences might arise. You're playing with power, so try not to hurt anyone.

Sunday, September 12 (Moon in Scorpio) Mercury goes direct in your third house. Any confusion, miscommunication, and delays, especially with relatives and neighbors, start to recede into the past. Things move smoothly. You get your message across, and everything works better, including computers and other electronic equipment.

Monday, September 13 (Moon in Scorpio to Sagittarius 9:52 a.m.) Yesterday's energy flows into your Monday as Pluto goes direct in your seventh house. That takes the heat off a relationship. You're not so introspective about it, and you have the opportunity to integrate what you've learned more directly into your life.

Tuesday, September 14 (Moon in Sagittarius) Mars moves into your fifth house. You put out a lot of energy as you seek the pleasures of life. It's a good time for an active, energetic sex life. There's a tendency to be impulsive or fickle. It's also a time to show off your creative talents.

Wednesday, September 15 (Moon in Sagittarius to Capricorn 5:30 p.m.) Yesterday's energy flows into your Wednesday. You're innovative and creative; you communicate well. Enjoy the harmony, beauty, and pleasures of life. Remain flexible, warm, and receptive. Your attitude determines everything.

Thursday, September 16 (Moon in Capricorn) The moon is in your seventh house. The focus turns to relationships, business and personal ones. You feel a need to be accepted. You're looking for security, but you have a hard time going with the flow. Be careful that others don't manipulate your feelings. A legal matter comes to your attention.

Friday, September 17 (Moon in Capricorn)   Your ambition and drive to succeed are highlighted. Your responsibilities increase. You may feel stressed and overworked. Self-discipline and structure are key. Other earth signs, a Taurus and a Virgo, play a prominent role. Maintain emotional balance. Don't forget to exercise; don't ignore the domestic scene.

Saturday, September 18 (Moon in Capricorn to Aquarius 4:35 a.m.)   Service to others is the theme of the day. Offer your advice and support. Be sympathetic and kind, generous and tolerant. Do a good deed. Visit someone who is ill or in need of help.

Sunday, September 19 (Moon in Aquarius)   If you are planning on making a major purchase, make sure that you and your partner are in agreement. Otherwise, you could encounter intense emotional resistance. An interest in metaphysics plays a role in your day. You could be dealing with a mystery.

Monday, September 20 (Moon in Aquarius to Pisces 5:15 p.m.)   It's another power day. You attract financial success. You have a chance to gain recognition, fame, and power. Be aware that fear of failure or fear that you won't measure up will attract tangible experiences that reinforce the feeling.

Tuesday, September 21 (Moon in Pisces)   Your mind is active, and you yearn for new experiences. You can create positive change through your ideas. A publishing project goes well. Publicity and advertising are emphasized.

Wednesday, September 22 (Moon in Pisces)   You turn inward. You seek universal knowledge, eternal truths, and deep spirituality. Deep healing is the theme of the day. You're compassionate, sensitive, and inspired. It's a good day to remember your dreams.

Thursday, September 23 (Moon in Pisces to Aries 5:47 a.m.)   You reap what you've sown related to your career. If you've done the groundwork, you gain a promotion or an elevation in prestige, and you're admired by fellow workers. Best to avoid emotional displays in public.

Friday, September 24 (Moon in Aries)   Yesterday's energy flows into your Friday. It's a great time for initiating projects, launching new ideas, and brainstorming. Be aware that emotions can become volatile. You're passionate but impatient. Imprint your style, but avoid reckless behavior.

Saturday, September 25 (Moon in Aries to Taurus 5:17 p.m.)   It's time to get organized. Clean out your garage, your attic, or your desk. Be methodical and thorough. Control your impulses. Stay on task. Persevere to get things done.

Sunday, September 26 (Moon in Taurus)   The moon is in your eleventh house. Friends play a significant role, especially a Capricorn and a Virgo. Take a look at your goals; make sure that they're still an expression of who you are. You work well in a group of like-minded people.

Monday, September 27 (Moon in Taurus)   Try to avoid any tendencies toward stubborn behavior. You might be feeling somewhat rigid in your thinking or inflexible in your opinions. Help others, but pay attention to health issues. It's a good day for physical activity. Get out and enjoy the fall weather.

Tuesday, September 28 (Moon in Taurus to Gemini 3:12 a.m.)   You work best on your own. Keep your own counsel. Secrets, intrigue, and confidential information play a role. Investigate activities taking place behind closed doors. Knowledge is essential to success. Gather information, but don't make any absolute decisions until tomorrow.

Wednesday, September 29 (Moon in Gemini)   You might feel a need to withdraw and work behind the scenes. A troubling matter from the past could arise, or something related to your childhood could play a role. It's a great day for a mystical or spiritual discipline. Your intuition is heightened.

Thursday, September 30 (Moon in Gemini to Cancer 10:47 a.m.)   The month ends on a number 9 day. Finish what you started. Clear up odds and ends. Make room for something new, but don't start anything until tomorrow. Look beyond the immediate. Take an inventory of where things are going in your life.

OCTOBER 2010

Friday, October 1 (Moon in Cancer)   The month starts out with the moon in your first house. You're sensitive to other people's feelings. You may feel moody one moment, happy the next, then withdrawn and sad. You focus on how the public relates to you. Your self-awareness and appearance are important. You're dealing with the person you are becoming.

Saturday, October 2 (Moon in Cancer to Leo 3:22 p.m.)   Finish what you started. Visualize the future, set your goals, and get to work. Accept what comes your way. It's all part of a cycle. Use the day for reflection, expansion, and concluding projects. It's a good day to make a donation to a worthy cause.

Sunday, October 3 (Moon in Leo)   Mercury moves into your fourth house. There's strong mental activity in the home. Homeschooling a child is a possibility. Alternately, you're thinking a lot about selling your home or remodeling.

Monday, October 4 (Moon in Leo to Virgo 5:00 p.m.)   It's a number 2 day. Partnerships are highlighted. Use your intuition to get a sense of your day. Be kind and understanding. Don't make waves. Don't rush or show resentment. Let things develop.

Tuesday, October 5 (Moon in Virgo)   The moon is in your third house. You're probably going from place to place, taking care of your everyday needs. Get in touch with others,

293

especially relatives or neighbors. You'll have some things to talk about. Be careful while driving.

Wednesday, October 6 (Moon in Virgo to Libra 4:52 p.m.)   Tear down the old in order to rebuild. Be methodical and thorough. Revise; rewrite. You're in the right place at the right time. Missing papers or a lost object is recovered.

Thursday, October 7 (Moon in Libra)   There's a new moon in your fourth house. It's a good time to begin a new project, especially one related to your home. A doorway opens, possibly one allowing you to work at home. Your home life is important. A parent plays a role. You feel close ties to your roots.

Friday, October 8 (Moon in Libra to Scorpio 4:52 p.m.)   Venus goes retrograde in your fifth house. Sit back and reassess things, especially related to a romantic relationship or your creative efforts. Avoid starting a relationship or beginning a creative project.

Saturday, October 9 (Moon in Scorpio)   Yesterday's energy flows into your Saturday. Investigate, research, and dig deep. Ponder what's going on. Be aware of things happening in secret and of possible deception. Control issues might arise. Forgive and forget; try to avoid going to extremes.

Sunday, October 10 (Moon in Scorpio to Sagittarius 7:09 p.m.)   Be courageous. Open your mind to an approach that could bring in big bucks. Expect a windfall. Business discussions go well. You have a chance to gain recognition, fame, and power.

Monday, October 11 (Moon in Sagittarius)   The moon is in your sixth house. It's another service day. If someone in your home environment could use a hand or needs your advice, be there for that person. Help others, but dance to your own tune. You improve, edit, and refine the work of others.

Tuesday, October 12 (Moon in Sagittarius)   You see the big picture, not just the details. Abundance plays a role. You're restless, impulsive, and inquisitive. Spiritual values arise. Worldviews are emphasized. A publishing project gets a boost.

Wednesday, October 13 (Moon in Sagittarius to Capricorn 1:17 a.m.)   Take care of loved ones. Cooperation is highlighted. Avoid criticizing and complaining. Don't make waves. Don't rush or show resentment. Let things develop.

Thursday, October 14 (Moon in Capricorn)   Yesterday's energy flows into your Thursday. Relationships, either personal or business, play a big role in your day. A legal matter comes to your attention. Stay focused. Self-discipline and structure are key.

Friday, October 15 (Moon in Capricorn to Aquarius 11:24 a.m.)   Get everything organized. Fulfill your obligations. Control your impulses. Emphasize quality. You're building foundations for an outlet for your creativity.

Saturday, October 16 (Moon in Aquarius)   The moon is in your eighth house. The feeling of security is an important issue with you. Your experiences are intense. You have a strong sense of duty and feel obligated to fulfill your promises. It's a good time to get involved in a cause aimed at improving life for large numbers of people.

Sunday, October 17 (Moon in Aquarius to Pisces 11:52 p.m.)   Some of yesterday's energy flows into your Sunday as you make yourself available to help others. You offer advice and support. Be sympathetic and kind, generous and tolerant. Focus on making people happy.

Monday, October 18 (Moon in Pisces)   The moon is in your ninth house. You're a dreamer and a thinker. You're captivated by new ideas and philosophies. You may feel a need to get away. You feel restless and yearn for a new experience.

Tuesday, October 19 (Moon in Pisces)   Keep track of
your dreams, including your daydreams. Ideas are ripe. Your
psychic abilities are enhanced. You're compassionate and sensitive, but you tend to be easily influenced by others.

***Wednesday, October 20 (Moon in Pisces to Aries 12:24
p.m.)***   Mercury moves into your fifth house. You express
yourself in a dramatic way. There's also a tendency to play
mental games. You could be more analytical in your view of a
romance. Try not to be overcritical with children.

Thursday, October 21 (Moon in Aries)   The moon is in
your tenth house. You are concerned with your reputation related to your career; you seek recognition for what you do.
You get along well with the public. Your feelings are domi-
nated by your desire for achievement.

***Friday, October 22 (Moon in Aries to Taurus 11:31
p.m.)***   There's a full moon in your tenth house. Energy
expended on your career pays off. You gain an elevation in
prestige. You're warmer toward coworkers, but don't blur the
boundary between your private and professional lives.

Saturday, October 23 (Moon in Taurus)   The moon is in
your eleventh house. Friends play an important role in your
day, especially a Pisces and a Scorpio. You find strength in
numbers. You find meaning through friends and groups, especially if you're united in a common cause.

Sunday, October 24 (Moon in Taurus)   Health and physical activity are highlighted. Go hiking, have a picnic, and
get out into nature. Enjoy the fall weather. It's a good time
for cultivating ideas, especially for practical things. You're
highly sensual and opinionated. Try to avoid any stubborn
behavior.

***Monday, October 25 (Moon in Taurus to Gemini 8:48
a.m.)***   Change and variety are highlighted. Approach
the day with an unconventional mind-set. Take a risk. Think

outside the box. Promote new ideas; follow your curiosity. A change of scenery would work to your advantage.

Tuesday, October 26 (Moon in Gemini) The moon is in your twelfth house. Think carefully before you act. There's a tendency to undo all the positive actions you've taken. Avoid any self-destructive tendencies. Be aware of hidden enemies. Work behind the scenes.

Wednesday, October 27 (Moon in Gemini to Cancer 4:15 p.m.) You investigate a secret matter. Look behind closed doors, dig deep for information, or just observe what's going on. You detect deception and recognize insincerity with ease. Go with the flow. Maintain your emotional balance.

Thursday, October 28 (Moon in Cancer) Mars moves into your sixth house. You're a hard worker. You get things done. Fellow workers might get annoyed by your aggressive behavior on the job. Control your temper. Don't be so concerned about details and getting everything perfect. It'll all work out.

Friday, October 29 (Moon in Cancer to Leo 9:39 p.m.) It's time to complete a project. Clear your desk, and make room for something new, but don't start anything. Spend some time in deep thought. Consider how you can expand your base.

Saturday, October 30 (Moon in Leo) You're dealing with money issues. You may be dealing with payments and collecting what's owed to you. You equate your financial assets with emotional security. You identify emotionally with your possessions or whatever you value. Look at your priorities in handling your income.

Sunday, October 31 (Moon in Leo) Use your intuition to get a sense of the day. Marriage could play a role. The spotlight is on cooperation. Your emotions and sensitivity are highlighted. Focus on your direction and your motivation. Where are you going and why?

Monday, November 1 (Moon in Leo to Virgo, 12:51 a.m.)   With the moon in your third house, you might be thinking about your behavior in the past related to your brothers and sisters. Your communication was probably erratic, and that affects your relationships. Control your emotions around siblings. Cooperation is highlighted.

Tuesday, November 2 (Moon in Virgo)   Take care of details, especially related to your health. Exercise; watch your diet. Stop fretting. It's a good day to write in a journal. You write from a deep place with lots of details and colorful descriptions.

Wednesday, November 3 (Moon in Virgo to Libra 2:19 a.m.)   Partnerships and cooperation rule the day. Use your intuition to get a sense of your day. Be kind and understanding. Don't make waves. Show your appreciation of others. There could be some soul-searching in regard to relationships.

Thursday, November 4 (Moon in Libra)   The moon is in your fourth house, your native home. Emotional issues that arise relate to the domestic scene. You could be feeling possessive of loved ones. It's a good day to retreat to a private place for quiet meditation. Find a new way to beautify your home scene.

Friday, November 5 (Moon in Libra to Scorpio 3:16 a.m.)   Get organized. Focus on advertising and publicity. Be adventurous. But also be methodical and thorough. You're building a creative base for the future. A romance plays a role in your day and could distract you from your goals.

Saturday, November 6 (Moon in Scorpio)   You get a fresh start on something new that exemplifies your creative abilities. With Neptune going direct in your eighth house, things related to shared money or resources move along smoothly. Pay attention to any matters related to taxes, insurance, or legal dealings.

Sunday, November 7—Daylight Saving Time Ends (Moon in Scorpio to Sagittarius 4:28 a.m.)   Don't forget to exercise and watch your diet. Attend to details related to your health. Make a doctor or dentist appointment. Your personal health occupies your attention.

Monday, November 8 (Moon in Sagittarius)   Now Mercury joins the moon in the sixth house. Your mental abilities are strong, and you're analytical about a health matter or something you're working on. You're methodical and thorough. Help those in need, but don't overlook your own needs.

Tuesday, November 9 (Moon in Sagittarius to Capricorn 9:37 a.m.)   You get an opportunity to expand and grow. Be courageous. You're playing with power, so be careful not to hurt others. Be aware that others in power may be watching your moves.

Wednesday, November 10 (Moon in Capricorn)   The moon is in your seventh house. Your partner allows you to expand your horizons. Material gains are likely, especially through marriage or a partnership. You and your spouse or partner work well together and succeed at whatever you are doing.

Thursday, November 11 (Moon in Capricorn to Aquarius 6:33 p.m.)   It's a number 1 day. You're at the top of your cycle. You get a fresh start. Get out and meet new people; do something you've never done before. You make connections that others overlook. Stress originality.

Friday, November 12 (Moon in Aquarius)   The moon is in your eighth house. You feel obligated and responsible to help others. You flow with social currents. You could get involved with a group that seeks to improve living conditions for certain people.

Saturday, November 13 (Moon in Aquarius)   You pursue the deeper mysteries in life now, such as life after death or reincarnation. Your psychic abilities are enhanced. Follow any intuitive nudges, especially related to whatever you share with another person. Issues of the day could include matters of sex, death, rebirth, rituals, and relationships.

Sunday, November 14 (Moon in Aquarius to Pisces 6:25 a.m.) Be practical with money. Take time to revise and rewrite. Be methodical and thorough. You're at the right place at the right time. Missing papers or objects are found.

Monday, November 15 (Moon in Pisces) The moon is in your ninth house. You're feeling restless; you have a strong emotional need to stretch your intellect. It's a good day to plan a long journey or sign up for a seminar or workshop on a subject close to your heart. A person born in a foreign land might play a role in your day.

Tuesday, November 16 (Moon in Pisces to Aries 7:00 p.m.) Focus on making people happy. Be sympathetic, kind, and compassionate. Diplomacy wins the way. Do a good deed. Avoid scattering your energies. Domestic purchases are highlighted.

Wednesday, November 17 (Moon in Aries) You're extremely persuasive, especially if you're passionate about what you're doing, selling, or trying to convey. You gain recognition in the workplace. It's the perfect time for launching ideas or initiating projects.

Thursday, November 18 (Moon in Aries) With Venus going direct in your fifth house, you're attractive to the opposite sex. You're popular and well-liked. You do well in any artistic endeavor. Meanwhile, Jupiter goes direct in your tenth house, which means you have the opportunity to expand your career into new areas and to get a raise or a bonus.

Friday, November 19 (Moon in Aries to Taurus 6:05 a.m.) Clear up odds and ends. Take an inventory of where things are going in your life. Accept what comes your way. It's all part of a cycle. Make a donation to a worthy cause. Make room for something new.

Saturday, November 20 (Moon in Taurus)   Friends play an important role in your day. It's a great time to socialize. You also get along well with members of a group, especially if you're working together on a project for the common good.

Sunday, November 21 (Moon in Taurus to Gemini 2:46 p.m.)   There's a full moon in your eleventh house. You reap what you've sown related to your wishes and dreams. Social consciousness plays a role. Examine your overall goals. Those goals should be an expression of who you are.

Monday, November 22 (Moon in Gemini)   It's a good day to work behind the scenes and to avoid any conflict. You could be dealing with a matter from the past that has returned to haunt you. Keep your feelings secret. Follow your intuition.

Tuesday, November 23 (Moon in Gemini to Cancer 9:14 p.m.)   Persevere to get things done. Clean a closet, clear out the attic, or reorganize your garage. Tear down the old in order to rebuild. Be methodical and thorough. Missing papers or objects are found.

Wednesday, November 24 (Moon in Cancer)   The moon is on your ascendant. You get recharged for the month ahead, and this makes you more appealing to the public. You're physically vital; relations with the opposite sex go well. The way you see yourself is the way others see you.

Thursday, November 25 (Moon in Cancer)   Yesterday's energy flows into your Thursday with the moon in your first house. It's all about your health and your emotional self—how you feel and how you feel about yourself. Your feelings tend to fluctuate, but your thoughts and feelings are aligned. You're particularly sensitive to other people's feelings.

Friday, November 26 (Moon in Cancer to Leo 2:01 a.m.)   It's a number 7 day. You become aware of confidential information, secret meetings, and things happening behind closed doors. You investigate like a detective solving a mystery. Dig deep and gather information, but don't act on what you learn until tomorrow.

Saturday, November 27 (Moon in Leo)   The moon is in your second house. You identify emotionally with your possessions or whatever you value. It's not the objects themselves that are important, but the feelings and memories you associate with them. Look at your priorities in handling your income. Put off making any major purchases.

Sunday, November 28 (Moon in Leo to Virgo 5:34 a.m.)   Finish the month by wrapping up a project and preparing for something new. Take time to reflect on everything that's been going on. Strive for universal appeal. Spiritual values surface. Look for a way to expand your horizons, but don't start anything until tomorrow.

Monday, November 29 (Moon in Virgo)   The moon is in your third house. It's a day for taking short trips. As you move about in your daily world, your thinking is influenced by matters of the past, especially related to relatives. You communicate well, but control your emotions when you make your point.

Tuesday, November 30 (Moon in Virgo to Libra 8:16 a.m.)   Mercury moves into your seventh house. You communicate well with the public. It's a good day for advertising and promoting your ideas. You get along well with a partner, especially one who can match your wit and intellect.

DECEMBER 2010

Wednesday, December 1 (Moon in Libra)   The moon is in your fourth house, a comfortable place. Take the day off and stay home, or work at home. Find time for a home-repair project. You could be dealing with parents. You feel a close tie to your roots.

Thursday, December 2 (Moon in Libra to Scorpio 10:44 a.m.)   Cooperation and partnerships are highlighted. Use your intuition to focus on relationships. Don't make waves. Don't rush or show resentment. Let things develop. Show your appreciation of others.

Friday, December 3 (Moon in Scorpio)   Your emotions tend to overpower your intellect. Be emotionally honest. In love, there's great emotional depth to a relationship. You feel strongly attached to children. But eventually you need to let go.

Saturday, December 4 (Moon in Scorpio to Sagittarius 2:00 p.m.)   Emphasize quality in whatever you're doing. Don't get sloppy. Be methodical and thorough. Take care of your obligations. You're building a creative base for the future. You're at the right place at the right time.

Sunday, December 5 (Moon in Sagittarius)   There's a new moon in your sixth house. An opportunity comes your way related to service. You can help others and help yourself. With Uranus going direct in your ninth house, you get an exotic outlook related to education and long-distance travel.

Monday, December 6 (Moon in Sagittarius to Capricorn 7:17 p.m.)   Yesterday's energy flows into your Monday. Service to others is the theme of the day. You offer advice and support. Be sympathetic, kind, and compassionate. Diplomacy wins the way.

Tuesday, December 7 (Moon in Capricorn)   With Mars moving into your seventh house, there's powerful energy coming into a marriage or partnership. How that energy is used is up to you. Things could explode, or a relationship could flourish. However, for the latter to happen, you'll need to go with the flow, and that might not be so easy with all the aggressive energy you're feeling.

Wednesday, December 8 (Moon in Capricorn)   Yesterday's high energy flows into your Wednesday. Your ambition and drive to succeed are highlighted. Your responsibilities increase. You may feel stressed and overworked. Maintain emotional balance. Your domestic scene needs attention.

Thursday, December 9 (Moon in Capricorn to Aquarius 3:32 a.m.)   Complete a project. Clear up odds and ends. Visualize the future, set your goals, and get to work. Look beyond the immediate. Strive for universal appeal.

Friday, December 10 (Moon in Aquarius)   Mercury goes retrograde in your seventh house. That means you can expect some delays and glitches in communication over the next three weeks, especially related to friends and groups. It's best to relax and control your emotional reactions to situations.

Saturday, December 11 (Moon in Aquarius to Pisces 2:41 p.m.)   Cooperation is highlighted. Use your intuition to get a sense of your day. Be kind and understanding. Don't rush or show resentment, even if someone is nagging. Let things develop.

Sunday, December 12 (Moon in Pisces)   The moon is in your ninth house. You're a dreamer and a thinker. You can create positive change through your ideas. You impart knowledge and guide others in their intellectual development. You also may feel a need to get away. You yearn for a new experience.

Monday, December 13 (Moon in Pisces)   Yesterday's energy flows into your Monday. Keep track of your dreams, including your daydreams. Ideas are ripe. You're compassionate and sensitive to others' feelings. You can also inspire others with your positive thoughts. Focus on universal knowledge, eternal truths, and deep spirituality.

Tuesday, December 14 (Moon in Pisces to Aries 3:15 a.m.)   Approach the day with an unconventional mind-set. Release old structures; get a new point of view. Think freedom, no restrictions. Variety is the spice of life. You can overcome obstacles with ease.

Wednesday, December 15 (Moon in Aries)   Professional concerns are the focus of the day. Business is highlighted. Your life is more public. You're more responsive to the needs and moods of a group and of the public in general. It's a good day for sales and dealing with the public.

Thursday, December 16 (Moon in Aries to Taurus 2:49 p.m.)   It's a number 7 day. You work best on your own. Gather information, but don't make any absolute decisions until tomorrow. Knowledge is essential to success.

Friday, December 17 (Moon in Taurus)   The moon is in your eleventh house. You have deeper contact with friends, especially a Pisces and a Scorpio. Your sense of security is tied to your relationships and to your friends. You find meaning through friends and groups.

Saturday, December 18 (Moon in Taurus to Gemini 11:38 p.m.)   Accept what comes your way now. It's all part of a cycle. But don't start anything new. Take an inventory of where things are going in your life. Use the day for reflection, expansion, and concluding projects.

Sunday, December 19 (Moon in Gemini)   The moon is in your twelfth house. Unconscious attitudes can be difficult. Keep your feelings secret. It's a great day for a mystical or spiritual discipline. Your intuition is heightened.

Monday, December 20 (Moon in Gemini)   It's a good day for a change of scenery. Get out and have fun. How about a short trip to a new place? You're restless and likely to be contacting friends and associates while you're on the road. Watch your driving.

Tuesday, December 21 (Moon in Gemini to Cancer 5:22 a.m.)   There's a full moon and a lunar eclipse in your twelfth house. Emotions related to issues from your past arise. You gain clarity about things that have been buried in your life. You might even meet someone you knew in a past life!

Wednesday, December 22 (Moon in Cancer)   The moon is on your ascendant. You're feeling particularly sensitive. You're malleable, and you tend to change your mind on a whim. You're easily influenced by what others say, and you're responsive to the way others relate to you.

Thursday, December 23 (Moon in Cancer to Leo 8:51 a.m.)   Think freedom, no restrictions. Promote new ideas; follow your curiosity. Like yesterday, you're versatile and changeable. Variety is the spice of life. Be careful not to spread out and diversify too much.

Friday, December 24 (Moon in Leo)   The moon is in your second house. Money and material success are important to you and provide you with a sense of security. You feel best when surrounded by familiar objects in your home environment. Put off making any major purchases for a few days.

Saturday, December 25 (Moon in Leo to Virgo 11:15 a.m.)   You investigate, analyze, or simply observe what's going on. You quickly come to a conclusion and wonder why others don't see what you see. Maintain your emotional balance. Avoid confusion and conflicts. Go with the flow. Merry Christmas!

Sunday, December 26 (Moon in Virgo)   The moon is in your third house. You communicate well. Take what you know, and share it with others. Make sure you keep conscious control of your emotions when communicating, especially with siblings or neighbors. Your thinking might be unduly influenced by the past.

Monday, December 27 (Moon in Virgo to Libra 1:39 p.m.)   Look beyond the immediate. Strive for universal appeal. Spiritual values surface. Take an inventory of where

306

things are going in your life. It's a good day to make a donation to a worthy cause.

Tuesday, December 28 (Moon in Libra)   The moon is in your fourth house, your native home. Spend time with your family and loved ones. Stick close to home. You're dealing with the foundations of who you are and who you will be. A parent plays a role. You feel a close tie to your roots.

Wednesday, December 29 (Moon in Libra to Scorpio 4:50 p.m.)   It's a number 2 day. Show your appreciation of others. Help comes through friends and loved ones. The spotlight is on cooperation. Use your intuition to get a sense of your day. Be kind and understanding.

Thursday, December 30 (Moon in Scorpio)   Mercury goes direct in your sixth house, which means that any confusion, miscommunication, and delays that you've been experiencing related to your efforts to help others recede into the past. Things move smoothly, especially in your efforts to be of service to others. You get your message across, and everything works better, including computers and other electronic equipment.

Friday, December 31 (Moon in Scorpio)   The moon is in your fifth house. You're emotionally in touch with your creative side. There's great depth in a love relationship. You're emotionally tied to your children and pets. But make sure you allow them room to grow.

HAPPY NEW YEAR!

SYDNEY OMARR

Born on August 5, 1926, in Philadelphia, Pennsylvania, Sydney Omarr was the only person ever given full-time duty in the U.S. Army as an astrologer. He is regarded as the most erudite astrologer of our time and the best known, through his syndicated column and his radio and television programs (he was Merv Griffin's "resident astrologer"). Omarr has been called the most "knowledgeable astrologer since Evangeline Adams." His forecasts of Nixon's downfall, the end of World War II in mid-August of 1945, the assassination of John F. Kennedy, Roosevelt's election to a fourth term and his death in office ... these and many others are on the record and quoted enough to be considered "legendary."

ABOUT THE SERIES

This is one of a series of twelve *Sydney Omarr® Day-by-Day Astrological Guides* for the signs of 2010. For questions and comments about the book, go to www.tjmacgregor.com.